From the Heart of a Dancer

Daily Devotional

for Praise Dancers and Worshippers

by the

HALAL DANCE MINISTRY

Watersprings
PUBLISHING

From the Heart of a Dancer: Daily Devotional for Praise Dancers and Worshipers published by:

Watersprings Publishing

P.O. Box 1284 Olive Branch, MS 38654

www.waterspringspublishing.com

Contact the publisher for bulk orders and permission requests.

Printed in the United States of America.

ISBN-13: 979-8-9894494-7-7

Contents

ACKNOWLEDGMENTS

We, the Halal Dance Ministry & Family would like to thank you the reader for purchasing our devotional book that was truly a labor of love and commitment.

A special thanks to our church family Apostle Dr. Marlon Husbands, Prophetess Dr. Suzette Husbands, Elder Anthony Greene and the Sanctuary Empowerment Centre for always being there to support and encourage us.

Thanks to our editor, Raquel Griffith of Cubyss Communications, for tirelessly working to ensure that all devotions were edited. Thanks to our publisher, Watersprings Publishing, for seeing the vision and helping us bring it to fruition.

Finally, a big thank you to all the writers who made this devotional book possible.

January 1

KNOWING WHO HE IS MAKES OUR MINISTRY AUTHENTIC

*You ask, "Who is this king of Glory?" He is Yahweh, armed and ready for battle,
the Mighty One, the invincible commander of heaven's hosts!
Yes, he is the King of Glory.
Psalm 24:10*

Sometimes, we can be tempted to tie our identity to a particular ministry. But if we don't know our true identity in Christ, how will we be authentic in our specific ministry? To know our true identity, we have to read His Word, and then we will see that He says a great deal about who we are. We'll realize that not only is our identity in God, but that it is dependent upon who He is. When we know this, we can minister authentically. To minister through dance is a heightening experience; it has become part of my identity.

We often interact with a lot of different people who have different personalities and ways of doing things. When we try to do things the way everyone else does, we lose sight of our true identity. However, when we let God lead us, we'll eventually understand that our identity is in Him and Him alone. For God, there is no ideal dancer; there is only the dancer who allows him to minister through them.

I choose to believe what God's Word says about who I am. I am fearfully and wonderfully made. I am God's special possession. I am the head and not the tail. These things and more He said about His children in His Word, and they form the identity we have as His children.

Prayer

Dear Heavenly Father, may You continually show us, through Your Word, who You are and who You say we are. We sometimes listen to what people in our lives say about us and take that on as our identity. We must cement the belief that our identity comes from You alone. God, may what You say about us in Your Word be evident as we dance for Your honor and glory. In Jesus' Name, Amen.

Call To Action

Whether you minister in dance, song, poetry, teaching or evangelism, in whatever gift or talent you minister, know that your identity is in Christ and Christ alone.

Danielle Harewood

January 2

WHOSE IDENTITY DO WE CARRY?

So God created man in His own image; in the image of God He created him; male and female He created them. Genesis 1:27

I knew you before I formed you in your mother's womb. Jeremiah 1:5

Many people struggle with the word identity. Many are unsure of who they are and subsequently function in a false identity. Persons may identify us by our names or, at times, as someone's daughter or mother. Other times, they label us by our associations.

Because our true, God-given identity is in Christ, it overflows into our ministry. This principle extends to how we move our bodies, our approach, and attitude towards ministry, how we speak to persons, and how we carry ourselves, whether on or off stage.

Family, in whatever we do, onlookers should be able to recognize traits in us that resemble our Heavenly Father. His characteristics must be evident in every area of our lives. We have His DNA and His blood type. Therefore, we are ultimately identified as His. After all, God calls us His children, His very own.

Prayer

Father, we declare that our identity is in You and that we will look like You, carrying Your image and attributes so that people can recognize You in us. Father, I pray that our ministry will be an extension of Your DNA flowing through us. As individuals observe us, they will see You in us, our actions, and our ministry. May You cause these souls to become beneficiaries of the overflow of Your presence within us. We thank You, Father, in Jesus' name, Amen.

Call To Action

Every morning, take a few minutes to remind yourself of your God-given identity.

Debra Marshall

January 3

GOD CREATED ME

For we are His workmanship, created in Christ Jesus for good works, which God prepared beforehand, that we should walk in them. Ephesians 2:10

What is my purpose in life? Why am I here? How do I exist in this world? Who am I? These are some questions we've asked ourselves at some point in our lives. As a dance minister, I sometimes ask myself if this is what God has called me to be. Am I genuinely ministering in my dance to Him?

Ephesians 2:10 tells us that we belong to God, who has created us in His image for good things – ministry. My favorite part of this verse is that I no longer have to question if dancing is what I should be doing; I can now dance with the assurance that He has prepared the way for me to show forth His good works.

Thus, ministry should not only be directed towards persons in the audience but also to God. In my dance, I want my ministry to draw me nigh unto God, to worship Him and, mostly, to bring joy and pleasure to Him. I believe ministry is why God created me. When I think of being a work of God, I think of purpose. Therefore, I dance with purpose; I am doing what He has called me to do.

Prayer

Our merciful and everlasting Father, we thank You for creating us like Your Son, Jesus. You handcrafted us, and we thank You for preparing and establishing our lives beforehand. You knew us before we even knew ourselves. May we, as dancers, walk in the good works You have created for us, fulfilling Your purpose for our lives. Help us to know that we are Your creation. We bless You and praise Your name. Amen.

Call To Action

Always remember that God created you to worship Him; that alone is purpose. So, walk in the good works that He has prepared for you.

Eslyn Taylor

January 4

COMING TOGETHER

I am the vine; you are the branches. Whoever abides in me and I in him, he it is that bears much fruit, for apart from me you can do nothing. John 15:5

We all know the creation story. God separated the darkness from the light; He created the sky, the drylands, the sun and the moon, animals, and then us, people. But God didn't just create us to wander around the earth without a purpose. Instead, He created each of us uniquely with different gifts, talents, desires, and strengths to fulfill our lives and His will on earth. One of those gifts was the gift of dance, and God has given us the capacity to love dance and use it to minister to those around us.

The Bible verse above paints a picture of a tree with God being the branches and us being the vine. So, what does that make our ministry? It is the fruit. Even though there are different parts of the tree, we still consider it whole, right? That is how we must view our ministry and identity since we are extensions of God, and our ministry is an extension of us. Unfortunately, sometimes this is not the case, and our fruit grows in the wrong place. When this occurs, there is usually a disconnect between our ministry and our identity that must be bridged. How can that disconnect be bridged? Accepting Jesus as our Saviour and relying on Him to show us how to let our ministry shine through our identity. Once we do this, our identity and ministry will become extensions of the eternal branches found in Christ Jesus.

Prayer

Dear heavenly Father, I thank You for the gift of ministry, which is rooted in You. I pray that my ministry and identity align so that my ministry is an extension of who I am because who I am is an extension of You. I pray this in Jesus' wonderful name, Amen.

Call To Action

The act of ministry and identity are one and the same, but have they manifested that way in your life? Have a conversation with God today about how you can further align your ministry with your identity.

Gabrielle Blackett

January 5

ALL THINGS BRIGHT AND BEAUTIFUL

Therefore, if anyone is in Christ, he is a new creation: old things have passed away, behold all things have become new. 2 Corinthians 5:17

"Ok," you say. "A new creation? How is this possible? Our fingerprints have not changed."

Most countries, if not all, have a register of all births and baptisms. A person can also have a driver's license and a national identification card which says who he or she is – that's identity in the natural and physical. But there is another form of identification – your identity in Christ. What does this mean? How do we achieve this identity? This new creation speaks of a new spiritual life, a new way, a more exciting way made in His image.

How does a dancer identify with Christ? We have to know who Christ is to know who we are. We have to be able to minister in dance from a place of knowledge of the Word that Christ shines through us. His chosen vessels are the exhibits of who Christ is.

Knowledge of Christ gives you that boldness and assurance to step out and minister in dance even though you may be moving up in age, aware of negative comments others may make. It is that confidence I carried as I continued my dance journey. Knowing what God says about me encourages me to press on despite setbacks. When you know who you are and who you are connected to, no lasting fear will stop you from stepping out into ministry, regardless of age.

We must step back and allow the Holy Spirit to have complete control over our lives, believe what the Word says about us, and walk in obedience so that we can say, "Yes, Lord. Here I am. Use me."

Prayer

Heavenly Father, we thank You for choosing us to be Your representatives on this earth. May we be reminded that though You are not with us physically, You have sent the Holy Spirit to be with us and in us, working through us to achieve Your purposes, in Jesus' name, Amen.

Call To Action

Know who you are in Christ so that you can be effective in ministry.

Gurlain Applewhaite

January 6

IDENTITY IS WHO WE ARE

Before I formed you in the womb, I knew you, before you were born, I set you apart; I appointed you as a prophet to the nations. Jeremiah 1:5

We are all ministers in one way or the other. Once we serve people in any form, we are called ministers of the gospel. This scripture reminds us that He formed us from the womb and appointed us as prophets to the nations. We are all unique. No one on the face of this earth has the same fingerprints. Each one of us has a task to perform and a mission to fulfill. We must know that God deposited something inside of each of us to enable us to minister to others.

The word "minister" may sound deep, but if we always have the attitude to serve others, that is ministry right there. In our everyday lives, we should minister to everyone we encounter. Something as small as sharing a smile to something as big as "preaching the word" – all of this is ministry. There is no small or big ministry. As Christians, there is something that God has called each of us to do.

Prayer

Father God, please help us to walk always in Your purpose. Please do not let Your anointing ever leave us as we go about our daily routines. Let our lives reflect You in everything we do. Forgive us for not serving others and not reflecting Your qualities at times, in Jesus' Name. Amen.

Call To Action

Let us pause and ask ourselves some questions: Who am I? Am I representing Christ in my daily life? Can people see Jesus living in me? His identity should be shining bright in us. It is not easy because none of us is perfect, but God will help us once we surrender to Him.

Julie Greene

January 7

TAKE THE LIMITS OFF

Before I formed you in the womb I knew you, before you were born, I set you apart; I appointed you as a prophet to the nations. Jeremiah 1:5

Imagine that God had a purpose for you from your mother's womb. God is the one who formed you. He even knew you before you knew yourself. There is only one you; there is no carbon copy. Having understood this about yourself, you must know that there is nothing that God has equipped you for that you cannot do.

Everyone is called to minister in one form or the other. The Word of God shows us, in Ephesians 4:11-12, the five ministry gifts in the church known as the five-fold ministry – apostles, prophets, evangelists, shepherds, and teachers. These gifts are for the building up of the body of Christ. To some of us, this may sound like a massive task but let's not forget that He formed us for this, regardless of whatever ministry we are in or are going to do.

We must not limit ourselves by thinking we cannot or we are not good enough. If those thoughts come, rebuke them in the name of Jesus. The closer we get to Jesus and develop an intimate relationship with Him, the greater His identity will be seen within us. This way, we can minister even more effectively as others will see Jesus in our ministry.

Prayer

Father, thank You for choosing me to declare Your Word in the ways You called me to. I open my entire life to be fully used by You. Guide me, Lord, and help me, in Jesus' Name. Amen.

Call To Action

I challenge you to remove every limit you put on yourself from this day forward. Say to yourself and declare aloud, I *(say your name)* can do anything that God has called me to do, in the name of Jesus. Remember that He formed and created you for a purpose, and you should be open to Him fully to be used in any way He chooses.

Julie Greene

January 8

ON AND OFF STAGE

This, then, is how you ought to regard us: as servants of Christ and as those entrusted with the mysteries God has revealed. Now it is required that those who have been given a trust must prove faithful. 1 Corinthians 4:1-2

As a dance minister, my life must match my ministry. As I started ministering to God, it soon became clear that God gave me a special responsibility. People expected that the person who danced to the song that brought healing to their mind and whom God spoke to them through was an anointed person, carrying something special. Onlookers were convinced that it was not just a stage performance but God's grace over my life. It wasn't about me; it was God using me.

It is evident in this verse that God expects faithfulness in the lives of those given this type of responsibility. When I left the stage, and people interacted with me, they expected the same. They expected that my life and my ministry would line up. I knew God was just using me as a vessel for what He wanted to achieve in their lives. I knew that what they saw that was special in me was also in them. But it was clear that if God was going to use me in dance ministry, my responsibility to be the light and the salt was not just for the stage; it had to be present in my day-to-day life.

Prayer

God, You are my identity. Let my lifeline up with Yours, Lord. Draw me closer every day, oh God, to the perfection that can only be found in You. God, I desire to hear You say, "Well done." Fill me to overflow, in Jesus' name, Amen.

Call To Action

Ask God to reveal anything in you that does not give Him glory so that you can be a vessel of honor for the work He wants to do in the lives of His people, both on and off stage.

Laina Jacob

January 9

DID YOU GET A CALL?

Therefore, go and make disciples of all nations, baptizing them in the name of the Father and of the Son and of the Holy Spirit. Matthew 28:19

So many people talk about struggling to find their purpose, but the thing is, God made it so clear for us. As believers, we are to go out and make more disciples. As dance ministers, we have received that same call, and it's just that we do it through the medium of dance. We have gotten the call just like Samuel did in 1 Samuel 3, and we have decided to be obedient. So, what is stopping you now from doing the work?

Get out there, create movement, create choreography, and use social media to bless people through the gift God has given you. Additionally, where you feel you can improve, do the work. Your gift will make room for you, so use it. Do not think your gift is small. Don't compare, don't procrastinate, and don't wait for "the sign". Your gift is not meant for the four walls of the church. There are people outside of the church who need to know and understand that there is hope. What good is a dancer who does not want to dance? What good is a gift if it is never given? If you have heard the call, it is time to answer.

Prayer

God, I declare that the boldness of Peter will be upon Your dance ministers. I declare that they shall move as thus saith the Lord. I come against the accuser of the saint that would whisper in their ears and cause them not to be obedient to the call You have placed on their lives. I even come against delayed obedience. I declare that every gift will be activated to build Your Kingdom and glorify Your name. We will answer the call in Jesus' Name, Amen and Amen.

Call To Action

What is it that God has been speaking to you about doing in your dance ministry? What is it that you have found reasons to put off? It's time to get up, step out, and do it.

Laina Jacob

January 10

YOU ARE NOT LIKE WHAT?

But you are not like that, for you are a chosen people. You are royal priests, a holy nation, God's very own possession. As a result, you can show others the goodness of God, for he called you out of the darkness into his wonderful light. 1 Peter 2:9

Prior to this verse, the Word said that people stumble because they disobey the Word of God but not you! God has placed you in a class above. He has set you apart. You are now a VIP, sitting in first class. You are one of the people that the entire program needs to halt for until you arrive. That is the position you occupy in the Kingdom of God.

He has specially called you out. Yes, you! It was not by accident; you didn't happen to be in the ministry contributing what you are contributing. It was all God's design. When people are elevated on this earth, they change their behavior, walk differently, dress differently, speak differently, and interact with different kinds of people. You have been elevated by the King of Kings and the Lord of Lords.

Prayer

God, You have called me, You have accepted me, You have elevated me to Your Kingdom. Please help me not to walk the way I did before but to walk in a way that represents You always. Lord, when I fall, help me to get up and go again, knowing You love me, and You alone can strengthen me for this race. I honor and bless Your matchless name, in Jesus' name, Amen.

Call To Action

What is making you stumble? What is causing you not to act and behave like who God says you are? List the things you do currently that run contrary to who God says you are and burn them in the natural as you pray that they are burnt out of your life in the spiritual. Declare that you will be the opposite of whatever that list of things is for the glory of God.

Laina Jacob

January 11

ANSWER THE CALL

So Elijah went from there and found Elisha the Son of Shaphat, who was plowing with twelve yoke of oxen before him, and he with the twelfth: and Elijah passed by him, and cast his mantle upon him. 1 Kings 19:19-21

There are times when you must make sacrifices: practicing for long hours, repeating a move, exercising to keep fit and healthy, dancing although your feet hurt, and enduring even though you feel like giving up. Despite it all, you are called and that call requires sacrifice.

The Bible says that Elijah left the oxen and went after Elisha. I couldn't help but notice that Elisha was already working hard in the field. This tells me that when God is looking for someone, He checks you out in detail; He particularly looks at your heart. Even in 1 Sam 16:7, when God was looking for a king, He chose David because of his heart towards God. When we are called to ministry, it's a call to follow. It's a call to forsake all. It's a call of sacrifice.

Prayer

Dear Lord, help me to answer the call and to be diligent and committed to following through with the purpose and plans You called me to do. Please remind me that I should always surrender to Your perfect will in my life.

Call To Action

Search your heart and find three things you need to work on to help you become more committed to dance ministry.

Maxine Butcher

January 12

WHO AM I?

For Thou hast possessed my reins: Thou hast covered me in my mother's womb.
Psalm 139:13

Before I formed you in the womb I knew you, before you were born I set you apart;
I appointed you as a prophet to the nations. Jeremiah 1:5

There were times I wanted to dance just like ________, she made it look so effortless, and the choreography simply flowed. Her feet moved so gracefully upon the floor that I was mesmerized and enthralled by how she drifted across the stage. Watching her movements, I felt the urge to be her, wishing I could dance like that. Have you ever related to this feeling of wanting to be someone you're not?

I often had to remind myself that we all have different gifts, strengths, and traits. We all have characteristics or qualities that we may have inherited from our parents: their eyes, their smiles, and aspects of their personalities. We are all someone's son or daughter. We all have unique fingerprints that set us apart; isn't that amazing?

But the question remains: who am I? Am I just someone's son or daughter? I am more than that! I was in the mind of God even before the earth was made. I am one of God's creations. He has a plan for my life. Part of that plan is to dance for His honor and glory. I am a remarkable person; God says so.

Prayer

Lord, I declare that my identity is found in You. I was created for Your honor and glory; I am who You say I am, not who men say I am.

Call To Action

Learn Psalm 139:13 and Jeremiah 1:5 and speak it loudly over yourself.

Maxine Butcher

January 13

LINKED UP

You did not choose me, but I chose you and appointed you so that you might go and bear fruit, fruit that will last, and so that whatever you ask in my name the Father will give you. John 15:16

I love this scripture. Why? Because it tells me that despite how I feel about myself or how many mistakes I make, the all-knowing God still chose me; not only that, but He appointed me. When I first started dancing at church, it was a little intimidating doing so in front of the congregation. Not technically strong and still unsure of myself, I grew in my relationship with Christ and started understanding how He viewed me. Over time, my mind and heart began to be renewed in Him.

The intent was to dance the way God wanted me to. Seeing the triune that blesses and transforms made it essential that people be ministered to. It was required of me to bear fruit that would last. I became mindful that ministry and identity are linked, so I had to take my eyes off myself and set them on what my Father says about me. My identity was and is in Him.

There is good and bad fruit; trust me, what is in the heart shows up in our words and actions. We can't be out there doing as we please and expect that God will bless our ministry or the things we do. Things may go well for a while because the Lord is gracious and merciful, but there will come a point where a cut-off happens, and ministry will suffer. Remember, when faced with situations, your decisions will bear fruit, affecting how you see yourself and how others see you and your ministry.

Prayer

Father, help me to understand my identity in You so that I can appreciate the ministry that is required of me. I want a better relationship with You, and I am available for your glory. Amen.

Call To Action

I will commit to striving daily to please God in my words, thoughts, and actions because I understand this not only affects my ministry but how others view Him.

Orissa Fitzpatrick

January 14

IDENTITY CRISIS?

So God created mankind in his own image, in the image of God he created, male and female he created them. Genesis 1:27

When I think of what goes into creating something, my mind goes to these questions:

1.   What brought on this thought?

2.   What emotion or emotions were involved?

3.   What is the function?

4.   How should it look?

God knew all these answers, but what stands out more is that He wanted us. Can you imagine that? The all-knowing, all-powerful God wanted me. Now, we get all excited when someone we hold in high regard shows an interest in us, and it makes us feel so special that we believe we can do or accomplish anything. How much more value should we put on our Creator doing such? I've often heard, "I wish I could dance like her," or "This person is better at this than me." Envy and sometimes jealousy step in. Is it natural? Of course. Do we keep and operate in it? No. In those times, we have to remind ourselves of these truths:

*   Emotions that speak to the opposite of the Christ-likeness in us are lies from the enemy.

*   Be honest with yourself about how you feel and acknowledge it for what it is. You are not in competition.

*   Remind yourself of your strengths. There is so much more in us than we realize. Bring to memory what the Lord says about you.

The devil wants to keep us in an identity crisis because it prevents us from doing the work and the will of the Lord. The reality is that, too often, we allow it to happen. Get back what is rightfully yours and minister the life back into people and situations. What did God do? He created you in His image.

Prayer

Father, I thank You for creating me in Your image, for thinking of me even at the beginning of time. You are my true identity, not what the world says, not what I say, but what You say. Strengthen me daily to carry out Your will. I am grateful that I am not in an identity crisis. Amen.

Call To Action

Say, sing and believe these next few sentences whole-heartedly: "I will be what You called me to be. I say yes, Lord, I agree. My desire, passionately, is to be what you called me to be, and that's what I will be."

Orissa Fitzpatrick

January 15

ID CARD

<table>
<tr><td>

Ministry: Servant of Christ (Matthew 23:11)

Name: Written in The Book of Life (Revelation 3:5)

Address: (Temporary) Earth (Romans 8:18)

(Permanent) Heaven Bound (John 14:2-3)

D.O.B: Born again (1 Peter 1:23)

First Issue: Good Friday (Luke 23:43)

Place Issued: Calvary (Luke 23:33)

Expires: Eternity (John 3:16 & 4:13-14)

</td></tr>
</table>

Our Identity in Christ validates our Ministry in Christ. It allows us to operate and function on His behalf here on earth. We must never forget that our directives come from Him, and we are identified through Christ.

Ministry is what we do for Christ as we serve each other: "Let the Word of Christ dwell in you richly in all wisdom; teaching and admonishing one another in psalms and hymns and spiritual songs, singing with grace in your hearts to the Lord. And whatsoever ye do in word or deed, do all in the name of the Lord Jesus, giving thanks to God and the Father by him" (Colossians 3:16-17). We must never lose our identity in Christ fulfilling our ministry, but we must find our ministry through our identity in Christ. Let's not get it twisted.

Prayer

Lord, help me to remember that my identity is in You and that my ministry doesn't define me. It's simply what I do to serve others and You.

Call To Action

- Make a list of what you do (ministry) compared to what defines you (identity).

- ID>Ministry or Ministry>ID - Are they in the correct order?

Pierre Rock

January 16

WHO DEFINES ME?

See what great love the Father has lavished on us, that we should be called children of God! And that is what we are! The reason the world does not know us is that it did not know him. 1 John 3:1

The Word of God says that we are children of God, which means we are children of a King. The Word defines us, not man. We are who God says we are. He gives us our identity. We are a chosen generation, a royal priesthood created in His image. We are His workmanship, a new creation, fearfully and wonderfully made.

Often, we can become so caught up with what other people are saying about us that we lose sight of what God says about us. As dance ministers, you may have been told that you are not technical enough, don't catch on fast enough, and are not the strongest dancer. Have you let those words consume you more than God's Word? Shift your focus. Who will you let define you? Rewrite your definition today. Don't take your definition from www.whatpeoplesay.com. Instead, use the one that matters, www.whatGodsays.com._The latter one is the truth.

Prayer

Lord, remove the stain of every negative word spoken over me by others and wipe it clean with Your words. Show me clearly what my identity is in You, and let me walk and live in that identity. Let that identity come out in my ministry as I speak forth Your Word to others and show them who they are in You. Thank You, Lord, for every good thing You have blessed me with as a person and every good word You have spoken into my life, in Jesus' Name.

Call To Action

- Write as many scriptures as you can find about who God says you are.

- Write out daily affirmations to speak over yourself to remind you of who you are in Christ.

Rheanne Rock

January 17

HIS HANDIWORK

For we are God's handiwork, created in Christ Jesus to do good works which God prepared in advance for us to do. Ephesians 2:10

We are God's handiwork, which means that we are all created with a special design to work for God. We all have a task, which God will show us how to do once we ask. He is right there, waiting to answer and guide us.

Whenever I minister in dance, I feel like I am doing something dynamic for God. The feelings I get when I am ministering are ones that I cannot even explain. My hope and prayer are for other children to be inspired and get saved each time I minister. Ministry must bring about change in one way or the other. I desire that my identity always shows God's greatness not only in dance but in every area of my life. His greatness is so big and wide to me: He is, Healer (like how He healed my Mummy), Provider (like how He fed us when only my Daddy was working as my Mummy was sick), Saviour (like how I got saved at five years old), Listener (like how He always listens to my prayers), Comforter (like when I am afraid, I know He is there) and He sets people free.

Prayer

Lord, please help us as ministers to worship and praise You with our entire being. May Your identity always be seen in every aspect of our lives.

Call To Action

As the scripture mentions, God has created all of us to do something in His Kingdom. I encourage you to ask God to show you what He wants you to do. God has prepared you for it. We are all ministers of God; we were created to show other people the goodness of God.

Rhema-Jae Greene

January 18

THE EFFECTIVENESS OF MINISTRY AND IDENTITY

But ye are a chosen generation, a royal priesthood, a holy nation, a peculiar people; that ye should shew forth the praises of him who hath called you out of darkness into his marvelous light. 1 Peter 2:9

Sometimes, when we are called to dance, there is uncertainty about what that means. However, when we are chosen to represent God as ministers, we begin to understand that dance is not just about putting on nice garments but more about the power and presence of God moving through us. Ministering reveals our identity and draws people to the Kingdom of God. As the Holy Spirit gives us every opportunity to minister, know that we are the handiwork of God, created in Christ Jesus. Let us also remember that this call to dance is a spiritual one to bring people out of darkness into the light.

We must always be ready to give God excellence. Sometimes, we can fall short by letting people decide our identity, but that is a lie from the devil. Galatians 2:20 says, "I am crucified with Christ and it is not you who no longer live but Christ who lives in you". Since your life is not your own anymore, people should now witness who you have become and not who you looked like before. You are a new person.

Today, as you read this devotion, remember your life is a ministry within your identity in Christ Jesus. Through your ministry, strongholds can be broken, and healing can take place. Don't believe any lie the devil tells you because God has a purpose for you to fulfill through your identity. Ministry becomes part of who you are and not just what you do.

Prayer

God, thank You for choosing me and using me for ministry. May my life be a representation of my true identity in You. Amen.

Call To Action

- Ask God to help you know if you're called to dance.

- Let Christ be seen in your life.

- Always be ready to give your best.

Timeless Ministers

Call To Action

- Ask God to help you know if you're called to dance.

- Let Christ be seen in your life.

- Always be ready to give your best.

January 19

MINISTRY IS WHERE YOUR HEART IS

For where your heart is, there will your treasure be also. Matthew 6:21

Many different people define ministry in many ways, and it simply means where your heart is. You know that your ministry is a part of you when it becomes meaningful. It becomes an integral part of your life, and you are more committed and disciplined, making your love and passion for it rise to a different level. It suddenly becomes your baby, and what happens to it as you become more involved affects you more deeply than before. You also begin to place your most valuable treasures within it, such as your time, sacrifice, thoughts, prayers, love, and care. You serve it with joy, creating a change in your lifestyle and part of who you are as a dancer hidden in Christ. You are fearfully and wonderfully made and a true worshipper.

See your ministry as a part of who you are and who you will become. It will push you to grow spiritually and help you become a better you. It gives you a different mindset which causes you to take stock of how you operate as a believer of Jesus Christ. Your words begin to change, your thoughts begin to align with the mind of Christ, and your body and spirit now have new meaning and authority. You begin to see the true you that God has created you to be, and you find purpose. God has given us the gift of ministry, knowing that He has set us apart with the seal of the Holy Spirit to do the work for His Kingdom, according to Ephesians 1:13. So, being one with your ministry helps you discover the hidden treasure of your identity. Find your ministry, and there you can discover your identity.

Prayer

Lord, help me to intertwine with my ministry and let it become part of who I am and who You want me to be. Continue to reveal things to me as I discover my true identity. Help me to serve my ministry with joy and worship You in spirit and in truth, in Jesus' name. Amen.

Call To Action

- Become part of a ministry if you are not.

- Trust the leading of the Holy Spirit.

- Place a focus on your most treasurable qualities to discover your identity.

- Spend time with God.

Rhonda .A. Babb

Call To Action

- Become part of a ministry if you are not.

- Trust the leading of the Holy Spirit.

January 20

DO YOU KNOW?

Who hath saved us, and called us with a holy calling, not according to our works, but according to his own purpose and grace, which was given to us in Christ Jesus before the world began. 2 Timothy 1:9

Whether you believe it or not, something is missing from your life! Think about it; one day rolls into the next, and you have this void, a feeling of emptiness. You ask yourself, is this all there is to life? No, because you can feel something stirring inside you even though you can't quite put your finger on what it is. It is a longing for more that burns inside you, like a voice calling to another. But whose voice is it that's calling? It sounds vaguely familiar. Can it be the voice of the One who created me? The One who knew me even before I was formed? No, it can't be. Am I in denial? Yes, but the time has come for me to surrender. Hands up, I give in. Yes! Your call is the missing piece for me to become whole. My ways, my thoughts, my everything is Yours. My first ministry is to You. Knowing the pain and suffering You endured for me, I will answer the call.

Now what? Week after week, Sunday after Sunday, we meet to commune with each other so that I can get to know You. Well, You already know who I am. I worship, pray, and give, yet You say that You require more of me. Wait, what? Accepting You is not the only thing I am required to do? Can't I just stay here and talk with You? This feels hard. I am contented just doing "me" with no commitments that bog me down and tire me out. I love the way things are. I have the joy down in my heart; that's part of how I identify with You.

I want to be obedient, to show You how much You mean to me and to express my love for You in whatever You have for me to do. So, like Samuel, here I am. I give myself away for You to use me. Empty I came, and empty I will return, for I so want to please You. I want to be Your fisher of men, to complete every task to the best of my ability. Your accolade of "Well done, my good and faithful servant" is my heart's desire.

Prayer

All praise to the King of Kings. Thank You for dwelling in us and empowering us in Your love, in Jesus' name, Amen.

Call To Action

Know who you are and whose you are.

Sandra Britton

Call To Action

Know who you are and whose you are.

January 21

EXPRESS YOURSELF!

His master replied, 'Well done, good and faithful servant! You have been faithful with a few things; I will put you in charge of many things. Come and share your master's happiness!' Matthew 25:21

Chin up, head high; your catwalk awaits. The path is laid out before you, illuminated and pre-ordained, for you to begin expressing yourself. Our walk and purpose are the essence of who we were created to be. Our calling is right there before us, sometimes hidden by the blinding spotlight of humanistic accolades. If only we would seek after His Kingdom, thirst after His righteousness, and find our purpose. Seek, and ye will find, for He is waiting for you to be used by Him for His glory and honor. For all that we can be is hidden in Him.

Your ministry is your way of expressing yourself. So, begin to release and pour out all that is in you. He will fill you up again and again, just as He did with dedicated Dorcas, who was full of good works and almsdeeds. He did not see her gift of helping as any lesser in value than that of Peter's. She was mourned by those who saw her and were blessed by the things that her heart and hands could do. She was humble as she went about her business, pouring out what was placed in her. But she still had more, and her death spoke volumes; it screamed no, there is more. Her faithful friends mourned the woman whose cup wasn't empty; it was just turned down for a moment. So, whether your ministry is dance, song, action or just being a suitable help, identify with your "calling". Walk in it, strut your stuff, and express yourself.

Focus, perseverance, love, and laughter create everlasting memories that bring those around us closer to our goal of pleasing the one who gives us a crown. When our day is done and our time is spent, "Well done, my good and faithful servant" echoes through the streets of gold. And when the roll is called, and you are there, know, without a doubt, you have expressed yourself!

Prayer

Dear Lord, thank You for the unique gifts and talents you've bestowed upon us. Grant us the courage to express ourselves fully in service to Your Kingdom.

Call To Action

Embrace your calling with confidence, knowing that every act of kindness, every dance, every song, and every helping hand is a unique expression of God's love through you.

Sandra Britton

January 22

INTO HIS PRESENCE WITH THANKSGIVING

Let them praise His name with the dance; Let them sing praises to Him with the timbrel and harp, For the Lord takes pleasure in His people; He will beautify the humble with salvation. Psalm. 149: 3-4

When those who love God have accepted Christ and are grateful for what He has done for us, we can use our bodies by dancing to express how we feel without saying anything. It does not matter how we dance. What matters is that we show that we are pleased with God as He expects us to pour out our praise unto Him. God shows us that He is pleased with our praise.

In Jeremiah 31:4, God says, "I will build you up again, and you, Virgin Israel, will be rebuilt. Again, you will take up your timbrels and go out to dance." When I am feeling sad, angry, or afraid, my movements and the music I use may change, but God rebuilds me. When He does, He wants me to get up and praise Him. God will always build us up as we dance to minister to Him. No matter how we choose to praise God, He will always appreciate what we give, especially when we put everything we can into it.

Prayer

Dear God, receive my prayer of worship. I pray that my limbs will always be strong and able to worship You through dance. I pray that Your Spirit will continue to guide me and keep me on the path of a dancer and that I shall grow stronger in this ministry. Heavenly Father, I pray that when I worship, I can pour out my heart and soul unto You, in Jesus' name, Amen.

Call To Action

No matter your age, praise God.

Shiloh Springer

January 23

MINISTRY BECOMES WHO WE ARE

I am crucified with Christ: nevertheless I live; yet not I, but Christ lives in me: and the life which I now live in the flesh I live by the faith of the Son of God, who loved me, and gave himself for me. Galatians 2:20

What is ministry? Doesn't this question sometimes make you go "hmm"? When you internalize the word ministry, I agree that its weight can be a lot to digest. So, look at it as an inward meaning expressed through your outer body and your life – this is authentic living.

Ministry becomes the avenue through which we express ourselves. It comes through being in the secret place with our heavenly Father. Ministry can also be seen as an expression: a dove returning with an olive branch, letting us know it's a new beginning. When God's grace is sufficient, we can handle anything, no matter the season, because of our boldness and faith. Even when our hearts connect to God's heart, our dance becomes sweeter as the love of Jesus continues to cleanse and purify us for ministry assignments.

Through ministry, we can give God all the praises due to him. As our bags and cups overflow with testimonies, our lives become an accurate representation of what ministry looks like. Ministry, then, becomes who you are through salvation. As Galatians 2:20 says, "It is no longer I who live, but Christ lives in me being changed through faith in Jesus Christ."

Prayer

Lord, as my expression of ministry is seen through my life, I pray that it will be contagious and lives will be changed and ministered to, in Jesus' name. Amen.

Call To Action

- See yourself as an expression of ministry.

- Always be connected to the source.

- Become authentic ministers.

Timeless Ministers

January 24

MY IDENTITY IN CHRIST

I have been crucified with Christ. It is no longer I who live, but Christ who lives in me. And the life I now live in the flesh I live by faith in the Son of God, who loved me and gave himself for me. Galatians 2:20

About three to four years ago, I had a friend who told me that he did not believe in God. I was shocked, as I had never encountered anyone before who said they did not believe. I could not understand it and felt so sorry for him, so I said a quiet prayer in my heart for him.

God's love for us is everlasting, and I am grateful to know him as my Lord and Saviour. Knowing who I am in Christ has always been very important to me. God has created us in His image, and He knew us before we were formed in the womb. He expects us to worship Him.

He loves us very much; without Him, we would not experience life or love. God continuously provides us with the things we need, so we should be thankful. God has given us food, shelter, and a loving family. He also gave us talents that we should use to bring honor to Him. I am happy that I can share my faith in Christ through my dance.

Prayer

Dear God, I thank You for being a part of my life. I pray for all the children who are unsure of their identity in You and that they will accept You in their lives, in Jesus's name, Amen.

Call To Action

Share your faith with everyone you come into contact with today.

Trinitee Angus

January 25

STEPPING IN

And he gave some, apostles; and some, prophets; and some evangelists; and some, pastors and teachers; for the perfecting of the saints, for the work of the ministry, for edifying of the body of Christ: till we all come in the unity of the faith, and of the knowledge of the Son of God, unto a perfect man, unto the measure of the stature of the fullness of Christ. Ephesians 4:11-13

As children of God, we are called to minister in different ways so that the gospel can be proclaimed, the Kingdom can be built, and God can be glorified. Ministry has to come from the heart. Being a dancer for the Kingdom, I learned that when I minister, it is to bless people in such an impactful way that they want to follow Jesus. Ministry is a huge responsibility. Think about it as an important job interview, where you have to prove why you want the job and that you will do what it takes to keep it. Ministry is just as important to me. It means giving my all when I am on that altar to dance and win souls for the Kingdom of God.

Ministry starts by first knowing who you are and whose you are. God molded us in His likeness so that we may do His work. Do you know how special you are in God's eyes, that He called you from amongst the flock to do His good works? You are His special possession, treasured, irreplaceable, loved beyond compare, forgiven, set apart. It's time to step into your ministry and your new identity.

Prayer

Dear Heavenly Father, I ask that You help those struggling to discover who they are and where they belong. I pray that they will search for their true identity and find their calling within ministries. Oh God, my prayer for them today is that they search deep down. I ask that You remove anything hindering them from knowing their true identity or blocking them from their calling. Amen and Amen.

Call To Action

I challenge you to step into your purpose today. Step into your chosen identity.

Zariah Watson

January 26

AS YOUR FOOT GRAZES THE STAGE
(POEM)

And David danced before the Lord with all his might, wearing a priestly garment.
2 Samuel 6:14

That feeling

That release

That unbelievable power that washes over you

That feeling that God himself is dancing with you, moving your arms and limbs to the beat and words of the song.

The faces you see when the lights shine upon you

The reactions that you bring out

The souls you touch

The hearts you warm

The ministry you bring forth

That's all it takes

That's all it takes to make you completely fall in love with your ministry

and yet, with all of that

There is still so much more to uncover...

Zenaida R. Mayers

January 27

DO YOU SEE ME OR DO YOU SEE HIM?
(POEM)

For by the grace given to me I say to everyone among you not to think of himself more highly than he ought to think, but to think with sober judgment, each according to the measure of faith that God has assigned. Romans 12:3

When I take my stance

When I form my limbs into that first movement

When I first make eye contact with you

What do you see?

Do you see a beautiful dancer

Do you see the technique

Do you see a breathtaking garment

or

Do you see a woman of God?

Do you see a strong connection with Him?

Can you see Him?

Can you really see Him when I touch that stage to minister that song, that sweet, impactful song that should bring you to your knees?

That should fill you with overwhelming emotions that are so strong that you allow yourself to be ministered to?

or

Do you see a facade?

Can you tell when I come to deliver His message that I'm resisting

That I'm battling with myself internally on that stage

Can you see?

Zenaida R. Mayers

January 28

BRIDGING THE GAP

Because of the privilege and authority God has given me, I give each of you this warning: Don't think you are better than you really are. Be honest in your evaluation of yourselves, measuring yourselves by the faith God has given us. Romans 12:3

We can all agree that since we were able to think and reason for ourselves, we have asked ourselves three basic questions at various stages. At each stage, the answer was the same. Think about how many times you've asked these questions, and you'll understand what I mean:

1. Who am I?

2. Where do I belong?

3. What am I supposed to do?

We sometimes struggle with who we are in our personal lives and who we know we are called to be in ministry, not realizing that the two are inextricably linked. When God created you in your mother's womb, He knew the path He wanted you to take, who you would be and what you would become, and what area of ministry you would flow in.

According to Romans 12:3, we are not to think we are better than we are, but rather to compare ourselves to the faith that God has given us. When considering our lives and ministries, we should consider what God expects of us. We will all be at different levels, but in the end, it all comes back to God. When we evaluate ourselves according to God's standards rather than man's, we will notice that the line between ministry and identity is rather thin. Our ministry reflects our identity as dance ministers. When ministering, it is clear how much time we have spent in God's presence learning about Him.

Our personal and Christian lives are identical. I don't have a separate life for my identity and another for my ministry; there is only one me, just like there is only one you, and we must strive to be transparent in all areas. Is everything always easy? No. Will we make mistakes? Of course, and that's okay as long as we keep putting God first.

Prayer

God, thank You for working on my identity in You. As I continue to develop, it will overflow into my ministry, and people will see You flowing in me always in the name of Jesus. Amen.

Call To Action

Make an effort to keep a real relationship with God. Be honest with yourself. Your life is being planned by God. You are valuable. So stand up, take stock of your life, and get to work.

Orissa Fitzpatrick

January 29

THE JOURNEY

For this reason I remind you to fan into flame the gift of God, which is in you through the laying on of my hands. For the Spirit God gave us does not make us timid, but gives us power, love and self-discipline. So do not be ashamed of the testimony about our Lord or of me his prisoner. Rather, join with me in suffering for the gospel, by the power of God. 2 Timothy 1:6-8 - Ministry

Therefore if anyone is in Christ, he is a new creation. The old has passed away. Behold, the new has come! 2 Corinthians 5:17 - Identity

What is identity? Identity is the fact of being who or what a person or thing is. This means that you know who you are, and no one has to tell you. When we find our identity in Christ, it is exactly who He has set out for us to be, and nothing or no one can change that. There is strength in knowing your identity in Christ because then the devil can not use that against you, but you can use it against him. How do we learn the truth about who we are? To know who we are, we must change the way we think about ourselves and the things we say to ourselves.

What is ministry? Ministry is the work or vocation of a minister of a religion. This is the role ministers in the church have to perform as their act of service or, as we say, their calling to give God praise and bring people to His kingdom, such as roles of dancers, singers, intercessors, and so on. As dancers, this applies to us as we carry such a high mandate in our church for Christ. We take our ministry very seriously because we know who we are in Christ. Every move we make, and every song we dance to speaks to someone's circumstance and situation, and as we move, we break those strongholds, we break those yolks and set people free.

The journey of finding myself is still an ongoing one, but God continues to show me everyday bits and pieces of where I am going and where I am supposed to be. This causes my ministry to grow drastically, whether it be by seeing new moves, a new song or seeing new visions for my ministry, I know that this is the path that I am supposed to be taking.

Prayer

Dear Heavenly Father, continue to show us every day who You want us to be, may we not go looking to find ourselves in the wrong places, may we not go looking for validation from worldly things that are to be defined by men, but may we cling to You and dig deep into Your work. May we walk with You so we may know who and whose we are. In Jesus' name, Amen.

Call To Action

- Read inspirational scriptures every day.

- Speak life into every situation and react Godly.

- Prophesy over your life that you know who you are.

- Pray and ask the Lord to cover your ministry.

Jaida Roberts

January 30

SELF-REALIZATION - WHO WE ARE IN CHRIST

We are God's handiwork, created in Christ Jesus to do good works, which God prepared in advance for us to do. Ephesians 2:10

A tragic event in life can provoke deep introspection. Why me? Do I even matter in this world? What is my purpose in life? Who am I, really? Most people find it extremely difficult to answer these questions, which can be overwhelming. All too often, we base our identity on external forces instead of realizing who we are in Christ. We define who we are through our achievements, titles, physical appearance, interests, beliefs, or relationships. It can be risky, though, to define who we are by these attributes because life is filled with unpredictable, uncontrollable events. Tragedies happen, and they can shatter our sense of self if we do not realize who we are in Christ.

Understanding who we are in Christ can help us develop a growth mindset, where we see challenges as opportunities to deepen our connection with God. According to Ephesians 2:10, when God created us, He did so with precise plans for our lives. He brought us into this world with a purpose: to know Him, to glorify Him, and to engage in good works. This means as ministers in Christ, it is our duty to dance, walk, and live in a way that honors the One whose creation we are.

Indeed, trials will inevitably arise in life! However, we do not have to redefine who we are in light of difficult situations. We are chosen, we are forgiven, we are redeemed, and we are loved. We, therefore, stay connected to the source and let the Christ within us reflect who we are.

Prayer

Heavenly Father, I give You all the praise, honor, and glory. I give thanks for Your love, which remains unwavering. You are good in moments of joy and times of trial and tribulation. You have never failed me. You have called me according to my purpose. Fill me with discernment and true faith to accomplish all You desire of me. In the mighty name of Jesus, Amen.

Call To Action

Our identity should reflect the image of God, who created us. Practice these actions:

I - Immerse yourself in the scripture

D - Discover your God-given purpose

E - Engage in worship

N - Normalize praying

T - Testify to the goodness of God

I - Ignite your faith

T - Trust God's plan for your life

Y - Yield to Yah

Akia Brathwaite

January 31

WHO ARE YOU IN CHRIST?

In Christ Jesus you are all sons of God through faith. Galatians 3:26

God made us in His own image! Whether short or tall, big or small, red or yellow, black or white, we are made in God's image. Genesis 1:27 says God created man in His own image, so do not let anyone make you feel less than you are. God is King, and He is our Father, so we are all royalty.

We are God's handiwork. In Genesis 1:26, God said, "Let us make man in our own image, according to our likeness." Never allow anyone to diminish your worth, for in God's eyes, there is no superiority based on appearance. We are all sons and daughters of God, for he has given us hands and feet, so we should use them to worship him. Even if circumstances limit your abilities, like dancing, find comfort in knowing that you are still a child of God.

Prayer

Lord, help me to know that no matter what, I am a child of God. In Jesus' name, I pray, amen.

Call To Action

When you wake up in the morning, repeat this affirmation, "I am a king/queen, created in God's image, I am fearfully and wonderfully made."

Shaquonna Rock

February 1

LOVE COVERS

Hatred stirs up conflict, but love covers over all wrongs. Proverbs 10:12

Love is a key principle of biblical ethics. The general idea here is often repeated in the Old Testament (Leviticus 19:18; Proverbs 15:1). It is also cited in the New Testament (James 5:20; 1 Peter 4:8). In short, what we learn is that revenge-seeking never comes to a good end; it only multiplies anger and escalates a cycle of retaliation. Choosing to respond in love, instead, is far more powerful.

When people despise each other, they try to hurt one another. They argue and tear each other apart. This tragedy can even occur within a group of believers. Hatred divides and disrupts fellowship. It destroys a congregation's testimony and causes unbelievers to discredit Christianity. Hatred serves the Devil. Love, on the other hand, covers faults and sins. It is important to note that this verse does not refer to ignoring sin or "covering it up"; instead, it is about how love keeps trying to find common ground and ways to work together. It waits patiently for an offender to see the error of his way and repent. It is willing to forgive in so far as this is possible and reasonable. Love leads us to pursue unity (John 17:21).

Prayer

Dear Heavenly Father, thank You for the gift of love. I pray that we may love as You love and not forget that love conquers all evil sent to strike us down.

Call To Action

Whenever you find yourself with many reasons to hate and despise someone, remember Jesus' words to forgive.

Danae Niles

February 2

THIS IS LOVE
(POEM)

And may you have the power to understand, as all God's people should, how wide, how long, how high, and how deep his love is. May you experience the love of Christ, though it is too great to understand fully. Then you will be made complete with all the fullness of life and power that comes from God. Ephesians 3:18-19

A love we cannot explain

A love that is clearly seen even in our pain

A love that is deeper than the ocean

And wider than the sky

A love that pierces even the darkest hearts

Even the darkest souls

A love that breaks down the toughest walls that we put up

A love that mends our broken hearts

A love that turns our mourning into dancing

A love that calms all our fears

This never-ending love

His never-ending love.

Prayer

Dear God, thank You for Your precious unwavering love. I pray that those reading this prayer will know the wonderful agape love of God. I pray that we will never forget it, even when we are going through the toughest battles. Help us know that You are always on our side and that your amazing, unconditional love never fails. Even if we stumble or fall, help us remember that Your love is always there and is indeed a never-ending love.

Call To Action

Let us never forget the love of Christ Jesus, our Saviour, who died on the cross for our sins. He is the perfect example of love: giving us comfort when we need it, listening and answering our prayers, providing for us, and protecting us. All of these things and more show us that He truly loves us. We can always ask God to show us how to love Him and others in the correct way.

Danielle Harewood

February 3

THE UNMEASURABLE LOVE OF GOD
(POEM)

Until then, there are three things that remain: faith, hope and love—yet love surpasses them all. So above all else, let love be the beautiful prize for which you run. 1 Corinthians 13:13

This gift of God's love makes me want to sing

Makes me want to raise my voice

Makes me want to dance.

I'll lift my hands

I'll give you thanks

I'll give you praise

This gift of God's love makes me want to shout from the highest rooftop

Makes me want to shout from the highest mountain

Running, telling friends and telling foes

This gift of God's love makes me want to, in turn, love others.

Your unmeasurable love,

Making me lose all sense of fleshly emotions and desires

Filling my soul with all want and desire to please you.

Prayer

Dear God, your love is so powerful and profound. It truly is an unmeasurable love. Thank You that Your perfect love casts out every single fear that we may have. I pray that Your love will give us the confidence we need to face every situation, trial or problem we will have in this life. Thank You for such a love as this, for we know we aren't worthy of it. Yet, You give it to us so freely. Help us,

God, to never forget Your unmeasurable love. In Jesus' Name, we pray. Amen.

Call To Action

Think about the wondrous love of God today. I mean, really think about it. His love knows no bounds. Think about how this supreme, awesome God made the heavens and the earth. He has this agape love for us, giving us everything we need and more and always coming to our rescue. Think about how the King of Kings and the Lord of Lords is actually interested in and deeply cares for us. Think about every little blessing that He provides.

Danielle Harewood

February 4

LOVE CONQUERS ALL

Who shall separate us from the love of Christ? Shall trouble or hardship or persecution or famine, or nakedness or danger or sword? Romans 8:35

Sometimes, we can be plagued with an issue for many years. As an older, less experienced dancer, it was not always easy for me to "catch" the choreography. I often wanted to give up and say that dancing was not for me or that God did not call me to be a dancer. Nevertheless, the love my fellow younger dancers showed me helped me develop more confidence and belief in myself. Sometimes, it was just a hug or an encouraging, "You are going to get it" that helped.

This love made me think of the woman with the blood issue that touched the hem of Jesus' garment. This woman was persecuted, called unclean and endured hardship despite spending all her money seeking help from doctors. Yet she believed that if she could only touch the hem of His garment, Jesus would heal her. I believe that when she touched the Hem of Jesus' garment, the power that left Him was love.

As dance ministers, the love that Jesus has shown us is the kind of love we should have for others. A hug or an encouraging word can go a long way to healing and restoration. Today, may you know that love does conquer all. It can be a physical touch or an encouraging word that can heal, repair, build up and, above all, unify us.

Prayer

Abba Father, I thank You for Your love, the purest we will ever know. May Your love continue to shine through us in our dance as we give You glory, honor and praise. Let nothing we face separate us from Your love. In Jesus' name. Amen.

Call To Action

So, let the love of God flow out of you today and every day, no matter your situation. May your situation never separate you from the love of Christ.

Eslyn Taylor

February 5

WHAT'S LOVE GOT TO DO WITH IT?

Do everything in love. 1 Corinthians 16:14

Love is a word often split easily from our lips. Sometimes, we can fall in and out of love at the drop of a hat, but do we really know what love is? Do we even take the time to see the damage we have done before moving on to another love? You may be wondering what love has to do with dancing, and I can say that it has everything to do with it.

Firstly, you must love what you are doing. I have seen many dancers pass through my dance ministry who loved to dance, some of whom initially could dance and others who could not. What was common among them all was that they loved the Lord. I have found that the ones who have stayed generally love the Lord.

Kirk Franklin has a song called "Love", and he sings that love is a word that comes and goes, but few people really know what it means to love somebody. For our dance to glorify God, we must have a real relationship with Jesus. As we remember the love that Jesus has poured out on the cross for us, may it show forth not only in our dance but also in how we live and interact with each other.

If anyone asks you what love has to do with dance, you can say everything because Jesus said, "Do everything in love". Therefore, if you see another dancer messing up their steps or forgetting their choreography, do not ridicule them; show them love. Love can go a long way in building that person's confidence.

Prayer

Father, I thank You for your unconditional love for us. We are nothing without You. Thank You for dying on the cross for my sins. Let my dance always show forth Your love. Let my heart overflow with love for You and others. In Jesus' Name. Amen.

Call To Action

Remember that God loves you and died for you, that love is the basis of humanity. Without it, we are nothing. Therefore, in everything you do, do it with love.

Eslyn Taylor

February 6

LOVE, ACTUALLY

Let all that you do be done in love. 1 Corinthians 16:14

Let's talk about love. I started dancing when I was just five years old, and every time I dance, I feel like I'm discovering it for the first time all over again. Dance is a love language given to us, and when I dance, I understand what it feels like to be loved by someone bigger than myself. However, I quickly understood that while I loved to dance, dance wasn't just for me to hold to my chest, unwilling to share it with anyone else. No, I had to share my love. I realized, "Okay, so sharing isn't so bad". Maybe I'd have to share it with one or two people, tops. Imagine my surprise when I found out I'd be sharing it with more than two people. In that first moment when I got to share my love, I felt the gravity of His love upon me, and the love I had intensified. Now, all I want to do is share love.

When God sent Jesus to die on the cross for our sins, that was His way of showing love towards us, and there are so many ways that we can now show love to each other. When we choose to be kind to that one person who isn't too kind to us, that is an act of love. Whenever we extend grace to someone we may think does not deserve it, that is an act of love. When we apologize after we have offended someone, forgive someone who has offended us, and provide safe spaces for those who have not yet received Jesus as their savior, that is love unfolding within us. Anything is an act of love when it comes from the heart.

Prayer

Dear God, thank You for showing me the ultimate example of love. I pray that You will help me to show that same love to those around me. May I grow in Your love today, tomorrow, and forever. Amen.

Call To Action

Have you been exhibiting the love of God? Think of three ways to show your love to those around you this week and put them into practice.

Gabrielle Blackett

February 7

LOVE WILL KEEP US TOGETHER

This is my commandment, that you love one another as I have loved you.
John 15:12

Jesus commanded us to love each other just as He loves us. We can demonstrate that kind of love by how we relate to others. Our relationship with others is just as important to God as His relationship with us.

In dance ministry, being part of a dance group is challenging. Sometimes, there is conflict, and it hinders the flow of the Holy Spirit, decreasing the impact of our dance. Yes, you may get the cheers and kudos. But do we want to entertain or do we want to dance under the anointing so that the gospel will be communicated to those watching, resulting in souls saved?

Our negative feelings towards others affect us. Sometimes, we are in torment because we can't let go of our emotions even when the other person has moved on. What did Jesus say? "Love your neighbor" – that would undoubtedly include our enemies as well. And loving them means genuinely embracing them rather than being tolerant.

I recall a situation upon joining a dance ministry. While most people were very welcoming, there was one person whose attitude was very cold. She would even turn her head in the opposite direction when she saw me approaching. I remembered the saying, "Show yourself friendly if you want to win friends". So, I did just that. I decided to smile at her and greet her warmly each time I saw her, and she started to respond. If I had adopted the same attitude she initially had, there would've been no coming together as one.

Prayer

As we continue to strive towards that goal of loving each other, let us pray: Father, You are the God who is love and who told us to love. Even though it is hard to love those who hate us because You have commanded us to love, it is possible. Lord, help us to love all men. Mend our broken hearts and give us a heart to love totally and genuinely, in Jesus' name. Amen.

Call To Action

Let us continue to work on ourselves and our relationships so that we will come into alignment with what God requires of us.

Gurlain Applewhaite

February 8

THE DRESS CODE

And above all these virtues put on love, which binds everything together in perfect harmony. Colossians 3:14

Throughout this chapter, Paul mentions taking off negative traits and putting on those that are Christ-like. He clearly shows us the virtues that we are to clothe ourselves with. These virtues are compassion, kindness, humility, gentleness, patience, and forgiveness. But Paul emphasizes one in particular, "above all of these virtues, put on love."

As Ministers, love should be a part of our everyday dress code. The scripture says that we need to put on love, which implies that it takes effort and commitment; it is a daily necessity. When you are being attacked by the enemy or even a friend, the aim is to put on love and bless, not curse. It can be challenging at times, but we will clothe ourselves in love because we love God and do not want to disobey Him.

The verse states that after we are dressed in love, this brings perfect harmony (unity). Let's go back to the virtues:

Love is being compassionate.

Love is being kind.

Love is being humble.

Love is being gentle.

Love is being patient.

Love is being forgiving.

Once we understand love and practice love, then we are pleasing God. In life, difficult situations will always arise to test us. We may need to redress in love during the day if some of the virtues are not evident. For example, suppose you realize you are impatient in a specific situation; you can go to our Heavenly Father for help to exercise patience.

Prayer

Our loving God, we come to You as dance ministers. Firstly, we need to be clothed with Your robe of love. We cannot do it without You; we love You and desire to obey You. Please forgive us when we fall short in any of the virtues. Thank you for Your forgiveness. In Jesus' Name. Amen.

Call To Action

Ask God every chance you get to redress in love, and He will because He loves you.

Julie Greene

February 9

GOD FOCUSED

When we were utterly helpless, Christ came at just the right time and died for us sinners. Now, most people would not be willing to die for an upright person, though someone might perhaps be willing to die for a person who is especially good. But God showed his great love for us by sending Christ to die for us while we were still sinners. Romans 5:6-8

It has always been unexplainable in my mind how someone as great as God, the King of Kings and Lord of Lords, is so interested in me. It is even more amazing that He thought of me when I wasn't even interested in loving Him.

When I started dancing, I was so excited about bringing my gift before God through dance. It was not until I moved my body in time with the rhythm of the right song, with the right words, that I felt I was really communicating with God and sharing how much I loved Him. I loved to dance, and I loved doing it for the Lord.

One day, though, as I spent time with God, a switch flipped, and I fell out of love with dance and fell completely in love with God. My dance then became one of the ways I show my love for others and one of the best ways I show my love for God. The difference is that God can use me in multiple ways because I love him completely, and that love goes beyond dance.

Prayer

God, I love to dance, but I love You more than dance. I ask You, Lord, to use me in any way You see fit. I offer my body and my mind to You in service. Make this temple always fit for the Master's use. Make me fit for Your Kingdom's building up and Your people's edification. In Jesus' Name, Amen.

Call To Action

In your time with God this week, thank Him for the gift of dance but ask Him to fill you up and use you for whatever He wants to do on this earth. Let Him know He is more important than anything you can do for Him.

Laina Jacob

February 10

LOVE = OBEDIENCE

Be careful to obey all these commands I am giving you. Show love to the Lord your God by walking in his ways and holding tightly to him. Deuteronomy 11:22

We have so many ways that we show love to each other. We are usually very intentional in ensuring that we get that perfect gift, treat, or experience that shows a special person how much he or she means to us. Gary Chapman teaches how to show love in his book, *The Five Love Languages*. He teaches that you give based not on what you want, but on what the person would appreciate. Sometimes, this involves getting to know the person's likes and dislikes; other times, it requires guesswork. Conversely, we do not have to guess with God.

Obedience is how He knows that we love Him. 1 Samuel 15:22 makes it clear, "Obedience is better than sacrifice". We can do many nice things in the name of the Lord or unto the Lord, but you see obedience? That is how He knows for sure that we love Him. Just like we cannot give our loved ones gifts that *we like* to show them we love them, we cannot give God what *we feel like* to show our love for Him. We must listen to Him, follow His Word, and do what He commands. These are the true showings of our love for God.

Prayer

Father, I am sorry for the times I tried to show You love in my way, not Yours. I ask for Your forgiveness and mercy. Come into my life and help me to be obedient to Your will and way in my life. I step off my own path and step boldly onto the path You have for me. I will be obedient because I love You. In Jesus' Name. Amen.

Call To Action

What has God been speaking to you about? What have you delayed doing? Remember, delayed obedience is disobedience. Get back on track today. Show God that you love Him by doing what He says.

Laina Jacob

February 11

PURSUE LOVE

*"Love is the greatest", and we are to "desire spiritual gifts but to pursue love"-
words spoken by Apostle Paul. 1 Corinthians 13 and 1 Corinthians 14:1*

There were times when I felt hurt during rehearsal for a piece. Not being able to grasp a move and the other dancers making fun of me was hard. In those times, I did not feel any support or love. I could not show love, which, in return, closed me off from other dancers and affected how I danced. Because of this, I could not perform to the best of my ability. Have you ever felt like that?

I soon learned that I must pursue love; this is how I move forward to express myself in dance. Our gifts, talents, and worship must not be selfish but must be done in love for God, His church, and others. In 1 Corinthians 14, the believers were disorderly in their gifts in the church. Paul reminded them that love should be the motivation for using gifts. Likewise, dance should be done out of love and not for the elevation of self.

Prayer

Dear God, please help my heart be filled with love for Your people so I can use my gifts and talents to show my love through dance.

Call To Action

Think about a person you may not feel love for and reach out to that person in hopes of sharing love.

Maxine Butcher

February 12

IT IS HIS WILL

Be devoted to one another in love. Honor one another above yourselves.
Romans 12:10

If only it were that easy, right? People get on our nerves, and if we're honest with ourselves, we also get on people's nerves. In a dance ministry with only women, you can imagine the different personalities, the hormones raging, the sensitiveness, and the triggers of each person are present. These many differences can be a lot to take in and deal with, but we must because God accepts our differences and works with us. Therefore, we must show grace. The truth is that we will encounter difficult people along the way; that is unavoidable. But from the beginning of time, we were meant to be our brother's keeper.

I remember times when someone was being difficult or behaving out of character, and I initiated conversations with them to figure out what was causing that behavior. It didn't always bring about the intended result, but I enquired with a sincere heart. Sometimes, people are dealing with things from childhood to the present, and those issues can't be dealt with overnight. It's a process most of the time. Therefore, our first instinct shouldn't be a defensive stance but one of grace extended. The Word says that anyone who says they love God but hates his brother is a liar. Treat others as you want to be treated; it's honestly that simple. Do not let selfishness, deceit, and the "this is how I am" attitude get in the way of how we are to love each other.

Prayer

Dear Lord, create a clean heart and renew a righteous spirit within me so I can love others the way I am called to love. Let me be sensitive to their triggers so that I can help them come to a healthy place. Amen.

Call To Action

Be mindful of your words and actions when interacting with people.

Orissa Fitzpatrick

February 13

NOT DOING IT*

Do nothing from selfish ambition or conceit, but in humility count others more significant than yourselves. Philippians 2:3

What's your motivation for serving?

Is it for love or the likes?

Is it for love or the lights?

Is it for love or to shine bright?

If it's from a heart of rivalry or conceit to "outshine others" or gain likes, *me nah dweet.*

If it's just for the lights or to prove myself right, *me nah dweet.*

If it's only to hear "Yowww, daa wuz tight", ("Hey that was great" *me nah dweet.*

Instead, we should all serve in humility and dance from a disposition of gratitude, seeking to uplift others as we move. Every action should point others closer to the Source of our motivation and inspiration. It's a balancing act to be in the spotlight and simultaneously illuminate God's glory without keeping it for ourselves. We must always send it back to Him! Always!

Prayer

Lord, help me to always do it for the love and not for the likes. Let my disposition be this: if it's not for love me nah dweet.

Call To Action

Simply stated, let's all do what we do for the love and not the likes.

Pierre Rock

*Incorporates Barbados Slang

February 14

LOVE IS…

And we have known and believed the love that God hath to us God is love; and he that dwelleth in love dwelleth in God, and God in him. 1 John 4:16

Love is…a person.

Love is…a choice.

Love is…you.

Love is…me.

God is love. We've heard it, read it and seen it in His Word.

God is love, and we see this manifested in the person Jesus Christ, who is the perfect expression of love. When we choose Jesus, we are saying yes to becoming a person of love. We are choosing to dwell in love, and we are saying that love is living here in me. These choices encourage others to choose Jesus by choosing love, the love they see us express in our words and actions. Those actions come alive in our talk, dance and walk. Now, the question we have to ask ourselves is: Is anyone in my circle talking, dancing and/or walking with me?

Prayer

Lord, help me to become the "perfect" expression of Your love and to continue drawing others to You when they see Your love in me – in my talk, my dance and my walk. May they do likewise and talk with You, dance with You and walk with You.

Call To Action

Make the decision today that the persona of love will become a lasting reality in you and invite others to talk, dance and walk with Jesus through you.

Pierre Rock

February 15

DANCE IN LOVE

Whatever you do, work at it with all your heart, as working for the Lord, not for human masters, since you know that you will receive an inheritance from the Lord as a reward. It is the Lord Christ you are serving. Colossians 3:23-24

As dance ministers, I believe that most of us, if not all, can admit that at some point in our dance, we were more caught up with the movements and everything else happening around us than the ministry. I'll be the first to raise both hands and admit that sometimes I have to snap myself back to where the heart of my dance should be – a love for God and His people. Our movements should embody the Father's love for us as we pour that love onto others. When we dance in love, we set aside everything that is not of God. We lay aside the weight of sin that so easily besets us – unforgiveness, hate, jealousy, bitterness.

Free yourselves! Dance to the rhythm of God's heart. Let His heartbeat be felt through your hands and feet so those who look to your ministry for healing, hope, salvation and love may leave filled and refreshed. Move in love. Dance in love. For the One we worship is love.

Prayer

God, make our hearts pliable in the Master's hands. Remove any impurities that Your love may be shed abroad, free from any hindrances. When we dance, may it be out of a place of love from You so that we may show that love to Your people. Change our hearts, Lord, that our dance may be changed. We love You, Lord. Give us Your heart.

Call To Action

When you are dancing, whether in rehearsal or on the day of ministry, make a conscious effort to think about the condition of your heart. If your heart is not in the right place, talk to God and ask Him to help you shift your focus.

Rheanne Rock

February 16

LOVE WHO?

To love him with all your heart, with all your understanding and with all your strength, and to love your neighbor as yourself is more important than all burnt offerings and sacrifices. Mark 12:33

Love who? Even those difficult people? Love who? Even those who try to sabotage me and "stab me in the back"? Love who? Even those people who get "under my skin"? Love who? The haters and gossipers? Love them?

Yes, them! Love all of them. I've been in a dance ministry for over 14 years, and many have come and gone, all with varying backgrounds, perspectives, personalities, and ways of doing things. I have seen and experienced personality clashes and differences of opinion over these years, but does that mean the members of the ministry can stop operating in love? No, God views loving your neighbors as more important than the sacrifice of long hours you put into work on choreography.

He teaches us how to love, even those we deem "difficult" to love. If we are honest with ourselves, we have all messed up, said or done the wrong things, yet our heavenly Father is always waiting with open arms. Loving someone may not always be easy, but it is what God expects of us, and He equips us with His love. He doesn't only want us to focus on perfecting the "art of dance" but also on perfecting the "heart of love". So, love who? Love them, all of them.

Prayer

Father, help me to love as You do. Show me how to love even when I don't feel like it. Take away all hatred and anger from my heart and teach me the art of love. May Your love flow through my dance ministry and repair any broken relationships. When people look at me, may they see Your love. Amen.

Call To Action

- Write the names of any persons you find difficult to love.

- Ask God to show you how to love and how to show love to those persons.

- Pray for those persons sincerely.

Rheanne Rock

February 17

EVEN WHEN YOU DON'T FEEL LIKE

And this is love: that we walk in obedience to his commands. As you have heard from the beginning, his command is that you walk in love. 2 John 1:6

As a Christian, God wants me to love others which does not apply only to my friends. Even if I do not feel like loving people who mistreat me, I still have to because I want to please God and make him happy.

We can always rely on God's love. Sometimes at school, people may mistreat you, lie about you and may often say they don't like or love you, but you know what? God's love for us never changes.

Like others, I make many mistakes, and God still loves me. As a dancer for God, I cannot be ministering knowing that someone did something bad to me, and I refuse to forgive them and love them. God truly will not receive my dance.

I do not only tell them that I love them, but I also show them in many ways:

1. At home, I obey my parents all the time

2. At school, I share my snacks with my friends

3. At dancing, I help others after class if they do not know the moves

4. At church, I listen to the Word of God

5. At playtime at school or anywhere else, I help others who fall or trip up, and I do not laugh at them.

These are just a few examples of how I show love. Sometimes, it is very hard, but I really want to do what God says, which is to love.

Prayer

God, help everyone to show love all the time. Forgive them if they are not doing that in their lives. We will obey Your Word, which says to love. We love You, God, so we commit to obeying Your Word. Thank You for helping us in Jesus' Name. Amen.

Call To Action

I want to encourage you to not only say "I love you", but show love to everyone.

Rhema-Jae Greene

February 18

TRUE LOVE IS REAL

We know how much God loves us, and we have put our trust in his love. God is love, and all who live in love live in God, and God lives in them. 1 John 4:16

I used to think that I knew what real love was until I met this man. When I gave my life over to him in April 2009, I wept like a baby because of the joy I felt on the inside. I remember it like it was today. He called, and I felt this yearning and longing just to yield to His voice. It was as though something was pulling me towards Him, and I just couldn't say no. His love changed my life forever.

I was inspired, excited and overjoyed. I just couldn't keep God to myself. I was in love with Him, and He loved me. He gave me hope and made me brand new. My life began to take on a new meaning, and my love for people changed. I had to see them through a different lens, it was hard at times, but there was an expectation of me. I love because God is Love.

Something different was happening within me; I couldn't explain it, but I knew it was because of our connection and being a dancer for God. Soon, there were places I felt uncomfortable in and people I had to separate myself from. The separation took place without notice because I chose to follow Him, and He stayed with me from the first day I met Him until now. "Greater is he that is in us than he that is in this world", according to 1 John 4:4, a powerful verse just like His love for us. There is no better love than His because God is love, and only in Him can you find real, true love.

Prayer

God, I pray that this love I read about is one I can experience today. I need this love now. My life isn't where I want it to be, but I know You can change it. I thank You in advance for doing it, in Jesus' name. Amen.

Call To Action

- Surrender to the call.

- Receive Him as your savior.

- Follow Him with all your heart.

Rhonda .A. Babb

February 19

TO LOVE MEANS TO SACRIFICE

For this is how God loved the world: He gave his one and only Son, so that everyone who believes in him will not perish but have eternal life. John 3:16

God gave up His only son for you and me. He did it not only for our sins but to bring us into a relationship with Him so we will not perish, but we can have eternal life. It is a privilege to know that God did not just give up a son, but His only son for us. This sacrifice means that all of our sins have been forgiven. There is no condemnation. We can have eternal life with Jesus Christ.

As a dancer, one of the ways we can honor that sacrifice God made for us is by using our bodies to glorify Him. It won't always be easy to do because we come from a place of sin; that is why He has given us the Holy Spirit to lead and guide us in all we do.

Yes, I know you may be saying, "I messed up so many times," but He knows, and it doesn't end there. The Word of God says in John 1:9 that if we repent of our sins, "God is faithful and just to forgive us and make us whole again". That doesn't mean we should keep on sinning; it means that our love and commitment to Him and His for us is more than enough to help us do what is right.

So, what will be your stance today, knowing God's loving sacrifice for us? We need to honor that sacrifice today. Thank You, Lord, for the sacrifice You made not only for me but for this entire world. My heart is truly grateful.

Prayer

God, although I do not deserve what You did, I am genuinely grateful that You did it. Have Your way in my life and help me to be strong as I honor my commitment to You, in Jesus' name. Amen.

Call To Action

- Be controlled by the spirit and not the flesh.

- Honor Him with your body.

- Repent of your sins.

Rhonda .A. Babb

February 20

MY LORD, MY LOVE

For God so loved the world that he gave his only begotten son, that whosoever believeth in him, shall have everlasting life. John 3:16

Dear Diary, I saw him again today. It's been a while since I last saw him, and I had forgotten all about him. My thoughts were so far away that I didn't see him standing there with that warm smile that made me feel all toasty inside. It was happening; God was beginning to melt away the hurt, the pain, and the coldness of my heart. His arms outstretched, reaching for me, but not yet. I'm not ready. I have to know more about him even though I feel drawn to him. Just a glimpse of who he is, a tiny peek into his heart, a brief introduction because I was in a hurry. Oh, I missed seeing him standing there looking so regal and at peace in this place of chaos and destruction. How I wished I had the time to stay and chat, but it was time to go. I hope to see him again. So, with a smile and the wind, I was gone.

Oh! The pain and misery of this loveless, worldly marriage. I need to get out. I need him. He's different from all the others. I don't know. I'm so alone and unloved. No one cares, sigh, I think.

Dear Diary, there he is. Those kind eyes are drawing me to him. He's not my usual type, but there is something about him that I can't ignore. He's slowly drawing me in, and I'm falling. Every time I see him, those eyes speak to me, telling me I'm safe and protected. Dare I take a chance? Will I be hurt like the others before? My heart can't. I just can't give my heart again for it to be trampled on, but those eyes and that smile tell me I need to stop running away. He is slowly seeping into my heart. Oh my! I feel this knocking at the door of my heart, but dare I open it? Ugh, I don't know what to do, but I have secretly fallen in love. I'm a goner.

Dear Diary, seventeen years since I opened the door of my heart and let Him in, He showed all of who He is and then some. I am complete, a woman with a purpose and destiny. I can do anything because He is with me, by my side every step of the way: my Lord, my love, Your Majesty.

Prayer

Father, help us to love You as You love us, in Jesus' name, amen.

Call To Action

Love is the key; eat of its fruit.

Sandra Britton

Prayer

Father, help us to love You as You love us, in Jesus' name, amen.

Call To Action

Love is the key; eat of its fruit.

February 21

UNCONDITIONAL LOVE

This is love, not that we have loved God but that He loved us and sent His Son to be the propitiation for our sins. Beloved, if God so loved us, we ought also to love one another. 1 John 4:10-11

God loves the world so much that He gave us His only Son to be crucified on the cross for our sins. And because of that love, we can have eternal life. If we love God so much because of what Jesus did for us, as dancers, we can show Him that love by praising and worshipping Him through dance. And as we dance before Him, we need to put Him first in our lives. The more expression and strength we put into our dance, the more it looks complete. Otherwise, it would just be exercise.

God's love is just like a parent's love. My mother and family love me so much and would do anything to make me happy and ensure I'm healthy. God loves us just like that. But we should not only show our love to God, He wants us to love and care for each other and for each dancer in our group. It does not matter who they are or what they have done, we are to love them as part of our family.

Prayer

Dear God, we thank You and appreciate You for sacrificing Your one and only Son just for us. We thank You for truly loving us even though we sin against You. No one loves us more than You do or can do what You did for us. So, we say thank You again in Jesus' name. Amen.

Call To Action

Let us always remember that God loves us more than anyone else. So let us also love and care for each other, fueled by that love we consistently receive from God.

Shiloh Springer

February 22

WHAT IS LOVE?

Love is patient, love is kind. It does not envy, it does not boast, it is not proud. It is not rude, it is not self-seeking, it is not easily angered, it keeps no record of wrongs. Love does not delight in evil but rejoices with the truth. 1 Corinthians 13:4-7

The dictionary describes love as an intense feeling of deep affection. But do you know that there are actually eight different kinds of love?

1. Philia love - affectionate love, love without romantic attraction which occurs between friends and family.

2. Pragma love - enduring love, committed love.

3. Storge love - familiar love, natural love like a parent has for a child.

4. Eros love - romantic love, sexual love.

5. Ludus love - flirtatious love, found at the beginning of a relationship.

6. Mania love - obsessive, jealous or possessive love.

7. Philautia love - self-love but also a general love between friends, family and lovers.

8. Agape love - the highest form of love, the love between God and man.

As believers in Christ, Agape love is the kind of love we should have for each other. Agape love is what we find in 1 Corinthians 13:4-7. We need to love each other regardless of what a person can do for us or how they may treat us. Only then will we be able to experience the kind of love found in this Bible verse.

Prayer

Heavenly Father, thank You for the people You have placed in my life. Your word says that, above all else, we should have love, so help us love each other with the Agape love You show us daily. In Jesus' name, Amen

Call To Action

This week, let us think of ways we can show love and appreciation to others. Let us try doing simple things like helping with the dishes, making someone a meal or even giving a compliment.

Halal Teens

February 23

GOD'S LOVE FOR YOU

But God commendeth his own love toward us in that, while we were yet sinners, Christ died for us. Romans 5:8

Whoever does not love Jesus does not know Him because Jesus is love, and He loves you very much. He died on the cross for our sins because He loves each of us. You might say you don't like your brother or sister, but you like God; that shows God the opposite. You are supposed to love everyone even if they did something bad to you. You are supposed to forgive and forget and allow God to work on your heart and theirs.

We were all created to worship God. One of the ways I show my love for God is through my dancing. I recall that I've always enjoyed dancing, and I often feel God's presence through my dance. You can show your love to God in many ways, whether through dancing, singing, or helping others in need. God also shows His love to us in many ways, such as placing us in loving families, keeping us safe and waking us up every day.

Prayer

Dear God, thank You for dying on the cross for our sins. Thank You for showing love to us by helping us when we need help. Thank You for providing for our families and us. Thank You for keeping us safe and happy when we're sad. Amen.

Call To Action

As you go about your day and engage in various activities, think about ways in which you can show God's Love to others and how you can be more like Him.

Trinitee Angus

February 24

THE POWER OF LOVE

Love is patient, love is kind. It does not envy, it does not boast, it is not proud. It does not dishonor others, it is not self-seeking, it is not easily angered, it keeps no record of wrongs. Love does not delight in evil but rejoices with the truth. It always protects, always trusts, always hopes, always perseveres. 1 Corinthians 13:4-8

Love is a four-letter word and one of the most powerful emotions given to mankind. Love is an intense feeling of deep affection. God teaches us that love is patient, kind, not envious of one another, not boastful and keeps no wrongdoings in mind. This Bible verse perfectly defines love and what love stands for. As a Christian, you are taught to love your neighbor, love your brother and sister in Christ as God has loved you, with agape love, a never-ending love and a love that can conquer all odds.

Have you ever been in love? Do you know how it feels to have love consume you? I do. God's love is so powerful that it consumes me every single day. You may not see God's love, but it is there whether you believe it. God's love is the greatest love of all. His love fills this space that we never knew needed to be filled. God's love shows us what it means to be truly happy.

My love for dance is truly powerful. It has taught me to persevere and stretch myself beyond my limits, comfort zone, and boundaries. It has also taught me to be selfless within my dance. My love for the gift of dance is unmatched, and I thank God daily for it. Knowing that we can connect with God and feel His love is the greatest feeling; it stands the test of time. The power of God's love can transform, heal, set free, deliver, and most importantly, save.

Prayer

May I experience the limitless everlasting love of God, as He says in this scripture. May I feel Your love surround me. Father, let your love consume me and overflow me. I pray my walk with You continues to grow, and my love for You grows even more. In Jesus' Name. Amen

Call To Action

I encourage you today to keep reminding yourself that God loves you with everlasting love, and He will never give up on you. Let this be a reminder today and forever.

Zariah Watson

February 25

AGAPE LOVE

Long ago the Lord said to Israel: I have loved you, my people, with an everlasting love. With unfailing love, I have drawn you to myself." Jeremiah 31:3

Many of us can testify by saying God's love is really an Agape love. This kind of love is selfless, sacrificial, unconditional and stands the test of time. It extends beyond emotions and is more than a feeling or sentiment. The Lord said, in this scripture verse to the people of Israel, that He hath loved them with an everlasting love, with an unfailing love and man that gave me goosebumps! Just imagine that type of love.

Being a dancer, I grew to fall in love with the art of dance and how dancing makes me feel. Valerie King once said, "Dance is inward communication manifested outward", which has stuck with me. I fall in love with dancing every day because I know that something shifts in the atmosphere when I dance. I can save a life from the clutches of hell. I get to be unapologetically me and express my feelings in ways words can't.

God teaches you every day how He is not like man. Sometimes, I struggle with believing God loves me. No one is perfect. I, too, have sinned and fallen short. There are some days when I ask myself if God still hears me, if He knows how much I love Him if He sees me despite my past wrongdoings, and I know some of you have had the same thoughts and feelings. We've all been there. The Lord says in the verse above that He has loved us with an everlasting love, with an unfailing love, that He has drawn us to Himself. God loves you and He sees you. Even through your wrongdoings, He still loves you and cares for you. He wants you to make those wrongdoings right. He won't stop fighting for us, but we, too, must put in the work and fight back on behalf of Him because we love Him.

Prayer

Lord, occasionally, I listen to my negative thoughts, and I'm tempted to think You don't love me. In these moments, I am swiftly reminded that You revealed your unfailing, all-encompassing love by sending Your one and only Son into this world to die for us. Use me to love others, Lord, the way You love me. Amen and Amen.

Call To Action

Try using this devotional as a guide to show love as God showed His love for you. God loves you; never forget that.

Zariah Watson

February 26

MY FEELINGS FOR YOU

Above all, love each other deeply, because love covers over a multitude of sins. 1 Peter 4:8

Oh, so strong

Oh, so true

I feel you

I feel you in my choreography

I feel you in my movement

I feel you in the music you grace upon my ears

I love you not by obligations

I love you not because I was told to

I love you by my own choice

The gift of dance

What better way could I have possibly been given to show my love for you

To let you know

I'm. All. In.

I won't let you go

I won't give up on you, not this time.

Zenaida R. Mayers

February 27

WHAT IS LOVE?

Love is patient, love is kind. It does not envy, it does not boast, it is not proud. It does not dishonor others, it is not self-seeking, it is not easily angered, it keeps no record of wrongs. 1 Corinthians 13:4-5

Love isn't just a feeling, it's multiple acts displayed in everyday life to make you and others feel appreciated. As the scripture says, it's patient, meaning it waits; it's never in a rush; it's kind; it's helping others in any way possible. As a dancer, these very same attributes apply. Dance is a form of discipline and skill, and sometimes, we get so caught up in those two things that we forget that dance is also ministry, and it is done as a group.

Our mentality sometimes changes as dancers. We often focus on making our moves more pronounced than others. Sometimes, we even see another person struggling and refuse to give them any assistance. I, too, have been part of the "high horse crew", for lack of better words. Until one day, I was at rehearsals and couldn't execute a specific move. It was a struggle, no matter how hard I tried. Another dancer who was less experienced came over and helped me without hesitation. I paused and looked at her, and at that moment, I had a deep conviction from God, and He placed the above verse in my spirit. I left rehearsal feeling humbled. When I got home and opened my Bible, I landed on the same verse again, so I knew God had intentionally taught me something powerful at that specific moment. I'm saying this to say, never allow pride to be louder than love. In your day-to-day life, always act in love.

Prayer

Dear heavenly Father, I pray that You will position our hearts to perform acts of love without hesitation. May love become our day-to-day posture to assist others and accomplish what You have set before us.

Call To Action

Tap into love and let it flow out of you.

Be selfless today, and let love lead.

Perform an act of love today.

Jaida Roberts

February 28

GOD IS LOVE

Whoever does not love does not know God because God is love. 1 John 4:8

True love comes from God. God will always love us no matter what happens, even if we go astray. That same love God pours out to us, we should pour out to the world. We should show love to everyone we meet and interact with, not just select people. Even if people treat us or speak to us badly, let's show love. It might be hard, but God wants us to do it.

You must love and pray for those who mistreat you. The scriptures say that if you do not show love, you do not know God because God is love (1 John 4:8). God's love is the greatest example you can ever think of, and the example we should all follow. Loving God changes the way we love each other. Nothing can compare to the love of God. He loves us so much that He sent His Son to die for us.

When we dance, we should dance with love in our hearts for others. The love inside of us should be overflowing to the point that people can see our love for dance just by looking.

Prayer

God, I know You want me to show love to everyone, but some people are very hard to love. Teach me to love them like You do, Lord, amen.

Call To Action

Think of that person or persons who may have treated you badly, and the next time you see them, show love towards them.

Shaquonna Rock

March 1

HOPE ALIVE!

But those who hope in the Lord will renew their strength. They will soar on wings like eagles; they will run and not grow weary; they will walk and not be faint.
Isaiah 40:31

Hope is a motivator, a teacher, a healer, and an optimist. Hope is an essential requirement of being a successful dancer. But as dancers, what is our hope? We hope our ministry will impact others and, in turn, give them the same hope in God that we have acquired. We hope to look beyond our current struggles to know Jesus, our savior, is next to us as we go through our darkest moments. We hope that He will provide an escape. We hope to know that we will be rewarded once we put our faith in Him.

As dancers, hope gives us strength, courage, and boldness to take the stage, knowing that it is not us but He who is ministering through us. Furthermore, if our ministry is to give hope to others through our dance, we, ourselves, must have hope in God that He is who He says He is and that He will do what He says He will do. If you want to offer something to someone, you first have to possess that item, and the same goes for hope.

Prayer

Heavenly Father, we, Your humble servants, come before You today in need of hope. There are times when we feel helpless, and there are times when we feel weak. In those times, we pray for hope. We need hope for a better future. We need hope for a better life. Some say that the sky is at its darkest just before dawn. We pray that this is true, for all seems dark. We need hope, Lord, in every way. We pray to be filled with hope from head to toe, to bask in Your glory, to know that all is right in the world, as You have planned and as You want it to be. Help us to walk in hope and live our lives in faith and glory. In Your name, we pray, Amen.

Call To Action

Grow your hope in the Lord so that when the storms of life gather, you can withstand the winds. And having persevered, you will be ready to go with Him when He returns.

Danae Niles

March 2

OUR BLESSED HOPE

Looking for that blessed hope, and the glorious appearing of the great God and our Saviour Jesus Christ. Titus 2:13

Our mission as dancers is to give hope to our audience, believing that one day, they will look upon the face of the ultimate hope: the Blessed Hope, the Lord Jesus Christ our Saviour. To achieve great things in life, we often need help from others. We, dancers, are that help. Not everyone can find what they need alone, so we should prioritize reaching out and offering someone hope. We may not realize it yet, but we just might be the only way someone meets the Lord. We are the closest thing to Jesus some may ever see. When we dance, expressing our love for God, our audience becomes hopeful that, one day, they can be with our Saviour. Hope is a virtue that makes our life here on earth much easier while we await the return of the Lord. It keeps our reward in heaven in sight, always steering us in the right direction. We need hope if we desire to be with Him. He is our Blessed Hope.

Prayer

Lord, help us to be true vessels of You as we minister to Your people, desiring that they embrace Your hope and live in Your home. Help us not to lose track of what is to come; therefore, let us project Your hope through us as we touch lives abundantly. You are our hope and refuge when all seems wrong, when all is reduced to rubble, and when we lack hope. Help us to live in Your power of hope as we look forward to meeting You one day. You are our hope, and we trust in You. In Jesus' name, we pray, Amen.

Call To Action

Live pure and holy lives so that as you dance, your message of hope will be embraced by all who come into contact with you, and they will receive the gift of hope as they join you in looking toward the second coming of the Lord.

Danae Niles

March 3

A HOPE FOR THE FUTURE

And hope does not put us to shame, because God's love has been poured into our hearts through the Holy Spirit, who has been given to us. Romans 5:5

In this very evil world, it is important that we never lose hope. Now, more than ever, we need hope. So, do not let this world take it away from you. Cling to it. It is a tragedy when hope is taken from someone. Being in a state of hopelessness is a torturous place to be. Hopelessness can bring feelings of unease, agony, distress, even anxiety and depression. Nothing good can come from living a life void of hope. We need to hold on to the hope we have in God, the hope He gave us. Hope is one of the most powerful things in the world. When we continue to have hope, the devil cannot defeat us.

I believe that in order to always have hope, we must fully trust in God and His timing. To wait on Him and be patient. I know that sometimes we might feel like all hope is lost, but God reminds us that He only wants good things for us in Jeremiah 29:11. He tells us that He knows the plans that He has for us, plans to prosper us and not to harm us, plans to give us a hope and a future. I know that sometimes, when we hear someone say we should never stop hoping, we think... "Well, that's easier said than done," but if we just keep these words of Jeremiah 29:11 and the words of all the other promises our heavenly Father gave us in our hearts and minds, we'll never stop having hope.

Prayer

Dear God, I pray that You will bring comfort, peace, joy and hope to every hopeless soul in Your kingdom. We know that life is not easy and this race isn't either. So, we ask that You help us to always hope in Your promises to us, help us to remember that You have the final say and that no good thing will You withhold from those who walk uprightly. In Jesus' Name. Amen.

Call To Action

Hold on to the Word God gave you, this includes His promises in The Bible and the Word He has given you concerning your destiny and purpose.

Danielle Harewood

March 4

WHERE DO WE FIND HOPE?

May the God of hope fill you with all joy and peace as you trust in him, so that you may overflow with hope by the power of the Holy Spirit. Romans 15:13

We find hope in God's presence. When life feels out of control, turn to Him in prayer. "He alone is my rock and my salvation, my fortress where I will not be shaken. My victory and honor come from God alone" (Psalm 62:6-7).

We find hope in God's process, which seldom matches our own human understanding. Even in our pain, God is at work, sewing things together for good. This may not translate to our comfort; it's meant to transform us to be more like Christ (Romans 8:28). God uses our struggles to produce endurance, which produces character, which, in turn, produces hope (Romans 5:3-5).

We find hope in God's purpose for our lives. Every one of us has been created with a divine plan in mind. "'For I know the plans I have for you,' says the Lord. 'They are plans for good and not for disaster, to give you a future and a hope'" (Jeremiah 29:11).

Hope is not something we do. It's something we possess, gifted to us by God's eternal grace and the power of the Holy Spirit. Hope is the anchor for our soul (Hebrews 6:19); without it, we are incomplete (Proverbs 13:12). As dancers, what is our hope? Our hope is that our ministry will impact others and, in turn, give them the hope in God that we have acquired. That is, hope to know Jesus, our savior, is next to us as we go through our darkest moments and that He will make a way of escape. We have the hope to know that once we put our faith in Him, we will be rewarded. As dancers, hope gives us strength, courage, and boldness to take the stage, knowing He is ministering through us.

Prayer

Almighty God, You are our hope and strength. You are guiding us toward Your will, and we will follow You. We will walk in amazing Faith this day. We will lift Your truth up and pull down strongholds. We declare sickness will not triumph over us. We were created to be powerful and victorious. Today, we will walk in the power, purpose, and peace of Jesus Christ. We pray for hope. We need hope for a better future. In Your name, we pray, Amen.

Call To Action

Grow your hope in the Lord so that when life's troubles gather, you can withstand them. And having persevered, you will be ready to go with Him when He returns.

Destiny Niles

March 5

SOAR IN HIS HOPE

But those who hope in the Lord will renew their strength. They will soar on wings like eagles; they will run and not grow weary; they will walk and not faint.
Isaiah 40:31

This verse makes me think of a newborn baby bird now learning to fly. Every day, it practices fluttering its wings in its attempts to get off the ground. It must have gotten tired and grown weary at some point. Yet, that same bird will be soaring in the sky one day. I know the mother bird would have encouraged that baby bird along the way. Likewise, that encouragement is the hope that we, dancers, have in the Lord. We start a little timid, shy, and unsure of ourselves, but we put our hope in the Lord, knowing that He will strengthen us when we grow weary. We know that we will start to soar in our dance.

Soaring in my dance reminds me of when I was rehearsing for our dance production and was in five of the dance pieces. Some of the dances required "nuff" stamina, and some needed to be performed back-to-back. At one point, I wondered if I would ever get through, but I had to remember that God was my hope and strength. Well, let me tell you, the night of the production was a blur, and after ministering those pieces, I had so much energy. I was really soaring like an eagle. Putting our hope in God is trusting that He will take care of our every need. Trust the process, do not get weary when things are not going how we might like, and know that God will let us soar in His hope.

Prayer

My heavenly and gracious Father, thank You for causing my hope in You to renew my strength and allow me to soar. May I continue to dance and live without getting weary. I thank You today as You continue to lift me up. In Jesus' name. Amen.

Call To Action

Let the hope of the Lord be your strength in whatever you can imagine.

Eslyn Taylor

March 6

HOPE FOR THE FUTURE

Rejoice in hope, be patient in tribulation, be constant in prayer. Romans 12:12

Looking at the future may seem daunting sometimes and even uncertain. The Word of God says, "Rejoice in hope". When I think of rejoicing, I think of worshipping and dancing at church on a Sunday morning. Those pre-worship jitters creep in, but as the music begins and I start to worship, I remember that I need not be afraid of how I look or how people may see me. I rejoice in knowing that I am worshipping my God, who is my hope.

C.S. Lewis says, "A Christian's hope isn't an escape or wishful thinking, but something that a Christian is meant to do." As believers, we have a hope of eternal life and a future. With this hope, we can attack each day with renewed passion and strength. I know the future can be scary, with so many uncertainties and no one knowing what tomorrow holds. But know this: we have hope, not only in this life but in the next, which we can entrust to God. Our patience when we face tribulation, and the prayer life we lead will cement the hope of Jesus in our lives.

The road to the future will have its highs and lows and unpredictability along the way, but God has given us the road map for our future. We must rejoice in hope even when we can't see the end of the tunnel, be patient when our world seems to be spiraling out of control, and, most of all, be constant as we go to God in prayer.

Prayer

Father, I praise You for who You are. I thank You for giving us the blueprint for our future. May I always rejoice, be patient in trials and be prayerful as I wait on Your eternal hope. Have Your way in my life and my future in Jesus' Name. Amen.

Call To Action

No matter the uncertainties we see in our future, continue to look to God and rejoice in His hope.

Eslyn Taylor

March 7

I HOPE YOU...

Now faith is the assurance of things hoped for, the conviction of things not seen.
Hebrews 11:1

Quite arguably, the strongest force on earth next to love is hope. Hope is the driving force behind every unsure step that we take, and the truth is that we spend a whole lot of our lives hoping. Reflect on how often you started a sentence with "I hope". Now, there's nothing wrong with this. In fact, it's encouraged. If we aren't hopeful for the future, it is almost as if we have given up. You may be wondering, "Why is hope so important?" Hope is a healer and a motivator, and if we don't have hope, it can be difficult to move through life with our heads held high.

In dance, a lot of hope is expressed too: "I hope that I can get this move done," and "I hope that all of these dance rehearsals pay off and our ministry goes forth." I hope, I hope, I hope. That hope allows us to lift one foot after the other and try again after we fail because we hope the next time will be different. But where does this hope come from? The answer is quite simple, it comes from Jesus. As a popular Christian song notes, "In Christ alone, my hope is found (He is my light, my strength, my song)." May these words ring true in your life, for hope is just the beginning.

Prayer

God, I want to have hope, but sometimes it just seems so hard. I know that You died for me so that I could have life and life more abundantly. Part of that abundance is hope. May You always help me to have hope. Amen.

Call To Action

Practice having hope for the little things we may take for granted; this will help you have hope when bigger things arise.

Gabrielle Blackett

March 8

DAYS LIKE THIS

And now, O Lord, for what do I wait? My hope is in you. Psalm 39:7

H – Have you ever experienced the first rain after a drought? It has been miserably hot for as long as you can remember, and sweat runs down your back everywhere you turn. Then, the clouds burst out of nowhere, the sky cries, and the rain falls. Outside is nice and cool, finally, and you breathe a sigh of relief. You hoped the rain would fall soon, didn't you? Look, here it is. It probably did not happen right when you asked, but it still came.

O – Offer up your troubles to God and leave them. Yes, hope is important, but it is useless without the belief that God has it under control. Rest easy in the assurance that God has your back, always. You may not see it now, but He is always there.

P – Practice and patience are the equation for dance and hope. There is no shortcut from a life of hopelessness to one of hope. Along with being in the presence of God, you need to practice hopefulness and be patient as you grow.

E – Even your darkest days don't stand a chance against the beaming light of hope, and if that doesn't bring you peace, I don't know what will. There are so many beautiful reasons to have hope.

Prayer

Dear God, please show me how to have hope. Give me the patience and practice to make me stronger so that Your light of hope will shine on me even in my darkest days. Amen.

Call To Action

What is holding you back from a life of hope? Identify those areas and write down the ways in which you can change them and live a hopeful life.

Gabrielle Blackett

March 9

STANDING ON THE PROMISES OF GOD

The Lord is my rock and my fortress and my deliverer; My God, my strength, in whom I will trust; My shield and the horn of my salvation, my stronghold.
Psalm 18:2

The word hope is generally used when we expect a positive outcome to a situation, though it could go either way. Hope used in a Biblical sense speaks of an assurance believers have that things will not remain the same, and that is where faith comes in; it goes hand in hand with Biblical hope.

When we have hope in this present life, it can propel us to do what we know needs to be done. We can set goals and aspire towards them because we know that a positive outcome is possible. We believe we can realize our dreams. We may not be perfect dancers, but we believe that with regular dance training, we will move from the level we are at to one where it is a joy to behold because we are pleasing to the eye. We desire anointed dancers. Noticeably unpolished dancers can distract a congregation, so by improving our dance, we can improve our impact.

We can hope for a better life and prosperity, according to Proverbs 16:3. God's desire is for us to succeed and have a better life. But we also need to place our faith and trust in His promises. Our hope in God is not blind faith.

Prayer

God, You are God and God alone. We thank You for not having to go through this life alone using our own strength. We can stand on Christ, the solid rock to carry us through adversity and to reap success.

Call To Action

- Research the promises of God in the Word and meditate on them, for they are true.

- Let go of things and ideas that have held you back so you can triumph over your circumstances and see a brighter future.

Gurlain Applewhaite

March 10

ALL IS NOT LOST

And this is the will of Him who sent Me, that everyone who sees the Son and believes in Him may have everlasting life; and I will raise him up at the last day.
John 6:40

Hope is an optimistic attitude. In truly difficult circumstances, when we are at our lowest point, it may seem impossible to trust God for the future. In these times, God reminds us in 2 Corinthians 12:9-11 that His grace is sufficient to carry us through and assures us in John 6:40 that we have a brighter future ahead. When we have hope, it keeps us going no matter how difficult things are, for we know that He is working things out for our good. We have hope in our daily lives and something better to look forward to in the future.

Our dance ministries may comprise people of different ages, spiritual levels and skills. However, we are one body on the same mission. From time to time, dancers may become discouraged, but we have an obligation to offer hope and encouragement, especially as we all work on becoming better dancers.

There may be some dancers who do not see the bigger picture and, therefore, question the significance of the dance. Our duty as dance ministers of the Word is to instruct them on how we use our bodies to communicate the Gospel of Jesus Christ whilst we are here on earth, to share the joy that fills our souls when we think of what is ahead. Our hope is in Christ. We believe that when we die, that will not be the end. It doesn't end at the grave. We have the assurance that one day, He will return from heaven as He said He would and take us back to be with Him.

Prayer

Lord, Abba Father, we thank You for providing a way out for us in every circumstance, and we thank You that this life is not all there is, but there is the promise of everlasting life in Your presence. In Jesus' name. Amen.

Call To Action

- Never lose hope.

- Maintain a positive attitude always.

- Put your hope in God alone, not things or people.

- Take God at His Word.

Gurlain Applewhaite

Call To Action

- Never lose hope.

- Maintain a positive attitude always.

- Put your hope in God alone, not things or people.

- Take God at His Word.

March 11

GOD'S BETTER PLAN

"For I know the plans I have for you," declares the LORD, "plans to prosper you and not to harm you, plans to give you hope and a future. Jeremiah 29:11

God has a good plan for our lives, even though He does not show us every step of the way in advance. As we follow His guidance and let Him take full control of our lives, we begin to see the plan for our success unfold. When we do not commit our way unto God, things can go the opposite way of what we planned. Satan plans to deceive, cause us to fail and bring us discouragement.

We may make plans for our dance ministry, but as Psalm 127:1 indicates, "Unless the Lord builds the house, they labor in vain that build it". We see ourselves moving from ministering in-house to our congregation to ministering on national and international platforms, but how do we achieve this? We give God full reign over the ministry. We commit the ministry to God, make Him Lord over it and trust Him to guide us in the way we should go. Like John the Baptist in John 3:30, we must decrease so that God can increase and work wonders in our lives.

Prayer

Dear Lord, thank You for having a plan for our lives to bring success, for You know what is best for us. We are comforted that we do not have to navigate this life alone, working out our own plans and being unsure of the outcome. We trust Your plan, in Jesus' name. Amen.

Call To Action

- Always seek God's counsel before you make decisions.

- Turn over your plans to God, for He knows what's best.

- Trust God to lead you in the right way.

Gurlain Applewhaite

March 12

A TRUE HOPE

"For I know the plans I have for you," declares the LORD, "plans to prosper you and not to harm you, plans to give you hope and a future. Jeremiah 29:11

Jeremiah was speaking to the people as they were forced to leave Jerusalem for Babylon. There was so much turmoil (emotionally and physically) that it was a stressful time for the believers.

There was also a false prophet named Hananiah who gave false hope to the Jews. She told the people that God would relieve them from their suffering after two years and return them to their homes, a false prophecy Jeremiah heard and rebuked.

As Jeremiah did, we are called to share God's Word and remind others that there is hope in God. COVID-19 is still very present in our lives today. Many people have lost their jobs and cannot meet the various needs of their families, and many are depressed and have lost all hope. More than ever, this scripture verse gives us hope as Christians. When hardships occur in our lives, we are assured that we can always find refuge in the Word of God.

The enemy will use people to give us false hope, just like Hananiah did. COVID-19 seems not to be going anywhere anytime soon, but, like Jeremiah, we will take a stand by showing others that the God we believe in says there is hope. Not only is there hope, but His Word also says He has plans to prosper and not harm us. The trials and tribulations are just for a time, but the plans include giving us hope and a future. This implies that we will emerge with a great future after the season of trial and tribulation.

Prayer

Thank You, Jesus, for this reassurance that there is indeed hope. Even in these trying and difficult times, please help us to believe Your Word. Thank You for the bright future that You have ahead for us, in Jesus' Name, Amen.

Call To Action

Identify any areas of false hope in your life and seek God for His guidance.

Julie Greene

March 13

MY HOPE

Though he slay me, yet will I hope in him; I will surely defend my ways to his face.
Job 13:15

The Bible says that Job was "blameless" and "upright," always careful to avoid doing evil, yet he suffered so much pain and hurt. He lost his children and possessions and suffered such extreme afflictions in his body that he wanted to die. It was a sad position to be in, as Job did nothing to deserve this. We read that at one point, Job sat by a grave awaiting death, and with all of the anguish, he thought he would surely die. Further down in chapter 17, verse 15, Job is at the stage where he has lost hope in everything and everyone. The only one he knew that he could hope in was God.

The enemy uses anyone and anything to prompt us to lose hope. Often, he uses persons close to us to say or do things that cause us pain. As dance ministers, let us stand firm, knowing that whatever comes our way, no matter how hard it is, there is hope. We cannot depend on ourselves, but there is hope in our Father. In the darkest and most challenging times, let us cry out to God because in Him, there is hope.

Like Job, when I was at death's door in 2016-2017, it seemed as though there was no hope. Some doctors and nurses thought I was surely going to die. I was a "vegetable", but I had inner hope. My hope was not in the doctors, nurses or medication. My hope was in Jesus.

Prayer

Father, forgive us for not putting our hope in You. Help us to always remember that no matter how low we go, You are there with us. Thank You for this reassurance, God. We commit to putting our hope in You, in Jesus' Name. Amen.

Call To Action

What are you hoping for, or what have you lost hope in? Keep hope alive. Build that hope back up.

Julie Greene

March 14

THANK GOD!

But thank God! He gives us victory over sin and death through our Lord Jesus Christ. 1 Corinthians 15:57

We win! The victory is ours! Listen, you cannot only get excited about our victory over sin through Jesus at Easter. We have to be excited about God's sacrifice every day. Though we go through hard times, trials and disappointments, it is important that we are never distracted from the truth that Christ did it all, so we, once we stay faithful to Him, will win in the end. So, dance minister, it is okay to dance through that trial, praise through that circumstance, and wage warfare for your family and loved ones. Dance on the head of the enemy, man! Remind him whose you are and who you are. If it is necessary, dance to remind yourself as well.

Dance is not only beautiful, it is a weapon against the enemy's plans. So, getting knocked down will happen. You cannot be in a war and not get hurt, but what you do when you get that jab is what's important. Get up! You are predestined to win. If God is for you, who can be against you? If God is with you, who shall you fear? Keep fighting, and we'll win! Jesus is our hope.

Prayer

My hope is in You and You alone, oh God. I will praise You in the mountain and the valley. You guaranteed me victory when You sent Your Son; now, I live for You. Thank You, Daddy, for loving me with an everlasting love. Thank You for declaring that nothing can separate us. Thank You for all You have been and all that You are in my life. In Jesus' Name, Amen.

Call To Action

Whatever is trying to hold you down or keep you bound, please wear your praise garment and start to wage warfare as you dance this week. Make it your devotion time. Don't just sit and pray; get up, use all your weapons and fight. God is for you.

Laina Jacob

March 15

ABOUNDING IN HOPE

May the God of hope fill you with all joy and peace in believing so that by the power of the Holy Spirit you may abound in hope. Romans 15:13

There were times when God came through at the last minute. When we needed garments or worship instruments, God moved on someone's heart to provide the resources and open doors for our ministry.

There were times when I had a crisis within my family life that affected my dance. Truthfully, I would have preferred to sit in silence and deal with it on my own or take leave from dance, but it was during all this that God showed me amid my pain that there is hope.

Help - Ask for help and support if you need it. Never try to carry any battle alone. The Word of God tells us to bear one another's burdens. Ask God for someone you can talk to about what seems hopeless.

Open - Open your heart to love and support from others when life gets rough. Be open to advice and change. Make the necessary adjustments if needed.

Pray - Keep your face towards God. Speak to your loving Father. He will give you the needed grace to make it through any battle.

Encourage - Find someone else that you can encourage and stand in faith with. When we take our attention off ourselves, we see how God will work for us because we have put others first.

Prayer

Lord, we pray that in the midst of our battle, we will believe that Your joy and peace will keep our hearts and minds at rest by Your Holy Spirit.

Call To Action

Find one person to pray for and encourage them to have hope and not give up.

Maxine Butcher

March 16

HOPE IN GOD

Hope maketh us not ashamed; because the love of God is shed abroad in our hearts by the Holy Spirit which He has given to us. Romans 5:5

When I was much younger, I would go to concerts and see dancers dancing, and I would imagine myself on stage with my beautiful garments and flags. One day, to my surprise, my youth leader announced that she would be starting a dance ministry and wanted me to be a part of it. The rest, as they say, is history. I was hoping for something, and it came to pass.

So, hope makes us not ashamed. When trials come our way, sometimes, we stand alone; other times, our friends and family may stand with us to offer support and encouragement. We often hear these words, "Don't give up hope". If I stand in faith in God's Word, it will build hope in me. Hope gives us the inner strength to overcome our mountains. Hope allows us to see the silver lining behind every dark cloud. Hope says, "There's light at the end of the tunnel". Hope is an expectation of better things, giving us a feeling of trust in something or someone.

Prayer

God, let me never be ashamed. I put my hope and trust in You. Thank You for the love of God that is shed throughout my heart by Your Holy Spirit.

Call To Action

Think of something that felt too hard to continue, so you gave up on it. This time around, you'll be starting from a place of hope. Find the faith and hope to start again.

Maxine Butcher

March 17

GATHER IT

We remember before our God and Father your work produced by faith, your labour prompted by love, and your endurance inspired by hope in our Lord Jesus Christ. 1 Thessalonians 1:3

This scripture made me reminisce because it first talks about remembering. I was prompted to ask myself if I always "showed up" when necessary, pulled my weight or went beyond the call of duty. Colossians 3:23 says, "Whatever you do, do it as though you are working for the Lord". Ministry can get busy, and dance ministry can take it to another level with rehearsals, preparation for productions or pieces, being called to minister and all the other tasks that come with it. You get tired and weary, and I know for me, I sometimes wonder what the results will be.

As a former dance leader, the burden of ministry was heavy, and I didn't feel equipped. The results weren't what I expected in many areas; it was frustrating and disheartening, but I pressed on because I made a commitment not only to the Lord but also to those I was charged to lead. This was my mindset even before taking over the ministry. Through all the ups and downs, hope was always present for me. It was in the prayers we prayed, the pieces we ministered, the edifying of the dancers, the hope and inspiration for creativity. Unless we really think about it, we don't realize that hope is such a big part of our daily lives.

I want to encourage you to let hope fill your hearts and keep those dreams and desires alive. They might not always manifest, but there is something about having hope that lights the way and gives you something to believe in. So, gather it and plant those seeds of hope every chance you get.

Prayer

Father, thank You for giving me hope. I pray it will continue to be a source of inspiration when I am feeling low. May You remind me of the good things You have done so far in my life and the lives of others I know. You are my hope. Amen.

Call To Action

Trust and wait on the Lord.

Orissa Fitzpatrick

March 18

HOPE IS LIVING

Now the God of hope fill you with all joy and peace in believing, that ye may abound in hope, through the power of the Holy Ghost. Romans 15:13

Hope is living here simply because life brings hope. Strong's definition of hope is given in Greek as ἐλπίς, elpis, *el-pece'* from ἔλπω elpō, which is a primary word (to anticipate, usually with pleasure); expectation (abstract or concrete) or confidence; faith, hope.

Some say, "Do not set your expectations too high because you will set yourself up for disappointment". However, we should confidently set our expectations on the Most High, who always sets us up for *this appointment*. He always ensures that we get what is for us. Therefore, in life, we can patiently anticipate, with pleasure and confidence, what God has in store for us. We can also share this posture and position with others as we praise Him while waiting for its manifestation. When dancing, we can display (quietly or boldly) this confidence and hopeful expectation with our position, posture and praise, always leading our audience towards the One who gives us hope and fulfills it. He is Hope, and He is alive!

Prayer

Lord, may my position, posture and praise always reflect the faith, hope and confidence I have in You, leading others to pursue You with anticipation, pleasure, expectation and hope.

Call To Action

- Position: Align yourself with God.

- Posture: Always approach Him humbly.

- Praise: Bless the Lord at all times.

Pierre Rock

March 19

IN HIS SHELTER...PRAISE

God is our refuge and strength, a very present help in trouble. Psalm 46:1

There are moments in life when we are in a hard place. It seems like all there is around us is darkness and despair. In those moments, you may feel like all is lost and try to muster up whatever small glimmer of hope may be left, but it is hard. In the words of Judith Gayle, "Stay with God, in spite of what you see or feel. Stay with God, in spite of how things may appear. Stay with God. It doesn't matter what may come our way. There is only one place we are safe. Stay with God."

Imagine you are in the middle of a storm or hurricane, exposed, tossed to and fro, and someone is there calling you, willing and waiting to provide shelter. What would you do? I'm almost certain you would accept the source of refuge. The same rings true for us in our personal storms; God, our refuge, is there waiting for us to run to Him. Will we accept His help or continue trying to do it on our own? Accepting His help doesn't mean our situation will instantly be resolved, but it keeps our hope alive.

Might I suggest that while you wait, still praise? Speak to your spirit, command your body to praise God. He's still worthy, "Why are you cast down, O my soul, and why are you in turmoil within me? Hope in God; for I shall again praise him, my salvation and my God", Psalm 43:5. While you're waiting in His shelter...Praise! After all, praise is our weapon of warfare. Praise changes the atmosphere.

Prayer

Lord, help me to put my hope and trust in You through every storm and trial. Help me to have hope in the good times and the hard times. Give me the strength to never lose my praise, but prompt me to praise my way through every situation, in Jesus' Name.

Call To Action

Pause for 5 minutes, play a song that ministers to you, and give God your best praise.

Rheanne Rock

March 20

ULTIMATE HOPE

But I will hope continually and will yet praise thee more and more. Psalm 71:14

When I hear the word hope, I think and believe that whatever I face, God will help me. At first, when it was time to go back to school face to face, I was very afraid. I really did not want to catch COVID-19. I was obedient, followed all the protocols, and trusted God to keep me safe.

As a child, it is easy to rely on mummy and daddy, but at school, they are not there. So, I choose to trust God and place my hope in Him. Even when people do bad things to me, and I feel like I've been treated unfairly and I'm alone, I place my hope in Jesus.

We, children, often ask questions like, "Would COVID ever go away?" No one knows the answer, but one thing that is sure is that we have hope in Jesus. Once we obey His commandments and live for Him, He will continually protect us and give us hope.

At times, we may get tempted to do wrong, but there is hope for us. Our Daddy, named Jesus, is right there to help us through. My ultimate hope is to get to Heaven, so I will do what God wants me to do.

Prayer

Help us, Lord, to not look at what is going on around us but to always place our trust and hope in You. You are the ultimate One that will keep us. Thank You for giving that hope that only comes from You. In Jesus' Name. Amen.

Call To Action

I want to encourage you to always remember that no matter what you are faced with, there is hope. Things will happen in your life, but God will help you. It may appear that there is no hope, but as the verse says, there is hope, and we will praise God more and more.

Rhema-Jae Greene

March 21

HOPE IS AVAILABLE

"For I know the plans I have for you," says the Lord. "They are plans for good and not for disaster, to give you a future and a hope". Jeremiah 29: 11

Sometimes in our lives, we need that extra push, especially in difficult situations. We often don't know where to turn when the bills are due, cupboards are empty, and we have no idea what we should do next. I urge you to remember that our hope is in the Lord.

We, who know Jesus as our Lord and Saviour, can trust and know that our God is bigger than anything we face. We might not know when He will do what His promises say, but so long as we hold steadfast to the hope we have in Him, He will make a way.

One night, I had to minister in dance and lost my house keys. I began to get flustered, but the Spirit reminded me of the verse that says, "My hope is in the Lord", so I put my hope in Him that my keys would be found and nothing would stop me from ministering that night. In the end, I found my keys because God's Word is true and living.

God is the best person to put your hope in because He is not a man that He would ever lie. He knows whatever we need and whenever we need it, and He must always get the honor and glory. Don't stop hoping He will come through with that job or even that money to pay the bills, for He is God and God alone.

Prayer

Lord, my hope is in You, and I will continue to trust all Your plans for me. It can be hard sometimes, but I know You will make a way for me in Jesus' mighty name. Amen.

Call To Action

- Hold on to the promises of God.

- Always know there is hope.

- Trust God even when things seem hopeless.

Rhonda .A. Babb

March 22

HE WILL SEE YOU THROUGH

But blessed is the one who trusts in the Lord, whose confidence is in him.
Jeremiah 1:7

Having hope in God gives me the confidence I need to do all that God has placed on my heart to do. Sometimes, when I worship in dance, the rehearsal sessions can be challenging, but by hoping and trusting in God and surrendering my dance to Him, I know that He will see me through until the end, which brings me comfort.

So many bad things are happening in the world all around us, but God is asking us today to put our trust and confidence in Him. Sometimes, our friends, teachers and family may disappoint us, but God gives us hope.

Prayer

Dear God, I pray that we will always put our hope in You. Help us not to worry when things do not go the way we want them to, but help us look to You, call upon You, and never lose hope or take our eyes off You. Amen.

Call To Action

What do you think God's message of hope is for you today? As you go about your day, think about Jeremiah 29:11, which says: "For I know the plans I have for you," declares the Lord, "plans to prosper you and not to harm you, plans to give you hope and a good future."

Trinitee Angus

March 23

WHY SHOULD WE, AS BELIEVERS, HAVE HOPE

"For I know the plans I have for you," declares the Lord, "plans to prosper you and not to harm you, plans to give you a hope and a future." Jeremiah 29:11

This Bible verse is so meaningful and full of life. God has a plan for each and every one of you reading this book. Sometimes we feel like certain things are meant to harm us, or certain people or things come into our lives to ruin us, but that is not the case. You may think God doesn't know what He's doing, but He does. He is there behind the scenes checking things out, preparing a way for you that will give you so much hope and a future. You won't even remember that rough patch you went through.

I always ask myself, "How did you know you were meant to be a dancer?" God knew me before I got to know myself. God was already planning my future. He had plans for me to be His dancing prophet. He already knew I was going to be a warrior in His Kingdom. I used to ask myself, "Why me?". God asked me, "Well, why not you?" As believers, we need to be aware of our value to God. We need to have hope for today, tomorrow, next month, and the next few years to come.

We have to hold our ground and stand firm on what God says because sometimes the enemy might come and whisper things in our ears like, "You have lost that fire in you; you will no longer burn for God", or "You have lost your gift", you are nothing." Well, I am telling you today, enough is enough; stand your ground. Do you not know who you are? Are you unaware of your value? If so, I suggest you find and hold on to that hope quickly because the Lord is the hope of your soul. You'll find your strength and confidence in Him.

Prayer

Thank you, Oh God, for giving us hope. I pray that we will stay steadfast in You, that we will never lose sight of what is important and that we will never question the plans You have for us. In Jesus' Name. Amen.

Call To Action

I encourage you to listen to the song "Hope of My Soul" by Reverend Suzette Husbands on YouTube. I hope it speaks to you as it has to me.

Zariah Watson

March 24

HOPE IN GOD AND EVERYTHING WILL FALL INTO PLACE

I wait for the Lord, my whole being waits, and in his word, I put my hope.
Psalm 130:3

Waiting is a practice that seems counterproductive to most of us. The idea of waiting can be so tedious and long-term that you feel like giving up. You have all these unanswered questions, and it tends to frustrate you after a while. Trust me, I know; I have been there, and I had to take a step back and listen to God through his Word. You may think that God will give you what you are waiting for through someone, or it will just fall into your lap, but I have learned that you must dig into the Word.

We cannot just wake up one morning and pray for confirmation on something we have been waiting for without placing our hope in God. It does not work like that. You have to stay grounded in the Word and be available to hear God whenever and wherever. It is important that we not mix up God's words with the words we want to hear because sometimes we are so desperate to hear from the Lord.

Today, I encourage you to always place your hope in the Lord, even in your ministries. As a member of a dance ministry, I have learned that if you want your dance to reach higher levels and for the dance ministers to be aligned with one another, you must have hope, you must stay in the Word, you must pray for each other and the ministry, and, most importantly, you must wait. We, as a God-believing community, must learn to trust God. We must be willing to wait on Him and remember His timing is perfect and precise.

Prayer

I pray that we will maintain hope in You and hold steadfast onto the assurance that what we are praying for is already in the works. Teach us patience, oh Lord, that we may wait on You and wait for Your instructions. I pray that we will block out any words that are not from You or any confirmation that is not from You. May we only hear what comes from You. In Jesus' Name. Amen.

Call To Action

Wait, I say, wait on the Lord!

Zariah Watson

Call To Action

Wait, I say, wait on the Lord!

Zariah Watson

March 25

I NEED TO HOLD ON
(POEM)

For I know the plans I have for you declares the Lord, plans to prosper you and not to harm you, plans to give you hope and a future. Jeremiah 29:11

I need to hold on, I need to hold on, I need to hold on

It's slipping, it's on the tip of my fingers and yet still the touch is becoming unrecognisable.

I have to believe

I have to keep my head up

Held high

Higher than the clouds in the sky

I can't lose hope

Not now

I have to fight

I have to push

Get up

GET UP!

We can't stop here

There's still a chance

There's still hope that everything will fall into place

That He won't let us down

Give it all to Him

Put it all in His hands

He won't forsake us

He won't abandon us

So please

Just please don't give up Hope.

Zenaida R. Mayers

March 26

TO BELIEVE IN A BETTER MINISTRY
(POEM)

Then you will call on me and come and pray to me, and I will listen to you. You will seek me and find me when you seek me with all your heart.
Jeremiah 29:12-13

There's still a chance

A chance to be better

To be better than the ones before us

To bring Unity amongst the division

Unity to a strong ministry

To be a Family in each other

Not just in each other but in Christ as well

To understand

To take accountability

We must do better

We must become better

Our ministry is stronger than you think

It's more important than you think

We are God-sent

Disciples of God

To believe in a better ministry

Is to believe in each other

Is to believe in Him

Is to become, One.

Zenaida R. Mayers

March 27

GIVE HOPE A CHANCE

Those who hope in the Lord will renew their strength, they will soar on wings like eagles, they will run and not be weary, they will walk and not faint. Isaiah 40:31

Hope can be found in many things; some people put all their hope in their jobs, their friends and even their families, but 1 Timothy 4:10 says that we labour and thrive because we put our hope in the living God. Hope in God is a confident expectation of what is to come or what you want to happen. It allows you to set plans in motion to do or achieve something even though you don't physically see the way forward. The Word of God says you will soar and never get tired, which means you will prosper in all you do.

In dance ministry, we hope in more than one way: we hope to choose a dance that relates to the song, we hope to remember our routines, we hope to execute the dance well, we even hope there is no garment malfunction, but most importantly, we hope it changes someone's life and brings comfort to them, we hope it pleases and glorifies God, and we hope it brings souls to Christ.

I had always hoped to minister in dance one day. I would see myself dancing each time there was ministry. I would be dancing in the house a lot, and every time I attempted to join Halal's Timeless Arm, there would be some setback, some issue preventing me from getting started. One day, I said, no more, God, I am going to dance, come what may. I reached out to the leader of Timeless, and now here I am, ministering in dance for the Lord.

Prayer

Father, I thank You for blessing me with the gift of dance. I pray, God, that each time Halal ministers, it is pleasing to You, that it makes You smile, that souls will be saved, and that someone will find hope through our dance. We give You all the honor and all the glory that is due to You, Lord, in Jesus' name,

Amen.

Call To Action

God is our source of hope. Psalms 62:5-6 speaks to our trust in God's hope which gives us peace, and joy in the midst of our troubles. Romans 15:13 says there is boldness, strength, courage, endurance, confidence and patience to be had when we hope in God. Do not doubt. Give hope a chance today.

Lylah Browne

March 28

FROM HOPELESS TO HOPEFUL

May the God of hope fill you with all joy and peace in believing, so that by the power of the Holy Spirit you may abound in hope. Romans 15:13

It's easy to speak about hope when things are going well. It's easy to have hope when we're dancing on the mountaintop. But, those valley days, my my my… those valley days! Do I have a witness? Some days there's less hope than full hope. Some days, you can barely even conjure up a speck of hope, but God! That song, "Never Would've Made It," rings in my ears as I write this because, truly, we know that had it not been for God, we would've given up and walked away so many times.

Life can be so hard; every day we wake up, we do not know the challenges that may lie ahead. We see people walking around with smiles on the outside but open wounds of hurt, depression and despair on the inside. Have you been a source of hope for anyone who is feeling hopeless? Have you encouraged anyone today? Have you checked in on your friends and loved ones, even those who seem to have it all together? Allow yourself to be the instrument of hope God can use to help someone who's in the valley. So often, after someone commits suicide, we hear people saying, but what would make "so and so" do that; hopelessness made them do it. They felt like there was no way out. Be that source of hope to someone today. Offer the source of hope to them…Jesus.

Prayer

Lord, help me when I feel hopeless, and help me help those who are hopeless to be hopeful.

Call To Action

Check-in with a friend, co-worker, or loved one today or, better yet, right now.

Rheanne Rock

March 29

REJOICE!

Rejoice in hope, be patient in tribulation, be constant in prayer. Romans 12:12

Hope is a small, simple word to pronounce. Yet, it is also an impactful word that holds much weight. Hope is one of those words we need daily. When I look up the meaning, it says hope is a feeling of expectation and desire for a certain thing to happen.

We hope our prayers are answered.
We hope to live and not die.
We hope things work out for the better.
We hope to see the next day.
We hope to be recognized.
We hope to be married.
We hope for the job.
We hope for the school.
We hope for the bills to be paid.
We hope to be on time.
We hope to have a family.
We hope for the best for our children.
We hope to get in/out of situations.
We hope for the future.

Prayer

Dear God, thank You for reminding us that being hopeful is a good thing. We ask that You keep us hopeful in You before anything else. Help us to remember that once we do this, You will grant us the desires of our hearts according to Your will.

Call To Action

Listen to this Song, "You Keep Hope Alive" by Mandisa & Jon Reddick. Read Psalm 62:5-6 and Jeremiah 29:11.

Keisha Batson

March 30

WAITING IN HOPE

We wait in hope for the Lord; he is our help and our shield. Psalm 33:20

The definition of wait is to stay where you are, while hope means a feeling of expectation and desire for something to happen. When we wait in hope, we stay where we are expecting something to happen. When we wait, we also need to be patient with God. Sometimes, it can be hard to wait in hope for God. For example, if God promised you money or a job and you were waiting for months, staying hopeful can be a challenge.

Even if it seems like what you're waiting for is never going to happen, trust in God, and He will come through for you. If you look at the example of Sarai and Abram from the Bible, Sarai did not have a baby until she was 90 years of age. Ninety is a very big number. Can you imagine yourself waiting for ninety years for something? Some people would stop waiting. Sarai, on the other hand, was very patient and persevering.

God is calling you today to wait on Him, not to give up or get angry at Him, but to be hopeful. When you wait in hope, you can get more than you asked for. My encouragement to you is to be patient and wait in hope for God.

Prayer

Father, I know You want me to be hopeful, but sometimes it can be challenging. Teach me to be faithful to You and others, Father, Amen.

Call To Action

Make a ball out of paper; every time you are patient, add another piece of paper to the ball. Try to get your ball as big as possible this month.

Shaquonna Rock

March 31

WHERE CAN HOPE BE FOUND?

For I know the plans I have for you, declares the Lord, plans for welfare and not for evil, to give you a future and a hope. Jeremiah 29:11

Your back is against the wall. When it isn't one thing, it's the next. It feels like the weight of the world is on your shoulders. In that 1980's show, they would say, 'Who you gonna call? Ghostbusters!' So who are you gonna call when hope is nowhere to be found? Surely not Ghostbusters, but our Saviour, Father and Friend. He's an ever-present help in times of trouble.

So when you don't know where to find hope, you feel like you've looked everywhere, and it feels like you've tried everything possible, I encourage you to try Jesus. Make it a habit to try Jesus first, not last. If you were looking to buy a stove, would you go to a bookstore or clothing store first? No, so don't waste your time looking for hope where it cannot be found. Go straight to the one and only reliable source…Jesus!

Prayer

Lord, remind me daily, where my true source of hope is found. Amen.

Call To Action

Write down the times when God came through for you during a battle or a difficult period. Remind yourself that if He did it before, He can do it again.

Rheanne Rock

April 1

FAITHFUL AND TRUE

The master was full of praise. "Well done, my good and faithful servant."
Matthew 25:21

Faithfulness is remaining loyal to someone or something regardless of trials and tribulations. Being faithful to God requires us to submit our ways to Him, obey His word and listen to Him. We, dancers, have many ways we remain faithful to God without even knowing. Firstly, being committed to the ministry is the prime demonstration of our faithfulness. Paying subs and showing up to practice are also examples of demonstrative faithfulness to God. These examples might sound basic and routine, but they are simple and effective. Paying subs isn't always easy, as we, too, have challenges in our lives. However, we pay subs because we are giving back to the Lord, who once gave everything up for us.

Showing up for practices is required, but the things we do to meet that requirement show faithfulness. Dancers originate from all parts of Barbados, yet they all make the sacrifice to be in one place at one time to minister. That is faithfulness. In addition, we can be faithful by being true to ourselves and God by honoring and enhancing our relationships with Him. And just watch and see, when we remain faithful to Him, beautiful things happen: lives are changed, saved, and transformed.

Prayer

Dear Lord, we come to humbly ask You, How best can we serve You? What can we offer as an acceptable sacrifice to You? Help us to serve You without ulterior motives and solely for the reason of being faithful to You. Let our sacrifices as dancers be enough to satisfy You and enable us to maintain consistent services to You so that we can be qualified to receive Your blessings. This we pray in Jesus' name, Amen.

Call To Action

Stay faithful to God by displaying the many actions used to honor Him daily (like the ones listed above). Let God see clearly that we are loyal to Him and trust Him wholeheartedly. Just as He is faithful to us, we are faithful to Him.

Danae Niles

FAITHFUL GOD

But without faith it is impossible to please Him: for he that cometh to God must believe that He is, and that He is a rewarder of those who diligently seek Him.
Hebrews 11:6

Sometimes, we go through trials that are meant to test our faith. However, it is important to remember that these trials are also opportunities for our faith to grow. For example, when God brings us out of our trials victorious, which He always does, our faith in Him grows. Our trials and tribulations show us that He is indeed a faithful God.

We have to look to God whenever we speak about faithfulness because He is always faithful. In fact, the Bible says that He is faithful even when we are not. So, if we feel our faith is beginning to waver, we can look to the ever-faithful One and ask Him to strengthen our faith.

Sometimes God tells us a specific thing, and we believe Him, but then we let what others say sway our faith in what He has said. In these situations, it is important to remember that God is not a man that He should lie. We must also never lean on our own understanding but instead trust in God with all our hearts, for He is ever faithful.

Prayer

Dear God, we ask that You give us the faith we need to face every challenge we have in this life. We know that we can't be perfect, but we also know that without faith, it is impossible to please You, as the Scripture says. So today, we pray that You will strengthen our faith and multiply it. In Jesus' name, Amen.

Call To Action

I encourage you to look at your situations, challenges, trials, and tribulations from the perspective of faith today: faith in God and faith in His goodness, love, and sovereignty. Let that faith impact and affect how you see and interact with your situation, and remember that God gave us the faith to believe in His Son in the first place. Jesus is the author and finisher of our faith, not us. So, if we need our faith strengthened, we can always ask.

Danielle Harewood

April 3

FAITHFUL IN ALL

Well done, good, faithful servant. You have been faithful over a few things; I will set you over many things. Enter into the joy of your Lord. Matthew 25:21

Are you loyal to things that take you away from your faithfulness to God? Today, hit the reset button. When I get to heaven, I want Jesus to say, "Well done, my child, you have been a good and faithful servant". Don't we all want that? I don't want Him to say that I have been faithful only in the big things, but I want Him to say that I was also faithful in the small things. Sometimes, it is not always about doing a solo in a dance, but it's about those small things like being there and encouraging one another even when we're not chosen to be in the dance piece. It's about being committed no matter the role you are asked to play.

The Bible says that faithfulness comes from a place of trust and loyalty. Hebrews 11:1 says, "Now faith is a confidence in what we hope for and an assurance about what we do not see". As a Christian, it is essential to be faithful to God. It is one thing to believe in Him, but another to be faithful to Him. As you look inward today, know that God remains faithful to His children no matter your mistakes and lack of belief at times. He will set you over many things.

Prayer

Today, Lord, as we reflect on Your faithfulness towards us, may we also be faithful in the things You have given us. Thank You for the air we breathe, the hands we lift to worship You and the joy that is our strength. We thank You, Father, and bless You in no other name than the name of Jesus.

Call To Action

Remain faithful to God not only in the big things but in those small things that may seem insignificant. Hit that reset button today.

Eslyn Taylor

FAITHFUL TO BELIEVE

Faithful is the one who calls you, and he also will bring it to pass.
1 Thessalonians 5:24

By definition, faithfulness is about unfailing and unwavering loyalty to someone or something. God's faithfulness is shown to us daily in His protection, provision, guidance, and many other ways. God is so faithful that He does not need to do these things for us, but He does them anyway.

Unlike friends and family who may leave and forsake you because they are human, and we can't fault them for that, God will never do that, and that is one thing you can be sure of. Even when it feels like he has forgotten you, the truth is that he is preparing something better for you or preparing you for what you might have asked for.

As dancers, how can we show faithfulness to our craft? Faithfulness can show up as being on time, practicing and knowing the choreography, helping those who may need help with the choreography, and aligning yourself with the will of God before ministry so that He can speak through you. Why? Because this is a gift that God has given us, the best way to show our faithfulness to God through dance is by ensuring that we always do it from the right place.

Prayer

Dear Lord, forgive me for any time that I have doubted Your faithfulness towards me, and please forgive me for the times I have not been faithful to You. May I always be faithful to You and trust Your faithfulness to me. Amen.

Call To Action

Where does your faithfulness lie? Is it in Jesus? This week, be intentional in strengthening that faithfulness.

Gabrielle Blackett

April 5

GOD'S PROMISES ARE SURE

But the Lord is faithful, who will establish you and guard you from the evil one.
2 Thessalonians 3:3

In the book of Job, we see that Satan can only do so much as God allows. God is faithful and true to His Word. God will not leave us on our own. He will be there for us just as He was right there alongside Moses and Joshua in the many battles that Israel went through.

Even as we expect God to be faithful to His promises, we are also to play our part and be faithful to Him. He made a covenant, and all we must do is be obedient. Though we may stray at times and not spend time with Him in worship, prayer and thanksgiving, God remains committed to His promises.

Whatever we do in life, we should do it unto God. As dancers, we can show faithfulness in our commitment to attending rehearsals regularly and punctually. If we observe something that has been overlooked by those responsible, we can show we care by tackling that issue or assisting in completing it. Our talents or gifts should be placed at the disposal of the dance ministry, for we are all on the same path to reach the same goal – the success of the ministry in carrying out its mandate of saving souls through dance.

We need to show commitment to our church as a whole, for if we cannot or will not support our church in aspects such as regular attendance, support for other ministries in the church or support for projects undertaken by the church, then we have failed. Our dance ministry is not a separate entity from the church we attend, so overall support is needed.

As we continue our Christian walk, may we be ever mindful that God is still the same yesterday, today and forever. What He has done for others in the past, He can also do for us.

Prayer

Heavenly Father, forgive us for the times we have done things we should not have, as well as the times we did not do the things we should have. Thank You for Your constant faithfulness towards us in Jesus' name. Amen.

Call To Action

Let us be diligent and intentional in all we do, for whatever we do, we do it as unto God.

Gurlain Applewhaite

April 6

MAY WE BE FOUND FAITHFUL

Therefore we also, since we are surrounded by so great a cloud of witnesses, let us lay aside every weight, and the sin which so easily ensnares us, and let us run with endurance the race that is set before us, looking unto Jesus, the author and finisher of our faith, who for the joy that was set before Him endured the cross, despising the shame, and has sat down at the right hand of the throne of God.
Hebrews 12:1-2

We have the encouragement from the lives of those great men and women of the Bible and afterwards who pressed on and persevered to run the race with their eyes firmly fixed on Jesus. As children of God, we have a duty to stay the course and be faithful to Him, as He has proved Himself faithful to us. We must also be faithful to our ministry and our church. We can stand on God's Word and declare it as truth.

One of the most important aspects of the ministry is that we share the vision of the ministry's leader. We should also have God's purpose for the ministry in mind. Faithfulness is the foundation of any successful relationship, which entails sticking with our ministry partners during the good and bad times. When we hear outsiders bad-talking or gossiping about them, we should not tolerate it. It is incumbent upon us to show strong loyalty.

"Let us leave to those behind us. The heritage of faithfulness passed on through godly lives." - Steve Green, Singer

Prayer

Oh, Lord, help us to keep our eyes focused on Jesus so that at the end of the race, we can receive the prize and hear, "Well done, thou good and faithful servant." In Jesus' name, we pray. Amen.

Call To Action

Practice self-control, self-discipline and self-denial in all things.

Use your time and talents in the building of God's Kingdom.

Gurlain Applewhaite

April 7

A FAITHFUL SERVANT

His master replied, 'Well done, good and faithful servant! You have been faithful with a few things; I will put you in charge of many things. Come and share your master's happiness! Matthew 25:21

When you are faithful, this means that you are loyal. One who is loyal is unwavering, steady and firm no matter the circumstance. God is the ultimate faithful One, and as His children, we should also aspire to be faithful.

The first question to ask ourselves is, "Am I being faithful to God?" God has given us neighbors, co-workers, and friends who may be unbelievers but only hear or know about God through us. Are we sharing and letting our light shine so their lives can be impacted? If the answer is yes, then we are being faithful servants. If the answer is no, we have to pause and ask God for forgiveness and commit to sharing His gospel with all in our environment.

The second question to ask ourselves is, "Are we being faithful in the small things in life?" God has blessed us with finances to be used for His glory. Are we tithing and giving offerings? Let us not be bogged down with the lack of sufficient income. Instead, let us always remember the source of our income. Our faithful God is the ultimate source of our income.

God has blessed us with many talents that we should use to bless others. We should never get lazy or tired of being used by God. At times, we may feel like not using these talents, but we should always remember that there are persons who depend on our ability to be faithful. God will give us more when we are faithful with little.

Prayer

Father, our desire is to hear from You, "Well done, good and faithful servant". Forgive us when we lack faithfulness, and show us how to get back on track. Thank You, Father. In the name of Jesus, Amen.

Call To Action

Examine your life daily by asking the questions above.

Julie Greene

April 8

NO VOIDS

So is my word that goes out from my mouth: It will not return to me empty, but will accomplish what I desire and achieve the purpose for which I sent it.
Isaiah 55:11

There is peace in knowing that God stands by His Word. He is faithful. Sometimes, God would give you a song to inspire you to choreograph a piece to, but you are focused on preparing for a season at church or a scheduled time for dance ministry because you know God is using you to bless His people. In all the preparation, you forget that you, *too*, are one of His people. You forget that He can do His work while you are preparing the choreography and learning the dance. Sometimes, what you are doing is for you. So, in every rehearsal, you have to be open to the fact that God is using you for you and for others. His Word is always working, and He is faithful to carry out His work. Expect Him to always show up and do His work.

Prayer

Father, I know You are not a man that You should lie. Help me to trust and believe that as I operate in obedience to Your Word, You will faithfully carry out every plan and strategy You have. Lord, I declare that I will accomplish Your purpose for every ministry You assign me to send forth.

Call To Action

As you prepare for your next choreography or ministry event, remember that God is faithful to fulfill His word. Ask Him to move in you first as you prepare.

Laina Jacob

April 9

DO YOU SEE THE RAM?

Abraham looked up and there in a thicket he saw a ram caught by its horns. He went over and took the ram and sacrificed it as a burnt offering instead of his son.
Genesis 22:13

God will provide. He is faithful. A dance ministry has many needs, including those of the people in the ministry. You see, people have such gifts, but sometimes they aren't able to purchase garments because of their financial situations. They need garments, props, and space to rehearse, just to name a few necessities. What keeps some people focused is that with every prayer and need, they know that God will provide.

I have learned that He is always way ahead of us. Just when you think you are down to your last, God provides a ram. He lays it on the heart of people in the ministry to help, and sometimes He sends people that are not even connected to the ministry. We are our brothers' keepers, so we must pray and act together. Most importantly, we must keep our hearts open to God, to hear and to do His will.

Prayer

God, you are faithful to provide everything we need. We declare that there shall be no lack. Thank You for always sending a ram at just the right time. Thank You for being faithful. We hold on to every promise in Jesus' Name, Amen.

Call To Action

Is there something that God has asked you to do that you have delayed? Decide to be obedient to Him now. Step out and watch God be your provider. I dare you to trust Him.

Laina Jacob

April 10

MY CROWN

Be faithful until death and I will give you a crown of life. Revelation 2:10

Being trustworthy is essential as a dance leader to our pastors' vision for the church and dance ministry. As a former dance leader, I learned not to create my own vision but to submit to the vision laid out for the ministry by my pastors. They entrusted me to be faithful, and they were confident enough to rely on me to do so. My responsibility was to reflect the vision of my pastors through the ministry of the dancers, including dress code, movements and guidelines from leadership.

Being responsible and accountable before God first was my heart's desire. Out of this, I committed to being faithful to all that was entrusted to me. I learned faithfulness by serving others first and being willing to be committed to someone else's vision. God watches your faithfulness, especially when you are being faithful in little. Then He gives you more.

Prayer

Father, teach me how to be committed to our ministry's vision and be faithful to carry it out.

Call To Action

Visualize yourself three years from now. Write three goals you want to achieve by that time and then pray over them.

Maxine Butcher

April 11

WALK IT OUT

Now it is required that those who have been given a trust must prove faithful.
1 Corinthians 4:2

A heavy scripture, isn't it? One that calls for us to be responsible in our walk as believers, and let's be real; it isn't always easy, but it is absolutely possible. The Lord gives us many things to be responsible for, but what gets me about this scripture is that it says we have been given "a trust." Now, this says to me that the Lord sees trust as precious. He sees it as valuable. Yet He saw it fit to gift us with it. Can you imagine that? For a moment, think about what that says about you. Now, think about what it says about God. I know my God, and if He knows everything and is everywhere, this means He knows whether I will get things right or wrong. He knows whether I will drop the ball or run to the finish line with it, if I will put in the work or be lazy, if it will grow or die.

Friends, you will drop the ball, but pick that ball back up and prove yourself faithful to a faithful God. Now, here's the thing: just because we know that the Lord knows all and sees our shortcomings, it doesn't warrant the disposition of "it is what it is," nor should we be actively lackadaisical in our thinking or behavior. Don't lean on that thinking. Like everything else, we have a choice, so we must prove ourselves faithful. You have expectations from others; why shouldn't the Lord have them of you?

As a dancer, ask yourself how you can be faithful in the role you have committed to and consider that you are there to be used in various ways. 2 Timothy 2:13 says if we are faithless, He remains faithful, for He cannot deny Himself. I don't know about you, but this causes me to want to represent, for even though He is always faithful, I want to stand with Him and be counted as such. I want Him to say well done. I hope you do, too.

Prayer

Wonderful Lord, thank You for Your faithfulness. I ask that when I feel pulled not to be faithful, I remember Your Word and gain the strength to do what is right. Amen.

Call To Action

Make your resolve faithfulness.

Orissa Fitzpatrick

142

Call To Action

Make your resolve faithfulness.

WON'T HE DO IT!

The one who calls you is faithful, and He will do it. 1 Thessalonians 5:24

Say it with your chest. Say it again and again until you believe it. I love the Word of God, its power, strength and promises. It truly is food to my spirit. When the Lord called you, it was from a place of knowledge: knowledge of who you would be. Even as you read this, His heart chose you. Don't ever forget that. Don't give up when uncertainty comes and you feel like walking away. Grace is there to carry you. When nothing seems to be going right, and you feel misunderstood, listen to the voice of the Holy Spirit. You may be having difficulty remembering a choreography and may be feeling out of place but know this: you are not the first nor the only one who has been at this place. I certainly have been, but I knew it was where I was supposed to be and that I had to trust God to help me as I knew He would. Why? Because I know Him to be the Faithful One, a security that I lean on daily.

What are you worrying about that is causing your heart to ache? Are you experiencing lack in some form? Are you wishing for better, for a breakthrough? My dear friend, I ask this one thing of you: trust the one who chose you. He knows what He is doing, but just like He is faithful, we must be, too, because faith without works is dead.

The interesting part of this journey is that you will be amazed at the person you become. Do you want to find out? Then, trust the process of who you are becoming. Get the opportunity to look back and say, "I once was but...". God can and will establish you if you give Him a chance. He is sovereign. He is good. He is faithful, and His faithfulness is just one of the characteristics that make up who He is.

Prayer

Heavenly Father, thank You for Your faithfulness and for not letting circumstances break my desire to please You. I know You are building and improving me in Jesus' name. Amen.

Call To Action

Repeat after me, "I will begin to thank God for His faithfulness in every area of my life."

Orissa Fitzpatrick

April 13

FAITH-FULL-NEST

*Know therefore that the LORD thy God, He is God, the faithful God,
which keepeth covenant and mercy with them that love Him and keep His
commandments to a thousand generations; Deuteronomy 7:9*

*Yea, the sparrow hath found a house, and the swallow a nest for herself, where she
may lay her young, even thine altars, O LORD of hosts, my King, and my God.
Blessed are they that dwell in thy house: they will be still praising thee. Selah.
Psalm 84:3-4*

When we continuously dwell in the house of the Lord, especially by the altar(s),
we experience the fulfilling feeling of God's faith in operation to us and through
us. We must remember when we're dancing by the altar that our lives are to be
continuously presented as living sacrifices.

We're on an altar constantly (Romans 12:1-2), and "Blessed are they that dwell
in thy house: they will be still praising thee. Selah" (Psalm 84:4). When we
allow His presence to dwell in us, our nests are full and secure. We can display
our expressions of faith in multiple ways: praising, thanksgiving, supplication,
adoration, and charity, knowing God is faithful to a thousand generations.

Prayer

May my life be a constant display and testimony of Your faithfulness, Lord,
even in the "minute" things.

Call To Action

- Faith: Take at least one faith step today, however minute it may seem.

- Full: Let your life be full of praise and adoration for the Lord.

- Nest: Dwell in the Lord's presence continuously, and let His presence dwell
  in you.

Pierre Rock

April 14

FAITH-FULL-NEST...CONTINUED

Know therefore that the LORD thy God, he is God, the faithful God, which keepeth covenant and mercy with them that love him and keep his commandments to a thousand generations; Deuteronomy 7:9

Yea, the sparrow hath found a house, and the swallow a nest for herself, where she may lay her young, even thine altars, O LORD of hosts, my King, and my God. Blessed are they that dwell in thy house: they will be still praising thee. Selah. Psalm 84:3-4

It cannot be stated enough that our bodies are temples of the Holy Spirit (1 Corinthians 6:19), and His Faith-Full-Nest is on full display when we allow Him to dwell there freely, giving Him liberty to lead us. "Now the Lord is that Spirit and where the Spirit of the Lord is, there is liberty" (2 Corinthians 3:17). Our disposition of submission to the Spirit's leading allows Him to show and prove His faithfulness to us continually, for our "faith should not stand in the wisdom of men but in the power of God" (1 Corinthians 2:5).

Prayer

May our faith not stand in the wisdom of men but the power of God, and may our dance show forth a reciprocating Faith-Full-Nest to and from God.

Call To Action

- Faith: Take at least two faith steps this week.

- Full: Fulfill a promise or commitment you've been delaying.

- Nest: Be a place of security for someone this week.

Pierre Rock

April 15

THE EVIDENCE...THE PROOF...THE VERDICT

Now it is required that those who have been given a trust must prove faithful.
1 Corinthians 4:2

Are we faithful to what we have been entrusted with? Is there evidence in our lives of our faithfulness? When someone gives you a gift, how do you respond? What do you do with your gift? Usually, when one is given a gift, there is some measure of excitement and gratitude. God has given us the gift of dance; He has entrusted us with it. Therefore, He expects us to prove our faithfulness. He is looking for evidence of our dedication. Do not take your gift for granted by misusing it. Prove yourself faithful by living up to God's expectations of us as dance ministers. Some expectations can include:

- Treating your body as God's temple

- Expanding on and growing your gift

- Applying the Word to your dance

Let us be honest with ourselves. Are we proving faithful with our gift of dance? If we are, it should be evident in our lives. May those who come behind us find us faithful.

Prayer

God, we ask for Your forgiveness for any time we have been neglectful and unfaithful with our gifts as dance ministers. Change our habits to reflect the actions and words that You expect of us. Where we lack faithfulness to do what You have called us to do, renew and refresh us. May the evidence of our lives prove faithfulness in all You have entrusted us with. Amen.

Call To Action

After your introspection, identify at least one practical way to prove your faithfulness.

Rheanne Rock

April 16

COMMITMENT BUFFERING?

Do your best to present yourself to God as one approved, a worker who does not need to be ashamed and who correctly handles the word of truth. 2 Timothy 2:15

What is your commitment level? We should constantly examine ourselves and determine if we are truly committed to the ministry God has called us to. Each member of a ministry brings something unique that no other person can bring. What are you doing with what God has equipped you with?

We *do not* have to be the ministry's leader to take the initiative. Be on time, show up, and do what we are called to do with 100% effort. After all, we are doing it for the Master. When we show commitment to His ministry, our ministry, we show commitment to Him. If we really think about it, why should we be begged or pleaded with to show commitment to a ministry that is an instrument and means by which we serve God and bring others to God? Who are we doing it for? Surely not the leader of the ministry. We do it for the King! Is He worth your time, effort, sacrifice, and commitment? If the answer is yes, how can you show this more? Let your commitment level be 100%, not constantly bu…ff…er…ing.

Prayer

Lord, help me be more committed to the things of God than the things of this world. Shift my mindset where it needs shifting, and show me how to put You first in every area of my life. Help me find joy in working in Your Kingdom because it is not about me, God, but about Your Kingdom and giving unto You what you are more than deserving of. Lord, forgive me for every time I have said yes to the things of the world and no to You. Solidify my commitment to You and the ministry You have placed me in, in Jesus' Name.

Call To Action

Be intentional in displaying your commitment; start this week by thinking of and executing at least one task for your ministry.

Rheanne Rock

April 17

PROVING FAITHFUL

Now it is required that those who have been given a trust must prove faithful.
1 Corinthians 4:2

Sharing His Word

God trusts us to share His word with others. For example, if someone does not know about Jesus, I will talk to them about God and His Word. If they do not have a church to go to, I will invite them to come to my church. I will also teach them how to please God and be obedient to those in authority.

I shall continue to try to be obedient to my teachers and parents. My parents require me to do chores every Saturday, and, at times, to be honest, it is hard. At school, we children are given many commands and are supposed to obey them.

Showing Love

During COVID, a lot of children did not have snacks as their parents could not afford them. As Christians, we can take extra snacks and give them to our teachers and let them distribute the snacks to those in need.

<u>Being Faithful to God</u>

As children of God, we should spend time in His Word and in prayer. This is the best way to commune with Him directly. His Word will show us how to be faithful, using the talents He gave us for His glory. I am a dancer, and, at times, I do not feel like dancing. Then God reminds me it is not about me. He gave me this talent to bring glory to His name. I want to be proven faithful to Him. I really want God to be pleased with my life and what I do.

Prayer

Help us, God, to be faithful in all we do on this earth. May our lives be examples of faithful ones. In Jesus' Name. Amen.

Call To Action

God is a faithful God, and as the verse says, He requires us to be faithful. To find out how to be faithful, use His Word to help you.

Rhema-Jae Greene

REMAIN FAITHFUL

Remain in me, and I will remain in you. For a branch cannot produce fruit if it is severed from the vine, and you cannot be fruitful unless you remain in me.
John 15:4

Being faithful speaks about commitment. Sometimes, when situations occur and your faith is tested, you know if you're committed or not. God sometimes finds ways to test you to see if you will stay faithful to Him; He uses trials and challenges to see if you are still standing faithfully on the solid rock.

I remember being told I was not qualified to be on a team. I was lost as to what more I needed to have because I thought I had everything I needed: my attitude, character, knowledge, and skills, but it seemed not to be enough. It was heart-wrenching, but God always has a plan. Sometimes, things might seem confusing and unbelievable, but do you know what God's response to us is? "Which team do you prefer to be on, mine or man? Will you remain faithful to me, although things may not turn out how you want them to?" God waits for us to pass the test of faithfulness.

God always knows what is best for his children, and as His Word says, "A branch cannot produce fruit if it has been severed from the vine". So, it might seem like man has severed you, but God always remains faithful so long as you keep your commitment to him. Whether you are a dancer using your body to glorify Him or a gardener raking the leaves in the yard, His faithfulness is still the same because He is true to His Word. So, as you reflect on choice, choose to remain faithful to God daily.

Prayer

Lord, I stay committed to my faithfulness for You, and I pray that nothing will sever me from Your vine in Jesus' name. Amen.

Call To Action

- Be committed.

- Stay connected to the vine.

- Ask yourself whose team you will be on.

Rhonda. A. Babb

April 19

VOWS

For God so loved the world that he gave his one and only Son, that whoever believes in him shall not perish but have eternal life. John 3:16

With this ring, I thee wed, and as a symbol of my love to you, I will send My Son to shed His blood for you, to bear all of your sin and shame, and to become a joint heir with Christ Jesus and have a just reward. I fashioned you as my masterpiece so that my purpose for you can be fulfilled. I will always be by your side, for better or worse, even if you put other gods before me. In sickness and in health, for by my Son's stripes, you are healed. I know what's best for you in the good times and bad. I will never leave you nor forsake you. I will remain loyal and true to you. As the sun rises and sets, so is my faithfulness to you. Don't you see how I wake you up every morning and provide for you? My love is great, and so is my faithfulness.

I take you as my Lord and my God, to have and to hold, for You have done great things for me. I, too, pledge to be faithful and loyal to only You. No one can compare to You, for Your faithfulness shows when I praise You, smile, and even when I'm angry. Your heart and arms are always open. You understand me like no one can. My promise to You is to hope for the things I cannot see, for You are not a man that You should lie. All that I ask is that I will believe like Abraham, even unto death. Your Word is more than a bond; it has the power to create. When You say something, nothing can hinder it, and that is just who You are. I can depend on You for anything and everything, even if I give nothing.

I join you together with the truth of His Word, as there is nothing that He cannot do. He is faithful and true. Know the ancient of days is with you through the storms and He will never leave you nor forsake you.

Prayer

Thank You, Father, for Your faithfulness that is seen when we arise to embrace a new day. In Jesus' name, amen.

Call To Action

Confess your sins. He is faithful and just to forgive us and cleanse us from all unrighteousness.

Sandra Britton

FRUIT BOWL

But the fruit of the Spirit is love, joy, peace, forbearance, kindness, goodness, faithfulness, gentleness and self-control. Against such things there is no law.
Galatians 5:22-23

An apple a day keeps the doctor away, is how the saying goes. This saying suggests that once we eat an apple daily, our bodies will remain healthy, and we won't or shouldn't need a doctor. Apples support a healthy immune system, aid in digestion and, among other things, perform an antioxidant activity. Generally, all fruits are healthy for our bodies and are a good source of food. There are some fruits we love and some we may hate or dislike. Fruits should be a part of a healthy diet, for when we eat them, they help us eliminate what the body doesn't want and put in what it needs.

Just as our bodies need physical sustenance, our spirit also needs sustenance. A spiritual fruit keeps the enemy away and brings our flesh into subjection. To achieve this, we must water and feed our spirits daily just as we would a tree in our backyard. We faithfully water and nurture the tree, waiting and hoping, knowing it will bear fruit. Just like the One who created the tree is faithful in commanding the tree to bear fruit, He is faithful to us, and we can trust His Word. He is reliable and loyal through our good times and bad. For when He says a thing, we need to believe that His actions match His words. His faithfulness shows up in the sunrise and the sunset. He is trustworthy.

Prayer

God, we put our trust in You and acknowledge that You are God. We love You and place our hands in Yours. In Jesus' name, Amen.

Call To Action

God can still the waters and calm the seas. Place your hands in His.

Sandra Britton

April 21

BE FAITHFUL

For the Lord loves the just and will not forsake his faithful ones they will be protected. Psalms 37: 28

When you show faithfulness to God, you receive a gift. What's that gift? It's protection. You will be protected forever. Faithfulness is when you show faith to or in someone. Faith is also trust. When you trust God or have faith in Him, you trust Him with your life, which shows faithfulness. However, if you take back your life, then where is the faithfulness? We have to trust God with our lives, fully. He knows best.

I once had to dance, and I was extremely nervous. Someone quickly reminded me that I should be full of faith and trust in God. Sometimes, it may seem hard to have faith in God. If you're waiting for a miracle, it may be days, months, or even years, but you must remain faithful. It might seem hard and unbearable when going through those times, but trust God, keep the faith, never give up, and remain faithful.

A woman in the Bible had an issue of blood for many years. When Jesus was walking by, she touched His clothes and was healed. When I think about that story, I say to myself, "Wow, she had lots of faith to have waited that long". What she did sets a great example for us to follow. Another aspect of faithfulness is patience. Like that woman, stay faithful, stay patient, trust God. Our heavenly Father is the perfect example of faithfulness, and He expects us to be faithful just like Him.

Prayer

Lord, help me to have faith in You no matter what. Help me to be faithful and full of faith in Jesus' name, Amen.

Call To Action

Ask God to give you the faith you need for every challenge you face.

Shaquonna Rock

April 22

ENDURANCE AND FAITHFULNESS

No temptation has overtaken you except what is common to mankind. And God is faithful; he will not let you be tempted beyond what you can bear. But when you are tempted, he will also provide a way out so that you can endure it. 1 Corinthians 10:13

Have you ever felt like life was too burdensome and too much for you to bear? Well, you're not the only one. It's easy to feel like nothing is going your way and that God does not hear you when you pray. Scripture tells us that God would never put more on us than we can bear, and everything works for the betterment of us. Scripture also tells us that God always provides a way for us to exit our situations.

As dancers, we must remember that God called us to be ministers of His Word. While it may feel like the price of being a minister is expensive and heavy on our shoulders, it is in those moments we must remember that we were hand-picked by God. His faithfulness is why we are able to stand under the anointing of ministry. We were called by God to reach those in a way that they would understand and to open doors for them to also feel the faithfulness of God.

Prayer

Dear God, help us to always seek Your face, for it is there that we will see Your faithfulness. Forgive me for all the times You have shown me Your faithfulness, and I have taken it for granted. May my life be a living testament to Your faithfulness and hand over my life. Amen.

Call To Action

How many ways has God shown you His faithfulness? Write out the ways that God's faithfulness is showcased in your life, and thank Him for it.

Halal Teens

April 23

FAITHFULNESS IN MINISTRY

But the Holy Spirit produces this kind of fruit in our lives: love, joy, peace, patience, kindness, goodness, faithfulness. Galatians 5:22

This scripture verse describes what those in Christ should expect to see flowing from their lives when they let the Holy Spirit lead them. These are all characteristics of the fruit of the spirit.

Let us now look at the fruit of "Faithfulness"; this represents a kind of endurance driven by trust. In the Spirit, Christians can keep going in the right direction, even when facing a difficult situation. Although we don't fully understand all God is doing, it does not mean He cannot or will not work things out for our good. Remember, Jesus proved this on Calvary; it was His sacrifice for us. So, how we live our daily lives in this walk is justified through Him.

Our faith is not blind. God creates things out of what we cannot see. In our ministry, we need that kind of faith. Trust produces obedience that will result in God's blessings and approval of us as ministers. We must remember that with the help of the Holy Spirit inside of us, we can do anything, for it is He who leads, guides and directs us in all truth.

Sometimes, we doubt our ability to minister in dance, but we need to believe and put our trust in God and pray because, through Him, things can change. He will be there for us. His faithfulness isn't dependent upon our works. All He requires is a willing heart to bring about the incredible fruit of the Spirit in our lives.

You should aim to please God with a faithful spirit. Be someone who sees their ministry as service unto the Lord Himself, who has undertaken it out of gratitude in his/her own life and heart, and no matter how tough it gets, will not quit. Only God knows exactly what our best is, and we can trust Him to equip, correct, challenge, grow, and humble us when we step out in faith.

Prayer

Lord Jesus, may my Faith in You and Your abundant promises be ever-increasing each day. Help me to keep my Faith in You despite my circumstances. As a minister, may You strengthen me daily as I step out in Faith.

Call To Action

- Pray from a faithful heart.

- Allow God to reveal greater insight to you.

- Minister from a heart of faithfulness.

Timeless Ministers

FAITHFULNESS TO GOD

So be careful to do what the LORD your God has commanded you; do not turn aside to the right or to the left. Walk in obedience to all that the LORD your God has commanded you, so that you may live and prosper and prolong your days in the land that you will possess. Deuteronomy 5:32-33

The Bible tells us in James 4:8 that when we draw near to God, He will draw near to us. That is an example of obedience, commitment, and devotion to God. You must always be faithful and committed to God because you will never know when He will return to this earth. When we are on the right path, walking in obedience to God, He promises to prolong our lives.

To be faithful to God, you must listen to Him, do what He says, spread the Word to as many people as possible, and worship and pray to God daily. When you think you have done something wrong or were not faithful to God, you can ask Him for forgiveness and not do it again. When I am dancing, I am committed to it because dancing is worshipping God, and it shows God that I love Him and am faithful.

Prayer

Dear Lord, help me be faithful and committed to You every day so that I can have eternal life and live peacefully in Heaven. Amen.

Call To Action

God calls us to be faithful to Him first in all we do. Let us make it a daily activity to show our faithfulness through dance, conversation with friends, and obedience to our parents.

Trinitee Angus

April 25

HOW CAN WE PROVE WE ARE FAITHFUL?

Here is a trustworthy saying: if we died with him, we will also live with him, if we endure, we will also reign with him. If we disown him, he will also disown us; if we are faithless, he remains faithful, for he cannot disown himself.
2 Timothy 2:11-13

Faithfulness comes from a place of trust and loyalty. This scripture explains how God shows us faithfulness when we have been faithful. When we die in Christ, we will also live with Him. This means that as a Christian, when you commit yourself to God, live as a Christian, and follow His will, when this earth is no more, you will be alive with Him on this new earth (Heaven). If we endure temptation and shut out all aspects of sin and the enemy, we will also reign with Him for eternity.

Jesus is faithful to us, but when we disown Him in front of others, He will also disown us. His Word says, "But whoever disowns me before others, I will disown before my Father in heaven", so your relationship with God is essential. You have to be committed and faithful to God in everything you do, even in your designated ministry. For instance, being faithful to the call of dance as part of my ministry means that I need to stay consistently in the Word of God. This is not only so I know what I am talking about, but it gives my heart exposure to every word of Scripture.

Spend time praying for your ministry, confessing your sins, calling on God to purge and purify us and keep away temptation. Lastly, be your brother's keeper. If you see a fellow minister in your ministry struggling, help them along the way. Be there for one another, don't speak ill words towards each other and watch and see how your ministry will flourish.

Prayer

Father Lord, I pray that in everything we do, we remain faithful to You, faithful to our ministry and faithful to Your will. In Jesus' Name. Amen.

Call To Action

Remain faithful to the Lord your God, and He shall be faithful to you!

Zariah Watson

April 26

I TRUST YOU
(POEM)

Now faith is the assurance of things hoped for, the conviction of things not seen.
Hebrews 11:1

I trust you

I mean why wouldn't I?

Why wouldn't anyone?

I have Faith in you.

I have Faith in us.

I have Faith in the unknown

I'm taking that first step

Me

I'm taking that first step with you.

I'm taking that first step to believe in

You

To trust You.

My Gift

The gift you've given me was not for a season

It was not a mistake

But a blessing

A blessing to not be taken for granted

I understand now

I believe it now

I am a Dance Minister of The Most High

And I am a force to be reckoned with

Because without you

Without my Faith in you

I would just be another dancer

Heavenly Father,

I am loyal to You.

Zenaida R. Mayers

April 27

STOP WAVERING! HE'S FAITHFUL

Let us hold fast the confession of our hope without wavering, for He who promised is faithful; Hebrews 10:23

Are you tossed to and fro like the branches on a tree? We all go through a valley of decisions every day. If we reflect and confess, we'll know that we often waver, fluctuate, and are unsteady or indecisive. Our peak and valley moments are opportunities to turn our wailing into dancing. God remains faithful; He doesn't waver. If we are unfaithful, He still abides forever. God's character is consistent through all the changing scenes of our lives. Once God has spoken it, He will do it.

God has called believers to walk in faith, trusting Him and His Word in every situation. Just recently, I had to make a decision whether to further my studies, not knowing how the program would be funded. At this juncture, I halted between two opinions but chose the road which led to believing that all things are possible with God. Surely, my belief in His Word led to the performance of His faithfulness yet again in my life. Never forget that He's faithful through the ages.

Prayer

Heavenly Father, we thank You for Your faithfulness in our lives. In these uncertain times, Your faithfulness helps us not waver but believe as we stand upon Your promises.

Call To Action

Examine your life story and journal God's faithfulness in action for a week.

Trena Millar

HE IS

For if we died with him, we will also live with him. If we endure, we will also reign with him. If we deny him, he also will deny us. If we are faithless, he remains faithful. He can't deny himself. 2 Timothy 2:11-13

I know there are times when we begin to wonder about the character of God. When things aren't going how we want them to, we question who God is, how He operates, and why He lets things happen. The fact of the matter is that He is sovereign, meaning He has the right to exercise His rule and power over His creation – us. It's His kingship. He is supreme and He is God, who embodies the triune – Father, Son and Holy Spirit.

During difficult times, we may not understand the whys of things that happen. However, we must be at a place where we trust Him with everything, for He is faithful. He sees all, and He knows all. In all that is going on, the Word says He remains faithful. I don't think we will fully understand the character of God with our finite minds, but we must aim to do so. His ways are higher than our ways, and His thoughts are higher than our thoughts. What you know or hear about His character, trust it, know it, understand it, and be consumed by it because, in this knowledge, your heart will shout that He cannot deny Himself. His character is who He is, completely.

Prayer

Heavenly Father, I thank You for always being faithful. Even in times of doubt, You remain true to who You are. As I learn more about You, I pray that Your characteristics will take root in my heart, causing me to grow and become stronger in You.

Call To Action

I will commit to learning about the character of God.

Orissa Fitzpatrick

April 29

NOTHING CAN COMPARE TO GOD'S FAITHFULNESS

Because of the Lord's great love we are not consumed, for his compassions never fail; They are new every morning great is your faithfulness. Lamentations 3:22 -23

Great is Your faithfulness, O God my Father – there is no shadow of turning with You. Nothing changes You or Your decision to love us. Your love is incomprehensible. John 3:16 says that You gave up Your only Son, Jesus Christ, to die for us, to take on the sins of the world. His love for us is constant, never changing, and devoted to our needs.

He is true to His Word and always keeps His promises. He is loyal, dedicated and trustworthy. Man loves and disappoints. Man proclaims one thing and shows something else. Only God is truly faithful. He has proven Himself time and time again in both word and action. He is always there to pick us up, carry us and guide us. Great is His faithfulness.

John 14:1 says don't let your heart be troubled; believe in God. Believe also in me. To be faithful to something is to be devoted to it, dedicated, committed, and loyal. To be faithful means to be trustworthy and reliable. God calls us to be faithful, first and foremost, to Him. God wants us to be devoted to Him, loyal to Him, and committed to Him. So, no matter the situation or storm, we should always be faithful to Jesus and our calling. As praise dancers, we are committed to offering our temples as living sacrifices to prepare an atmosphere of worship to the glory of God. Our purpose is to magnify the name of the Lord through our dance.

Prayer

Dear Lord, no matter the trials that await us tomorrow, may we never forget the blessings You have shown us. Help us to cling to You as our Anchor. Help us remember Your steadfast love and faithfulness for us in all things in Jesus' name. Amen.

Call To Action

- Stay committed to your calling.

- Remember to hold fast to the confession of our hope according to Hebrews 10:23.

- Trust in the faithfulness of God.

Laura Phillips

April 30

A SNAPSHOT OF FAITHFULNESS

Well done, good and faithful servant! You have been faithful with a few things; I will put you in charge of many things. Come and share your master's happiness!
Matthew 25:2

It's easy to say we must be faithful to God, but really, what does faithfulness look like? When we're faithful to God, we are committed to Him; we trust that He will take care of us and are willing to follow wherever He leads. After all, faithfulness is one of the attributes that Christians must have according to Galatians 5:22-23, "But the fruit of the Spirit is love, joy, peace, forbearance, kindness, goodness, faithfulness, gentleness and self-control. Against such things there is no law".

Now, let's be real for a bit. Faithfulness is believing our life looks like a complete mess yet trusting in God to work it out. It's scoring below 40% on an important test, yet trusting God because He gives wisdom and knowledge. It's having a difference of opinion with others at work or in ministry, yet trusting God to work it out in our favor. It's God promising us something when we don't think it possible, but still trusting Him to fulfill the promise.

If we take a quick look at Abraham and Sarah in Genesis 18-21, God told them they would have a son, but as we know, Sarah was barren for many years, and both of them were indeed very old. Sarah lacked faith in God and took matters into her own hands by getting a woman for her husband so they could have a child. This, of course, was not what God had in mind, but when they eventually put their faith in God, Sarah ended up bearing the son that God had promised them.

Having faith in God might be easy for some and hard for others, like Sarah, but as you mature in Christ, this will become a routine part of life. Remember, despite what you may go through or what you're presently facing, keep reading His Word, keep praying to God, remain active and involved in ministry, and keep going to church because all these things help you in your walk of faithfulness to God.

Prayer

Gracious Father, thank You for Your unwavering faithfulness. Help us understand that faithfulness is a deep trust in Your promises, even when life seems chaotic. Strengthen our faith, especially in moments of doubt and uncertainty. May we be like Abraham and Sarah, ultimately placing our trust in Your timing and plans. In Jesus' name, we pray. Amen.

Call To Action

Embrace the journey of faithfulness. In both the seemingly mundane and challenging moments of life, trust in God's promises and remain committed to Him.

Charlene Hinds

May 1

THE POWER IN YOUR PRAYER

Then they cried to the LORD in their trouble, and he delivered them from their distress. He made the storm be still, and the waves of the sea were hushed. Then they were glad that the waters were quiet, and he brought them to their desired haven. Psalm 107:28-30

Prayer is powerful. When we make the Lord our first resort, seeking Him in prayer, the power of His presence is released in our lives. Prayer is one central way we communicate with God. It is not just about getting our needs met; God calls us to pray in order to develop and deepen our relationship with Him. The power of prayer is simply what the Lord can do for us when we ask with open hearts and open souls.

When you find yourself in unknown situations and see no way out, you can depend on the power of prayer. God is always there to help you, but that help needs to be activated. If you sit in despair and loathe your situation, it will only get worse, but when you call on Jesus with an open mind and an open soul, your prayers will be answered if it is in His plan for your life.

Some people underestimate the power of prayer because sometimes it doesn't "work". We see it this way because we pray, and the prayer isn't answered. You must think, "Is this prayer out of selfishness or do I need what I am praying for?" After thinking about that, you start to understand that God answers prayers according to what you *need*.

As powerful as prayer is, there is one thing that neither prayer nor faith can do. Prayer cannot supersede or override the will of God. You can pray as much as you want, for as long as you want, and with as much faith as you can muster, but it will not change what God has willed you to do. For this reason, one of the most powerful weapons in prayer is the agreement with God's will. Not only are we encouraged to pray God's will be done – think of the Lord's prayer – we are also assured that when we pray according to God's will, He will do what we are praying for.

Prayer

Father, help us to understand the power of prayer. Help us learn how it can further our relationships with You and give us something to fall back on when all seems discouraging. In Jesus' name, I pray, Amen.

Call To Action

Remember the power of prayer the next time you find yourself in a helpless situation and nowhere to run. Call out to God and you will be delivered.

Danae Niles

May 2

ON MY KNEES
(POEM)

For this reason I am telling you, whatever things you ask for in prayer (in accordance with God's will), believe (with confident trust) that you have received them, and they will be given to you. Mark 11:24

Here on my knees again

Bowing before you again

Entering into your gates with thanksgiving

And into your courts with praise

Blessing your Holy name

Making my request

Asking for protection and provision

Amongst other things

Being honest with what's on my heart

And what's on my mind

Speaking to you first thing in the morning

Speaking to you nightly about my day

Realising that you answer every request

Seeing a change in my day after

Seeing a change in my life after

Realizing that if I stand still for a moment

Or sometimes longer

You'll speak too.

Prayer

Dear heavenly Father, I pray that we will make time to pray with You every day. May we come to You honestly with open hearts and minds, ready to receive clarity, knowledge and wisdom about our situations. Dear God, may we not forget to come to You, thanking You for who You are. You said in Your Word that we just have to ask, and You will give. Help us to know that You always answer our prayers, whether the answer is a yes, no or wait. Help us to always remember that prayer is a powerful weapon that changes things.

Call To Action

Prayer is described as talking to God. You don't have to use big words or phrases. Tell our Father whatever is on your heart and mind today. Whatever you need, ask Him. Whatever you feel, tell Him. No matter how much of a mess things are in life, telling our Heavenly Father will bring you peace that passes all understanding. So, take time today to pray to our Heavenly Father.

Danielle Harewood

May 3

HE'S THERE

Be careful for nothing; but in everything by prayer and supplication with thanksgiving let your requests be made known unto God. Philippians 4:6

Sometimes, our situations in life can cause us to be anxious, and it's in these moments that prayer becomes even more important to us as Christians. When we talk to God, we begin to see situations more clearly. When I go too long without talking to the Father, it feels like something is missing. I start to feel a bit more anxious and on edge. When this happens, I ask myself when was the last time I prayed. I go to God and tell Him my worries and troubles, and I leave His presence feeling wiser, stronger, and clearer. I believe that dancing for our Father is a type of prayer. Yes, dancing can be praise and worship, but we also talk to God when we dance unto Him.

He is our king. He is also our friend and our counselor. Being able to come to the King of Kings and Lord of Lords and tell Him exactly what you're feeling is an honor. He's always there waiting for us to talk to Him, ready to listen. You can tell Him everything about your doubts and fears, what you're excited and happy about, and what happened during your day. You can also talk to Him about who He is to you, thanking Him for all He's done for you. If you need wisdom and understanding while reading His Word or dealing with life's situations, talk to Him.

Prayer

Dear heavenly Father, we thank You for Your grace and mercy. We thank You that we can approach You without feeling guilty or ashamed. Thank You that we can come to You any time we want, and You'll be there, ready to listen and help us in our times of need. Thank You that we can always be honest with You about our feelings. I pray that we'll always make time for You. In Jesus' name, Amen.

Call To Action

Don't stop praying. Pray when things are good, and pray when things are bad. If you want to start praying but don't know where to start, read Matthew 6:9-13 for guidance.

Danielle Harewood

May 4

PRAYERFULLY THANKFUL

Continue steadfastly in prayer, being watchful in it with thanksgiving.
Colossians 4:2

Remember when you were a new Christian or were going through something, and others would tell you, "Just pray about it"? I don't know about you, but it would frustrate me sometimes because I did not know how to pray. When I did pray, I was always anxious for my prayers to be answered. This verse tells me that I must be constant in my prayers and thankful as I wait for the Lord to answer my prayers.

I remember when we had to minister at another church and the choreography was not coming together. The dancers were not giving their best, so our leader asked what was hindering us in our dance. We had a little "pow-wow" session and ironed out some of the issues, but we also had to pray daily leading up to the actual ministry. At every rehearsal, each dancer had to say what they were thankful for in relation to being a part of the ministry, followed by a prayer of encouragement.

God truly answered our prayers; the choreography came together. Our prayers were manifested through the dance, touching the hearts of those who witnessed it. This situation reminded me that although I can constantly be praying to God, I must do it prayerfully.

Prayer

Father, today I just want to thank You that, although my prayer might not be perfect, You understand and know what's in my heart. May I always be thankful for whatever the outcome of my prayers may be. Thank You for always listening and answering. In Jesus' Name. Amen.

Call To Action

Remember to give God thanks in every situation because you don't know who will be blessed.

Eslyn Taylor

CALLING ON JESUS

Then you will call on me and come and pray to me, and I will listen to you.
Jeremiah 29:12

Nicole C. Mullen released a smash hit on August 28th, 2001, entitled "Call on Jesus". It was such a powerful song for believers because it reminded us that all things are possible in any situation or insecurity we face when we call on Jesus. Those mountains will fall, chains will be broken, and God will come to our rescue. God says that when you come to Him and call on Him (pray), He will listen to you. Isn't that an awesome God and a testament to how powerful our prayer can be when we come to God? Sometimes, we might not always get the answer we want to hear, but you can guarantee that He will answer in time.

As a dance minister or worshipper, our movements, whether with our arms, feet or a streamer, can be used to call on Jesus. The expression of our movements is a symbol of calling on Him. So, I raise my hand, stomp my feet, and twirl my streamer as my special way of calling on Jesus. I am assured that He is always listening.

Prayer

Our most wonderful God, we thank You for Your mercy and love. Thank You that You are always there when we need You. I may not always see when You answer my prayers, but I am reassured that You always have me covered.

Call To Action

Do not be discouraged when your prayers seem not to be answered. Remember that God always knows what you need, even before you do. Call on Him today.

Eslyn Taylor

May 6

I SAY A LITTLE PRAYER

Therefore I tell you, whatever you ask for in prayer, believe that you have received it, and it will be yours. Mark 11:24

Prayer is one of the many liberties of being a child of God. It is simply mind-blowing to know that we have an open line of communication to speak to Jesus whenever we want. We can humbly kneel before God and ask for something; if it is His will, He will grant it to us. It is also a wonderfully divine revelation that God, the Ruler of the universe, has appointed us to tell of His accomplishments as He does them for us. By praying to Him, receiving what we ask for, and telling others about His goodness, we are contributing to His will being done on earth as it is in Heaven. When we go to God and ask for something, it doesn't just end there. It then requires that we believe we have received or will receive what we have asked for.

There is no limit on what we can ask God for. It could be as small or as big as we want it to be, but we then have to believe in order for it to come to us. We can't pray to remember a part of the choreography we have been struggling with but continue to doubt ourselves during the process. That is not believing we have received what we asked for, and it blocks our blessing. As dance ministers, God can sometimes use us to deliver His answers to someone who is watching us, so it is important to align ourselves with the belief in receiving God's answers to our prayers. How can we tell someone to believe when we do not believe? My question today is, "Do you believe you have received what you prayed for?"

Prayer

Heavenly Father, I thank You for all the silent and verbalized prayers that You have answered. These are not taken for granted. God, I pray that You will always be my first line of defense in life and that whatever I ask will be mine in Your mighty name. Amen.

Call To Action

Ask the Lord for whatever you want and believe that it is already done.

Gabrielle Blackett

May 7

EVERYONE PRAYS IN THE END

The Lord is near to all who call on him, to all who call on him in truth.
Psalm 145:18

What is prayer? Prayer is how we express ourselves to God. We can do this by talking to God and asking Him for help, thanking Him for all He has done for us, and even just talking to Him like you would talk to a friend. Praying is an act of worship to God, and when we tap into prayer and intercession, we gain power over our circumstances.

In the Bible, God has shown us time and time again that all we have to do is open our mouths and pray to Him. We can ask for His help, guidance and blessing, and He will answer us. Do you understand how powerful that is? All we have to do is ask, and it is given to us. We never have to walk alone.

As dancers, we use songs to tell a story, but do you know that we can use our gift to pray to God? Our body is an instrument that talks for us when we don't have the words. God hears our hearts when we dance without us even opening our mouths. Sometimes, we are so broken down by life that it feels like we don't have the words, but we can close our eyes, play a song and dance. That act is enough for God to hear us and answer our silent prayers.

Prayer

Dear God, I pray that I will not only pray to You when things are bad, but even as things are good, I will constantly pray to thank You for all that You have done for me. Amen.

Call To Action

Take a moment to pray and thank God for all He has done for you.

Gabrielle Blackett

WHATSOEVER YOU ASK...

Delight yourself also in the Lord; and He shall give you the desires of your heart.
Psalm 37:4

What does it mean to delight yourself in the Lord? To delight yourself in someone means that you have come to know that person intimately; you know what they are like. They have a good track record, are trustworthy, and, most importantly, exhibit unselfish love towards you. Would we not say to ourselves, "Hey, this is where I want to be. I get such pleasure and joy being in this person's presence, and I would do anything to remain there?"

The psalmist David here encourages us to commit everything we have or do unto God. When we commit everything into His hands, we are telling God that we trust Him completely with our lives. Committing to God is how we delight ourselves in the Lord. And here comes the exciting part: He will give us the desires of our hearts. Wow! That is a fair exchange to me—a show of God's conditional will.

Sometimes, the levels we would like to reach in our ministry seem unattainable. But in order for God to give us what we desire, we must first ask. After all, Solomon asked for wisdom and received wisdom plus wealth (1 Kings 3:6-14). What is outstanding is that Solomon trusted and believed God to come through for him, and God did not disappoint. He gave him "over and above all he could ever ask or think".

Prayer

Father, we thank You for loving us and being concerned with everything about our lives. Forgive us, Lord, for our deficit of prayer, which You have established as a way of communication and relationship between us. May we look to You always as the God we can turn to, without reservation, in every circumstance, knowing that You hear us and will answer. Thank You for listening to our prayers in Jesus' name. Amen.

Call To Action

- Trust God with every aspect of your life and ministry.

- Fellowship with God and bask in His presence.

- Know that when we ask, God is able to give above and beyond what we require.

Gurlain Applewhaite

May 9

PRAYER AS A DAILY LIFESTYLE

And take the helmet of salvation, and the sword of the Spirit, which is the Word of God, praying always with all prayer and supplication in the Spirit. Ephesians 6:18

Paul encourages us to bring every situation we encounter throughout our daily lives to God. What is it about prayer that would have caused Jesus to pray for the whole night in Luke 6:12? Thinking on this alone should cause a change in our mindset and approach to prayer.

At some point, we realize that what we thought would've been fulfilling is really not so exciting. We learn that no one can help us but He who made us. It is then that we will humble ourselves and call out to God. There must be a reason we are required to "pray without ceasing" (1 Thessalonians 5:17). Not that we are to go a whole day on our knees praying, but it is the "posture of our heart" that is to be in constant communication with God. We must trust and depend on Him as we live out Psalm 91:1, "dwelling in the secret place of the Most High and abiding under the shadow of the Almighty".

Our dance ministry must be based on prayer. Things can only happen when we spend time in prayer. When we offer up our ministry and every dance minister to God, we allow Him to take His place as God over the ministry. Only then will we see transformation take place in the ministry and the lives of the ministers. This transformation requires cooperation on our part with God. We know that God hears us when we pray, but what we pray for must be in accordance with His Word so that His will is accomplished.

Prayer

Heavenly Father, thank You for the ways You have given us to know You. This allows us to develop the special relationship of a father and child. We do not wish to remain where we are. Give us a passion for prayer so that we may rise to higher levels in You. In Jesus' name. Amen.

Call To Action

- Be consistent in your prayers to release God's blessings over you.

- Invite God into your circumstances before you make decisions.

- Trust God and make Him your daily partner.

Gurlain Applewhaite

GATEWAY TO HEAVEN

And when they had prayed, the place where they had assembled together was shaken and they were all filled with the Holy Spirit, and they spoke the Word of God with boldness. Acts 4:31

What an amazing transformation in these disciples! After being threatened by the authorities for preaching in the name of Jesus, they called on the Most High God to intervene on their behalf (Acts 4:24-30). They weren't taken out of the situation; instead, the Holy Spirit empowered them to carry out their mandate.

There are so many instances in the Bible where God stepped in and answered the prayers of those who called out to Him. Those stories are there to give us encouragement that God hears us when we pray, and He responds. We can be assured of a favorable response as long as we pray according to His will. In reading and studying these passages, we should take note of the attitude of those praying. Our motive and attitude determine whether our prayers are answered.

As dancers, we may have dreams of ministering on the "big stage" before thousands and envisage many rushing forward to surrender their lives to God. Whatever we desire can be achieved through prayer if it aligns with God's Word. One significant thing which stands in the way of dancers going after what they desire is a lack of boldness. There is a time of preparation in which we should take the talent God has blessed us with and seek to present an excellent work until God releases us at His appointed time. Just as the disciples were filled with the Holy Spirit to do what they were commissioned to do, God will anoint us to do His work.

Prayer

Heavenly Father, we thank You for bestowing the gift of dance on us. We pray for a spirit of boldness to go forth and make a difference in Your Kingdom in Jesus' name. Amen.

Call To Action

- Expect God to answer our prayers as you commit to obeying His will.

- Be free of all physical and spiritual bondages.

- Be always willing to give your best to God so that He will bless you with more.

Gurlain Applewhaite

May 11

GET UP

*Peter sent them all out of the room; then he got down on his knees and prayed.
Turning toward the dead woman, he said, "Tabitha, get up." She opened her eyes
and seeing Peter she sat up. Acts 9:40*

Prayer is a mighty weapon that all of us need as His children. When we are consistent with prayer, it releases the supernatural power of God in our lives. God is the same God today as in Peter's times. We have the same authority as Peter, and we learn that Peter had an attitude of praying and believing. Earlier in this chapter, we read about what the people in Lydia saw while God used Peter to heal Aeneas, who was bedridden for eight years. He said, "Jesus Christ heals you, get up and take your mat".

Let your character and appearance draw people to us to receive healing. As Peter continued traveling, two disciples heard he was nearby. They sent for him. Tabitha (known as Dorcus) had died, and they needed Peter to bring her back to life. Peter knelt and prayed. With the authority of the Holy Spirit, he turned to her and said Dorcus, get up. She opened her eyes and sat up. With all these miracles, they then turned to God.

God wants our lives to bring people to Him. In our lives, we can speak to any situation and command it to "get up". Whether a situation may appear dead in our lives, we believe God has given us the authority to bring it back to life. Yes, God has given us all we need. His Word has all the instructions to activate the anointing to speak life and healing to any situation that may come our way.

Prayer

Heavenly Father, we come before You. Thank You for the power of prayer You have given to us. Help us to use it daily. We shall speak and see You move in our situation and in the lives of others. Amen.

Call To Action

Let us go forward and use the power that He has invested in us.

Julie Greene

May 12

COMMUNITY POWER

Therefore confess your sins to each other and pray for each other so that you may be healed. The prayer of a righteous person is powerful and effective. James 5:16

Everyone comes into ministry from a different place and space in their life. They also come into ministry for various reasons. One thing is clear; however you come, if one person is out of alignment, I have seen God stop the entire ministry to pull that person back in. We cannot just dance and ignore that people are hurting. We cannot just dance and pretend that the sin is ok. God will not have it. We are to be there for each other in prayer and in works, so iron will sharpen iron, and we will see the power of God's answered prayers in our lives.

What a powerful experience to minister through. When you have this experience, you know that God has granted a prayer request to the ministry, to a member, to you! It is heart-warming when you are in a community that will not let you go, leave you behind, or give up until change comes. Shame and pride have no power in a community of love. Everyone just wants the other person to be the best they can be in Christ. That is the power of prayer.

Prayer

God, help us to always remember that You are the God that will go searching after the one. Help us to always respond prayerfully to the situations in our lives and the lives of our brothers and sisters. In Jesus' Name, Amen.

Call To Action

This week, make it a point to pray with one of the members of your ministry team. Pray until you see the change that is needed in their lives.

Laina Jacob

May 13

PRAISE PARTY

And at midnight Paul and Silas prayed and sang praises unto God and the prisoners heard them. Acts 16:25

Lord, show up! Let this dance minister to all who see it. After long nights of practice and preparation, now the moment of truth arrives. You dress and are ready to go on stage. You know you can only do so much that is humanly possible. You may have the right song, the right moves, and the right garments, but without the Holy Spirit touching the hearts of the dancers and audience, it's all in vain. So, you pray: "Lord, show up!" You see the response to the dance; you feel the presence of God. That feeling is all an answer to prayer because the Lord showed up.

The Bible tells us that after Paul and Silas prayed and sang praises to God, suddenly, there was a great earthquake, and the foundation of the prison was shaken. Immediately, all the doors were open and everyone was freed. What an answer to prayer! Praise empowers your prayers.

Prayer

Lord, help me to seek You in prayer, always, knowing that You have the answers to everything in my life that seems impossible.

Call To Action

Pray for someone you know and let them know that you are praying for them.

Maxine Butcher

May 14

LET'S TALK

Devote yourselves to prayer, being watchful and thankful. Colossians 4:2

Devoting ourselves to prayer can be a struggle sometimes, but why? How can we spend so many hours watching TV, doing other activities, talking on the phone or going through our many different social media accounts yet find it hard to find time to pray? Could it be that it doesn't bring pleasure like the other things? Is it something required that we deem unimportant even though we know it is? The irony is, how can we call ourselves part of someone, say we are representing them, and yet don't talk to them?

Prayer is there so that we can feel what we say we aren't feeling, which is God's presence. It's easy to do the external, to show up at dance rehearsals and say the prayer at the beginning or end when called upon. Sometimes, when a prayer session is called, we're there hoping that our name isn't called. We have to do better than that. How would you feel if the only time someone reached out to you was when they wanted something or just to give you a cursory conversation? The Lord wants and has so much more for us than what we settle for, hence why He wants to talk to us and encourages us to talk to Him.

I love it when I suddenly feel the presence of the Lord, and he wants me to pray or just be with Him. During this time, things are revealed to me to pray about or against. There are so many perks in devoting ourselves to prayer. There is such strength and peace that comes with it. I hope you are encouraged to change how you see prayer. Tap into the One who knows all.

Prayer

Heavenly Father, I know so many things are there to distract me and make me lose my focus on You. You are important to me, and I will make room for you. Remind me when I forget. Amen.

Call To Action

Do not wait until tomorrow; start now, "Father, let's talk."

Orissa Fitzpatrick

May 15

POP OFF DE WORD*

Wherefore also we pray always for you, that our God would count you worthy of this calling, and fulfill all the good pleasure of his goodness, and the work of faith with power: That the name of our Lord Jesus Christ may be glorified in you, and ye in him, according to the grace of our God and the Lord Jesus Christ.
2 Thessalonians 1:11-12

Knowing and using the Word of God is essential in maintaining an active and effective prayer life. We see it in scripture: "Thy word have I hid in mine heart, that I might not sin against thee" (Psalm 119:11) and "Thy word is a lamp unto my feet, and a light unto my path" (Psalm 119:105).

"Well if yah have yah Bible Lock, Pop off de Word, Rock off de Word, Pop off de Word" - DJ Nicholas - *Pop Off The Word*

The POP or Power of Prayer in our lives is reinforced by the Word of God. Is there any evidence of this POP in your life? We must constantly spend time in God's Word and reuse it consistently when in conversation with Him and others. This is where the POP is rooted and this is how we can confidently POP when dancing.

"Fast and pray, walk and pray… Fast and pray, laugh and pray… Fast and pray, ask and pray… To God Throne this a the One Way" - DJ Nicholas - *Prayer Closet*

"Prayer works… Prayer works… so mi send dem inna de sky like fireworks" - D.A Jay - *Prayer Works*

Prayer

May Your Word always be my guide, may it rest in my heart, Lord, and may its tenets always POP up in my conversations.

Call To Action

Practice the Power Of Prayer (POP) because prayer works.

POP Off de Word in your life and light it up like fireworks.

Offer up to God your prayers consistently this week.

Petition God on behalf of those who don't know Him as yet.

Pierre Rock

Incorporates Barbados Slang

THE CONVERSATION

But truly God has listened; he has attended to the voice of my prayer.
Psalm 66:19

Were you ever speaking to someone, whether in person or on the phone, only to realize the person had fallen asleep in the middle of the conversation and you were speaking to the air? Or have you ever called someone, and they either couldn't answer because their phone had no credit or the battery was dead? Have you called someone while they were busy, so they either rejected the call or merely ignored it? Whew! I am so glad that we have an ever-present God. We don't have to wait for an appropriate time to call Him. He is always available and ready to listen, but are we taking the time to be in His presence?

As dance ministers, it is important that we maintain a two-way relationship with God. One of not just speaking and asking but also listening. Listen to hear the song God wants you to use, the moves He wants you to make, the scripture He wants you to read, and what He is saying to you and/or your dance group. We each must take the time to listen to what God is saying to us and respond with obedience.

Prayer

Lord, I thank You that You are always there to answer when I call. Help me to answer Your call, too, Lord. Open my ears to hear Your voice clearly and understand what You are saying to me.

Call To Action

The next time you pray, don't just get up straight away. Take a few minutes to listen and also obey.

Rheanne Rock

May 17

ACCESS GRANTED

Elijah was as human as we are, and yet when he prayed earnestly that no rain would fall, none fell for three and a half years. James 5:17

As we clearly see, we don't need to be from another planet or even have superpowers. All we need is to be human, like Elijah, and pray earnestly. Things will happen if we pray earnestly. Let us take a look at what the word "earnestly" means:

1. Characterised by or proceeding from an intense and serious state of mind

2. Serious and intent mental state

3. A considerable or impressive degree or amount

4. Something of value given by a buyer to a seller to bind a bargain

5. A token of what is to come

Looking at the meaning of earnestly, we can tell that Elijah's prayers were serious. They were intentional and of great value. Through this same power of prayer, God clearly gives us access to Heaven. We can be sure that as we pray with understanding, we are able to bring circumstances under control as we connect our prayers to and through the Holy Spirit. If we compare our dance to prayer, we must understand that as dance ministers, we, too, must be serious and intentional, bringing value as we go on the stage to minister. We can have access to the heavens through the Holy Spirit, like Elijah. Prayer is not restricted to any one person; all humans can pray. We have access through the Holy Spirit to activate the power of our prayers today.

Prayer

Lord, I thank You that there is power in my prayers through the Holy Spirit. As I pray, I know that I can access Heaven and things can stop or change. Lord, help me to be earnest in my prayer. In Jesus' name, Amen

Call To Action

- Pray earnestly.

- Be serious.

- Be intentional about prayer.

Rhonda .A. Babb

May 18

PRAYER WORKS

Elijah was as human as we are, and yet when he prayed earnestly that no rain would fall, none fell for three and a half years. James 5:17

We see that all humans can use prayer in any situation due to the power it has. Based on this scripture, Elijah was human; he prayed that rain wouldn't fall for three years, and it didn't. Sometimes, instead of praying when things happen, our default mindset is to worry. We, too, have the power to pray, to stop things in our lives from happening and to be strategic in praying about their duration. Evidence in scripture shows how powerful prayer can be.

As dance ministers, prayer helps us to hear what God is saying and to understand what movement He wants to give us when we have to minister. Our prayers must be done earnestly. Earnestly means to let our prayers be specific, from a serious mind, of great value and of good quality. Our prayers should never lack substance or strategy. When we're serious about something, we plan, and we prepare so that we can get the best result; prayer requires the same purposefulness.

Prayer must be done by faith because, without faith, it is impossible to please God, according to Hebrews 11:6. The Word of God also says, in Matthew 21:22, you can pray for anything, and if you have faith, you will receive it. Prayer is a very important part of our Christian walk. We don't only need prayer to stop things from happening, but we need it to keep us strong in God's Word by faith.

Prayer

Lord, help us to remember that You have given us the power to pray not only to keep us strong, but to be used when we need to stop certain situations in our lives from happening. In Jesus' name, Amen.

Call To Action

- Pray earnestly, for it has power.

- Remember that prayer can stop things from happening, and prayer is for all humans.

Rhonda. A. Babb

May 19

HEAR, OH LORD, ATTEND UNTO MY PRAYER!

Therefore confess your sins to each other and pray for each other so that you may be healed. The prayer of a righteous person is powerful and effective. James 5:16

There is power when the righteous pray. Does that mean that God only hears the prayers of the righteous? No, for he also hears the sinner's prayer. So, what do I need to do for my prayers to be effective? Pray from a place of sincerity and there is nothing in you that the enemy can use against you.

You earnestly want God to show up on your behalf, whether it's a repentant prayer or a prayer for when life gets too much. You want a breakthrough in whatever situation that you are faced with, so approach the throne humbly but boldly. Be enthusiastic, hoping and believing that when you call on the name of Jesus, your situation will make a 360° turnaround. Be happy with the knowledge that our faithful God will do all that He has promised us in our lives when we pray. Pack your prayer with power and strength, whistling that arrow towards the prince of the air so that it will burst through the enemy's camp in the second heaven to reach the throne of God.

Enter into the realm of the spirit, for it is here that things first manifest. For we wrestle not against flesh and blood, so we must engage our spirit in the battle, remembering that the enemy is already defeated. Prayer is our knockout punch to produce our desired result when we ask for anything in Jesus' name. Shutting away in our prayer closets for prayer goes beyond our borders; it goes through time to the root of that stubborn tree to break bonds, loose fetters and move mountains.

So, keep your chin up, live morally good and fear God. Reverence Him, for He is Holy. As we earnestly and enthusiastically gather in our small groups, believing in breakthroughs, our prayers will be effective. God, who loves us so much that He sacrificed His only Son for us, will hear and answer from Heaven, "for the effectual fervent prayer of a righteous man availeth much" (James 5:16). We will get the victory!

Prayer

Our Father, we call upon You, the God of all creation, to hear our prayer and heal our land. In Jesus' name, Amen.

Call To Action

- Pray sincerely, earnestly, and enthusiastically from a righteous place of living and you will see the results!

- Read John 3:16 and Ephesians 6:12.

Sandra Britton

Prayer

Our Father, we call upon You, the God of all creation, to hear our prayer and heal our land. In Jesus' name, Amen.

STEP INTO THE RING

But seek first his kingdom and his righteousness, and all these things will be given to you as well. Matthew 6:33

Right hook, left hook, uppercut, knock out! Another title, another heavyweight gold belt, but I did not achieve this on my own. I eat right (read the Word of God), I exercise (talk to God daily) and I live well (walk righteously).

Living this life calls for much prayer to get us through from one day to the next, and to add insult to injury, our opponent walks around "flossing" like he is "a big man 'bout town". Don't be scared, don't let our opponent get the upper hand on us; we have to be vigilant, for he walks around like a roaring lion, trying to hinder our prayer life, trying to shut us up, to keep us bound and gagged. But we must not be silenced, for there is power in prayer and numbers. Because he knows what is in us, he will try anything to hinder us from calling in our reinforcements. He doesn't want us to win, but our title cannot be stripped away unless we let it.

Reading the Word of God is the manual for arming ourselves with God's sword. Talking to Him daily is putting His Word into practice, and living righteously will give us a powerful right hook and left hook to land that knockout punch. Set your mind like flint, put your dukes up and jab, jab, jab. There is power when you pray; the gag order is revoked.

Begin, to speak to the Lord with power, believing that you will receive what you ask for. Don't be fooled. Your prayer will be effective; it is a weapon that is not carnal but mighty through Christ, for it is through Him that the enemy is defeated. Know who you are and whose you are, for there is safety in numbers, "Where two or three are gathered together in His name, touching anything, it shall be done" (Matthew 18:20). So, line up with a prayer partner and jab, jab, jab, for we are more than conquerors through Christ.

Prayer

Help us, Lord, to stand firm in adversity; help us to understand that we are overcomers, in Jesus' name, Amen.

Call To Action

Get up and stand. Don't get knocked out!

Sandra Britton

Call To Action

Get up and stand. Don't get knocked out!

May 21

MAYBE I'LL PRAY

Is anyone among you in trouble? Let them pray. Is anyone happy? Let them sing songs of praise. James 5:13

What do you think about when you hear the word "prayer"? I think about speaking in tongues and big fancy words that I don't even know the meaning of. But prayers don't have to be as extravagant as you think, especially if that is what makes you nervous. Prayer is a conversation between you and God. The same way you talk to your friends, you can talk to God. Prayers are how we can thank God for his blessings, and how we can ask for forgiveness and help. We have 24/7 access to God through our prayers.

We may not realize it, but prayers aren't always verbalized. Some prayers are thought, some are sung, and some are danced. What is important is that we are aware and conscious of our intentions as we pray in our own ways. "The Blessing" by Kari Jobe is not a song that inherently sounds like a prayer. It does not start by saying "Dear Heavenly Father…" but it asks of God what we would ask in prayer, and it even has the word "Amen" in it. So, if it is as simple to pray as to sing a song, it can't be that hard.

Prayer

Dear God, I pray that I will have a heart so drawn to Yours that every word that I speak is a prayer over my life. I pray that in every circumstance, I will seek Your presence and Your advice. May I not only seek You in bad times but may I always thank You in good times, too. These things I ask in Your holy and precious name. Amen.

Call To Action

What burdens do you carry? Offer up all your burdens to God and leave them at the altar. Pray for what you want and what you need, and you will see a change.

Halal Teens

May 22

IT'S A GOOD THING!

Therefore confess your sins to each other and pray for each other so that you may be healed. The prayer of a righteous person is powerful and effective. James 5:16

Prayers are good. I believe in the power of prayers. Whenever I have a dance to perform or minister, I first pray that I remember the dance and not make any errors. When I pray, I ask God to help me with any situation and He answers me in His own time. When you pray to God, asking Him for what you desire, sometimes, your prayers don't come through right away; they come through when He thinks they need to come through.

If you don't know how to pray, you can ask God to help you pray, or you can just have a normal conversation with Him as if you were speaking to a friend. Prayer helps you develop a relationship with God. Prayer provides answers. Prayer helps you find direction in your life. Prayer gives you the strength to avoid temptation. I pray because I believe in the power of prayer and God answers my prayers. He will always be there to answer our prayers.

Prayer

God, help me to listen to You when You talk to me; help me to have patience. Please give me wisdom and direction in whatever I do and say in Jesus' name, Amen.

Call To Action

1. Let us practice this fun game to encourage each other to pray more.
2. Five-Finger Prayer Game
3. Thumb: Say a prayer for those closest to you.
4. Pointer: Say a prayer for school teachers and Sunday school teachers.
5. Middle: Say a prayer for the president and the country.
6. Ring: Say a prayer for a sick person or someone with a serious need.
7. Pinky: Say a prayer for yourself.

Trinitee Angus

May 23

A PRAYING FAMILY

Is anyone among you sick? Let them call the elders of the church to pray over them and anoint them with oil in the Name of the Lord. James 5:14

Have you ever heard or seen the quote, "A family that prays together stays together"? For me, the word "family" could include anyone important to you, not only people who are blood-related. Family can be a friend, a teacher, an elder, a pastor or even a dance teacher. The scripture tells us what to do; when we need a praying partner to pray for someone or we need someone to pray for us, we can rely on our elders, pastors, and friends.

Sometimes, we misunderstand how important prayer is and how important it is for someone to pray for us whenever we find ourselves in a predicament or a tough situation. Sometimes, we just want to be able to call someone and say, "I haven't had the best day, and I would like it if you could pray with me." It really is an honor and should be a privilege to hear someone say "pray with me" or "pray for me" because that one prayer can result in a positive outcome.

In dance ministry, praying for your fellow ministers is an integral part of showing love for one another. Sometimes, I used to sit and think, "Why are we praying when we should be dancing?" because I felt as though prayer was wasting time when we could have done our choreography. But now that I am wiser and more mature, I understand the power of prayer and that it needs to be done in order to further the ministry and to help out one another. Do not ever take the power of prayer and a praying "family" for granted because those are the people you need to lean on the most.

Prayer

Help us not to take our family and friends for granted, oh God. I pray that as they pour their prayers into us, You pour right back into them and fill them up. For they, too, deserve it. Amen.

Call To Action

Always remember that a family that prays together stays together.

Zariah Watson

May 24

BEING FAITHFUL IN PRAYER

If you believe, you will receive whatever you ask for in prayer. Matthew 21:22

Have you ever struggled with being impatient or just frustrated in prayer? I believe we can all testify to feeling a little disappointed when things don't turn out how we want them to, especially when it feels as though God didn't hear our prayers or He's just ignoring us. The verse above says, "If you *believe*…". In other words, God says if you believe in me, you will then receive whatever you ask for in prayer. You can't be unbelieving in God and then pray for the desires of your heart. If you don't believe in God, who are you praying to? Who are you running to when things get rough and you need a way out?

God is a God of truth. If God has said He will do something…. best believe He *will* do it. God's timing isn't our timing. God will show up when He thinks we need it and not when we think we do. We just have to be patient, stay in His Word, stay in prayer, and He will do the rest.

When dance ministers or any ministers are getting ready to do ministry, we always go to God in prayer. We always ask God for advice on how and what to do regarding ministry. We spend time in His Word searching for things that can help us so we can help others. A minister always prays before and after ministry. When you pray, you are setting the atmosphere for the smooth delivery of ministry. Prayer is an essential part of your walk with God. So, a word to the wise: never stop praying, never stop believing, because if we believe, we shall receive.

Prayer

Dear heavenly Father, I pray that when I no longer have anything to say with my mouth, you listen to my heart. Help me remain faithful in prayer to You that I may walk beside You forever and ever. Amen.

Call To Action

Be faithful in your prayers and keep at it. Just because you can't see it right now, doesn't mean God has finished writing your story. Be patient and wait, I say, on the Lord. Wait!

Zariah Watson

May 25

BEFORE YOU MINISTER
(POEM)

If my people, who are called by my name, will humble themselves and pray and seek my face and turn from their wicked ways, then I will hear from heaven, and I will forgive their sin and will heal their land. 2 Chronicles 7:14

Before you minister

Check yourself

Cover yourself

Because the devil is lurking

Watching

Waiting patiently for an opening

Any opening to disrupt and corrupt what is supposed to be ministered to His people.

Pray

You must pray

The power

The strength

The shift that happens because of Prayer

Is beautiful

It's necessary before you let the soles of your feet touch that stage.

Prayer

It allows Him to move through you

Speak through you

Minister through you

To become one with you

To protect you

To minister to you

This is not to be taken lightly

The devil works

He watches patiently for an opening

Any opening to disrupt and corrupt the blessing to be brought forth through you.

Zenaida R. Mayers

May 26

BEFORE YOU MINISTER PT.2 (THE PRAYER)

This is the confidence we have in approaching God: that if we ask anything according to His will, He hears us. 1 John 5:14

Prayer

Heavenly Father, I come to You as Your daughter, as Your humble servant. I pray that before I allow the soles of my feet to grace that stage, You cover me from the crown of my head to the soles of my feet. I understand You are using me right now to bring forth a message, to deliver a word to Your people that will take over. I give You full control of every move, every emotion, every limb in my body.

I pray that You protect me from any harm or any attacks of the enemy that will hinder me or any of my ministry team from laying a blessing on Your people. Even if it's just one, we treat that one soul that is crying out to You as a necessity, and we bless them and speak to them today that they will be lifted up to You. May hearts and souls be open to You and respond to You.

As I say this prayer with my whole heart, with the understanding of what I am about to do, I pray that You also minister within me, that I will not be held back or blocked, but that I will surrender myself completely to You in Jesus' name I pray, Amen.

Call To Action

Step into the confidence bestowed upon us by 1 John 5:14.

Zenaida R. Mayers

May 27

MAINTAINING A PRAYERFUL LIFESTYLE

You can pray for anything, and if you have faith, you will receive it.
Matthew 21:22

What is Prayer? Prayer is simply having a conversation with God on anything that is happening in our lives. Sometimes, we underestimate what prayer entails and how powerful it can really be. Prayer is one of the ways we communicate with God. There are times that we go through our storms or valley experiences, and going to God in prayer about it is the last thing we do when really and truly it should be the first. When life throws its hard balls at us, instead of sitting and wallowing in it, try praying and asking God to reveal what we are to learn from it.

As dancers, we are to make sure we live prayerful lives always. Our role is so vitally important that we must remain prayed up as we use our bodies to win souls for Christ and to usher in His presence. Our lives as dancing priests can be so transparent when we go out there to minister to others that we need to make sure that we are always walking in alignment with the plan God has for our lives. In order to do this, we need to be in constant prayer on every detail of our lives so that we cause no one to stumble.

Prayer is the most powerful tool we have as dancers to fight against the enemy. Prayer should be our default setting not only as dancers but as Christians. So, no matter what we go through in life, always remember to pray about it and wait on God for the answer. Ask God to help you to maintain that prayerful lifestyle, not being cliché about it but being intentional.

Prayer

Father God, I ask You to help me to remember how important prayer is in my life. Help me to remain focused not only in ministry but in every aspect of my life. Rekindle that flame of prayer and increase it where it needs to be increased in Jesus' name. I pray, Amen.

Call To Action

Prayer is not a method of escaping conflict, but rather a catalyst for growth in the face of conflict. Pray for values rather than things and for growth rather than gratification. Make your prayer intentional.

Alicia Olton

May 28

UNTO YOU, I RETURN

Then Job arose and tore his robe and shaved his head and fell on the ground and worshiped. And he said, "Naked I came from my mother's womb, and naked shall I return. The Lord gave, and the Lord has taken away; blessed be the name of the Lord. Job 1:21-22

I believe that one story in the Bible that everyone knows, besides the birth of Christ, is the story of Job. He was a praying man of God blessed beyond measure. We know the devil can throw anything to tempt us to fall and turn away from God. For Job, it was the worst of the worst: all of his children were killed along with his cattle, and leprosy ravaged his body. Even his wife and friends turned against him and told him to curse God. Instead of getting angry, Job's first instinct was to worship and pray to God. Wow, that is the power of prayer. The Lord heard him, healed him and multiplied his blessings. Can you imagine if what happened to Job, happened to you today? Would you be like Job or would you turn away from God?

What would be your response if your ability to dance were taken away from you because of a broken leg or arm or even a missing limb? I remembered a time I had to miss dancing for a couple of months due to surgery. I would come to rehearsals and watch the other dancers. I felt useless at one point, and I had to pray about whether I should continue. God said one day that He would return unto me what I had lost. That blew my mind. He showed me that although I could not dance, I could help with the choreography and garments, and videotape the rehearsals. I was not limited in the ways that I could praise Him.

Prayer

Thank You, Father, for the reminder of Your love towards us. Let us, when we are going through our storms, be like Job and say, "Blessed be the name of the Lord". Let prayer be always on our lips and in our hearts. Unto you, oh Lord, will I lift my voice to worship You always. Amen.

Call To Action

When you are going through trials and tribulations and the seas seem rough. Remember the story of Job and know that God will bring you out.

Eslyn Taylor

May 29

PRAY THROUGH IT

Let us then approach God's throne of grace with confidence, so that we may receive mercy and find grace to help us in our time of need. Hebrews 4:16

Even as I look at the topic for this devotion, I wonder if you see the two, power and prayer, going hand in hand. Prayer can cause a ripple effect of things that happen in our lives and in the lives of others. It's food to our spirits and peace to our souls. Do we actually see prayer as power? As children and servants of Jesus Christ, we can have conversations with the Lord with confidence, trusting that He hears and wants to help us.

He extends mercy, grace, comfort, strength, miracles, and all that we need. One thing we must understand is that even when we pray, the answer may not come right away, but we must not be defeated. I know that it is hard not to feel down, and things will weigh mentally and emotionally, but you must have faith and pray through it. Even if you don't have the right words and you sit in God's presence, know that the God you serve is faithful, and He knows what you are going through.

Get a friend or two and share with them what is happening, pray about it and try not to get anxious. Even if you do, you can pray about that anxiety, too. That's the beauty of prayer, you can come just as you are. Talk to Him because He is always ready to listen. The thing of it, too, is that He will answer if you are still, and sometimes He answers in the chaos. He is always there in our times of need.

Prayer

Father, thank You for giving me the opportunity to come to You whenever I feel sad, down, happy, uncertain or "messed up". Your grace gives me the power to move past my circumstances one step at a time. Strengthen me with each passing day as I lean on You. Amen.

Call To Action

I will pray on the mountaintop and in the valley.

Orissa Fitzpatrick

May 30

HOW TO PRAY

Rejoice always, pray without ceasing, give thanks in all circumstances; for this is the will of God in Christ Jesus for you. 1 Thessalonians 5:16

There are two different types of prayer: prayer from the heart and prayer from the ego. Prayer must be meaningful and not for show. People pray in different ways. Some people like to thank God first and foremost and then ask for what they want. Others jump right in and directly tell God what they want. Then there are people who come humbly and make their requests, saying, "God, I know I do not need this or that, but I really want it, please God".

The Bible teaches us how to pray. When you pray, it is just like talking to a friend. If you are still wondering how to pray, here are three simple steps. First, state any names you love to address God by, for example, "Lord, you are Jehovah Jireh, King of Kings, Lord of Lords". Then you thank Him for everything He has done for you. For example, "I thank You for my family, friends and everything You have blessed me with." Finally, you state your matter; for example, "I do not know which career to choose. Please help me." Then you listen to hear what God says to you. If you put all these examples together, you get a prayer. Remember to just pray by talking to God and being honest with Him. Don't worry about the 'how' too much. Start first by building your relationship with Him through prayer and conversation.

Prayer

Dear Lord, thank You for making it so easy to speak to You. Lord, please help me pray to You in Jesus' name, Amen.

Call To Action

Create your own steps to pray and start your prayer journey today.

Shaquonna Rock

May 31

NUCLEAR PRAYER

Therefore I tell you, whatever you ask for in prayer, believe that you have received it, and it will be yours. Mark 11:24

Before we take a look at the power of prayer, let's first figure out the meanings of power and prayer. Power is an interesting word which means the great ability to do, act or affect strongly while prayer is the way we talk or communicate with God. So, when we combine these two words, we wonder what our prayers can really do. God is our Father, and He's our main source of strength. Therefore, when we need something, He's the one who has the power to help us when we pray. Our prayers are like nuclear weapons. Nuclear weapons are considered the most powerful weapons on earth. These weapons can destroy whole cities, kill millions, affect the environment and compromise future generations. Our prayers are equally impactful, they have the power to damage the enemy's camp.

Prayer gives us power over temptation according to Matthew 26:4, "Watch and pray so that you will not fall into temptation. The spirit is willing, but the body is weak." Satan may tempt us, but our prayers can rip these temptations to smithereens and make us victorious over sin.

Prayer can also relieve anxiety. Philippians 4:6-7 says, "Do not be anxious about anything, but in every situation, by prayer and petition, with thanksgiving, present your requests to God. And the peace of God, which transcends all understanding, will guard your hearts and your minds in Christ Jesus." We need not worry and fret; all we need to do is pray and let God take care of everything.

Prayers can result in miracles and healing. If it weren't so, would God say this: "Is anyone among you sick? Let him call for the elders of the church, and let them pray over him, anointing him with oil in the name of the Lord. And the prayer of faith will save the one who is sick, and the Lord will raise him up. And if he has committed sins, he will be forgiven" (James 5:14-15). Our prayers are mighty weapons; we ought not to take them lightly. So, the next time you have an issue, pray.

Prayer

Heavenly Father, may my prayers be like nuclear weapons destroying everything the enemy has thrown my way. May they be so effective that I see miracles and healings because I have called on Your name. In Jesus' mighty name, Amen.

Call To Action

Commit to praying to God at least twice a day. Let prayer be your default when something good or bad happens.

Charlene Hinds

June 1

THE SHIFT *(POEM)*

Proclaim this among the nations: Prepare for war! Rouse the warriors! Let all the fighting men draw near and attack. Joel 3:9

The atmosphere is moving

The devil is trembling

The room is covered in His holy presence

The praise

The worship is at its highest peak

A mighty move

It carries you

It consumes you

It brings out the warrior in you

The soldier in you

This is a battle

This is a war

And we are fighting

Through our movement

You can hear it

In the drums

In the piano

In the guitar

In the singers

You can feel it under your feet

The ground is moving

It's shifting

In the atmosphere

We are at our highest peak, nothing can stop us now

We are consumed by the amazing power of God

It won't falter

It won't move

It's growing

It's getting bigger

It's getting louder than before

We won't hold back

Every movement is a fight

A fight for our lives, our souls, our hearts

And most importantly our Faith

and we won't back down.

Zenaida R. Mayers

BE STRONG

Be alert and of sober mind. Your enemy the devil prowls around like a roaring lion looking for someone to devour. Resist him, standing firm in the faith, because you know that the family of believers throughout the world is undergoing the same kind of sufferings. 1 Peter 5:8-9

We are surrounded by all kinds of temptations daily, but God has given us the strength to resist temptations from the devil, whether big or small. We are encouraged as Christians to always put on the full armor of God: the helmet of salvation, the breastplate of righteousness, the shield of faith, the belt of truth, the sword of the spirit and our feet prepared with the gospel of peace.

God has given us many gifts that we are required to use to bring honor and glory to His name. As a dancer, I can fight spiritual warfare through my dance in worship to God, who will then give me the strength to resist any temptations the devil may throw at me.

Prayer

Our Father who art in Heaven, hallowed be thy name. Thy Kingdom come, thy will be done, on earth as it is in heaven. Give us this day our daily bread, and forgive us our debts, as we also have forgiven our debtors. And lead us not into temptation but deliver us from evil for thine is the Kingdom, the power, and the glory forever and ever, Amen.

Call To Action

Engage in daily devotions with your family and friends.

Trinitee Angus

June 3

ARMOR UP FOR BATTLE

Put on the whole armor of God that ye may be able to stand against the wiles of the devil. Ephesians 6:11

Warfare is engagement involving war or conflict. The devil seeks daily to scheme against us, to deceive, destroy, disgrace and cause division. Therefore, our struggles are against the spirit of evil forces as it is in the natural, so it is in the spiritual.

In the natural world, soldiers are disciplined to train, study and strategize in preparation for battle against their enemies. As soldiers of the kingdom of God, we have been given full armor for our battles in the spirit realm. Therefore, being prepared is important because our enemy studies us to see the best way to launch an attack daily. We have to be militant in our approach, even if it means being camouflaged under the shadow of the Almighty.

You can stand firm and grit with the belt of truth. With steel-tip boots on your feet and the gospel of peace, may you have the protection of your heart where all emotions generate. With the shield of faith, cover your mind to stay focused. With the helmet of salvation, arm yourself with the sword of the spirit – the Word of God. Complete your preparation for battle with prayer. No devil can stand up to the truth in the Word of God.

2 Corinthians 10:4 lets us know that the battles are of a spiritual nature, so we need to fight in the spirit realm. Armor up and walk in the power and authority that was given to you as Kingdom citizens. Go forward by faith, armed with your sword, and tear down strongholds in the kingdom of darkness through your ministry.

Prayer

Almighty and merciful Father, help us stand firm in our faith, armed with Your words, to face our daily battles. Help us to understand the importance of putting on our full armor and always being prepared. Give us that militant spirit as soldiers of Your Kingdom so we can go forward fearlessly in Jesus' name, amen.

Call To Action

- As a dance minister, be prepared for ministry, fully prayed up and fully armored because no soldiers go to battle unarmed.

- Absorb knowledge of the kingdom of darkness, for this is important.

- Put on your armor daily as part of your lifestyle.

Timeless Ministers

June 4

NO RETREAT, NO SURRENDER!

Why art thou cast down, O my soul? And why art thou disquieted within me? Hope in God: for I shall yet praise him, who is the health of countenance, and my God. Psalm 43:5

Breaker, breaker 1-9. Breaker, breaker 1-9, come in. This is the helpline for when a soldier is out on the battlefield, the enemy is closing in, and he or she needs airborne help. They are calling out to the one who will fly overhead and drop bombs to defeat the enemy.

We, too, as dancers, have a helpline, a name above all other names to shout in triumph. In our garments of praise, we assume the position of worship: flags in hand to wave in the air and the enemy is decapitated, our feet to firmly plant in the belly of the enemy, our bodies as a living sacrifice, holy and acceptable in the sight of the Lord. This is a war of no retreat, no surrender.

You have the victory, so dance like it. Act like it, be the victory. Don't allow your spirit to be downcast, for we all go through challenges, but it's how we get through them that makes the difference. Begin to dance and feel the flow of the Holy Spirit through your limbs, through your heart, and through your mind. Release it all to God and yield to the power in you that can overcome, just as Jesus did on the cross, for you are called for His purpose, His pleasure. Don't you want to please the King?

For when we dance, we not only defeat the enemy, we praise our God, our Lord, our King. We shower Him with the love that is bursting inside of us. He gets our full attention as we adorn Him with our praise, worship, and love. He receives our attention, moves obstacles, and gives commands to his angels who have charge over us to help us fight and win. The enemy doesn't have a chance; he is outnumbered and out-maneuvered. The attention is not on him but on the creator.

Prayer

Father, we thank You for Your love. We praise and honor You. Even in this battle, we ask for Your strength. In Jesus' name, Amen.

Call To Action

Clothe yourself in the armor of God, put on your dancing shoes, take up your flag and worship with your weapon, for we will not retreat, or surrender.

Sandra Britton

June 5

RAINBOWS

I have set my rainbow in the clouds, and it will be the sign of the covenant between me and the earth. Genesis 9:13

A promise is a promise; there is no need to cross your fingers or your heart. It's just His Word manifesting in the sky with colors of beauty: blue, yellow, green, red, purple, orange, pink, and the list goes on. Our body is an instrument, vital in expressing movement. As we move, we create rainbows of light, color and war!

For we wrestle not against flesh and blood, but against principalities and powers. Our movement of praise and worship defeats the enemy. Our weapons of warfare are not carnal, but we can pull down strongholds with a flag of red for the blood that was shed at the cross to blind the enemy. A billow of orange roars, declaring that the Lion of the tribe of Judah is here as our shield, defense and strong tower. When the enemy comes in, a sea of blue will reveal who we are and whose we are, for we are royalty, joint heirs with Christ and seated with Him in heavenly places.

Stamp your authority and tread upon the serpents and scorpions, for you have the power to defeat our adversary through your dance with a rainbow of colors and an arsenal of instruments. Wave the white rag of victory and adorn yourself as the bride of Christ. Wait with the oil of joy instead of mourning. Don't let your circumstances get the better of you; you are no longer captive, for He has come to give life and give it more abundantly. You are not in chains, so be free to strike. Strike with every movement, strike with the wings of glory and one, two, three, twirl on the four winds of heaven blowing away like shaft the plans that won't prosper, as we are Christ's and Christ is God's.

Let's stand tall, heads high as champions and rejoice with our ribbons of color. Let's create rainbows filled with true promises that He manifests daily. He hasn't failed us yet. Believe that greater is in you, than he that is in the world! A promise is a promise.

Prayer

Dear God, we thank You for Your sure Word, which is Your promise that will not return to You void. In Jesus' name, amen.

Call To Action

Let your nay be nay and your yea be yea!

Sandra Britton

June 6

BE READY FOR THE WAR

For we are not fighting against flesh-and-blood enemies, but against evil rulers and authorities of the unseen world, against mighty powers in this dark world, and against evil spirits in the heavenly places. Ephesians 6:12

Warfare always seems present in our lives, and at times, there is a constant battle of the mind. We sometimes battle with finances, people, or problems, but the Word of God says the fight isn't against flesh and blood but against principalities in high places. We, as individuals, even have to war in dance for ourselves to keep our bodies under subjection to the spirit.

God tells us the battle is not ours; it is His. We not only fight the wrong person at times, but we also fight with the wrong weapons. We fight with anger, fear, words and attitude, but God is saying today to put on His armor which Ephesians 6:11 speaks of. These weapons are perfect because when the enemy is operating from a spiritual place, we can go in and war against him, knowing that we are fully equipped by God.

War doesn't happen because you are doing anything wrong. It happens because you are seen as a threat to the enemy. So, the enemy tries to attack you from different angles to get you frustrated, but the devil has no power. You have the power of the Holy Spirit, and He is all you need to fight every battle the enemy throws at you today. Put on the armor of God and say to the devil, "I am ready to fight because God has given me the weapons I need to defeat you, Satan. You are the loser and I am the winner."

Prayer

God, help me continue to win these wars against the enemy and let him know I am no loser. I am a winner in Jesus' name. Amen.

Call To Action

- Put on the correct armor.

- Use the weapons of God.

- Know that the battle is not yours.

Rhonda. A. Babb

June 7

WAR ON THE BATTLEFIELD

"Don't worry about this Philistine," David told Saul. "I'll go fight him!"
1 Samuel 17:32

We face giants every day in our lives, and sometimes, they seem way too big for us to defeat, so we back down. David is a great example that neither size nor age matters when you go to war on the battlefield.

David, who was just a boy on the battlefield, knew who he was fighting against. David saw that this giant was much bigger than him, but he never backed down. Look what he told the giant, "You come with all your weapons, no problem, but this is who I have and how I come". 1 Samuel 17:45-46 says, "I come in the name of the Lord of Heaven's Armies and the God of the Armies of Israel, the Lord will conquer you, and I will kill you and cut off your head." What confidence David spoke with. I could just imagine the giant holding his belly and laughing as David said these words, but he had no idea what was about to happen.

There is no giant that you or I can go to war with and not defeat today. Giants have nothing else but weapons and talk. If David, a boy, killed a giant who was ten times bigger than him, then we have no excuse. What are we afraid of? We, too, have the name of the Lord of Heaven's Armies and the God of Israel to back us up; all we have to do is get ready to fight.

Prayer

God, I thank You for reminding me that when I go to war, there is no battle I cannot win as long as I have Your backing, in Jesus' name. Amen.

Call To Action

- Be ready to fight.

- Do not go into a fight alone.

- Have confidence.

Rhonda. A. Babb

June 8

SAY YES TO GOD AND NO TO THE DEVIL

Therefore submit to God, resist the devil and he will flee from you. James 4:7

We should always say yes to God and no to the devil. If the devil tells you to cheat on a test and God says no, listen to God. It is not worth taking the chance to cheat even though your teacher is not looking. God wants us to be honest and not give in to the devil's lies.

If the devil says to be mean to the new girl at school and God says no, listen to God. As a child of God, our lives must always shine bright. Others might want to be mean to the new girl, but we will stand up for what is right.

If the devil says to break your mother's vase and lie that you did not do it and God says no, listen to God. It is understandable not to want to get into trouble, so we may be tempted to tell a lie. However, God wants us to speak the truth.

We should always listen to God no matter what the devil says. God helps us get through things. It is time we say thank you. We are not doing this for ourselves but for God our Father. Do you know when the devil tells you to do something and you do it, when you get in trouble, he will not help you? He will laugh even when you think he is on your side.

Prayer

Dear God, thank You for being with us. We know we can always say no to the devil and yes to You. Lord, we pray that we will grow spiritually in Your name. We hope that we can always be in Your presence, Lord. In Jesus' name. Amen.

Call To Action

Always listen to God, even if being obedient involves doing something hard.

Rhema-Jae Greene

June 9

SUIT UP

Finally, be strong in the Lord and in his mighty power. Put on the full armor of God, so that you can take your stand against the devil's schemes.
Ephesians 6:10-11

It's a war! A war, a spiritual war we're fighting, no guns, no bombs (in the words of John J -Elder Cheyenne Jacobs).

Imagine you're in a war in the middle of the battlefield. You have no armor. You're unprepared, sleepy and completely out of it. This could spell disaster for you on the battlefield. As dance ministers, we should always be ready, for the enemy surely is. We should not be caught "slacking". Satan is always waiting for us to drop our guard and go out exposed. We must remember that our armor is a necessity, not an option. As soldiers in God's Kingdom, we are fighting a battle daily against not flesh and blood, but principalities and powers.

When you have to minister in dance, can you honestly say you prepare for the war that will try to hinder the Word, or do you just prepare the choreography? Put on your armor so that you may withstand the devices of the enemy. During my years in a dance ministry, I have seen how the enemy attacks dancers, sometimes immediately after the ministry has ended. Do not only put on your spiritual armor for your sake but for the sake of your fellow dance ministers.

Prayer

Lord, I put on the full armor right now. I pray that the belt of truth will be buckled around my waist, the breastplate of righteousness will be in place, and my feet be fitted with the readiness that comes from the gospel of peace. I take up the shield of faith to quench all fiery arrows of the enemy and take up the helmet of salvation and the sword of the spirit, always praying in the spirit.

Call To Action

Make it a habit to put on your armor. Set an alarm or write a sticky note to remind you until it becomes a habit.

Rheanne Rock

June 10

THE SECRET PLACE OF GOOD WARFARE

Now unto the King eternal, immortal, invisible, the only wise God, be honor and glory for ever and ever. Amen. This charge I commit unto thee, son Timothy, according to the prophecies which went before on thee, that thou by them mightiest war a good warfare; Holding faith, and a good conscience. 1 Timothy 1:17-19

Let it be known that the only way we can possibly "war a good warfare" is through the King eternal, immortal, invisible, the only wise God, and the prophecies (promises) of God, which allow us to hold onto our faith and keep a good conscience. To help achieve this, we must make our dwelling in the secret place of the Most High, as Psalm 91 states:

He that dwelleth in the secret place of the Most High shall abide under the shadow of the Almighty. I will say of the LORD, He is my refuge and my fortress: my God; in him will I trust. Surely, he shall deliver thee from the snare of the fowler, and from the noisome pestilence.

He shall cover thee with his feathers, and under his wings shalt thou trust: his truth shall be thy shield and buckler. Thou shalt not be afraid for the terror by night; nor for the arrow that flieth by day; Nor for the pestilence that walketh in darkness; nor for the destruction that wasteth at noonday. A thousand shall fall at thy side, and ten thousand at thy right hand; but it shall not come nigh thee. Only with thine eyes shalt thou behold and see the reward of the wicked. Because thou hast made the LORD, which is my refuge, even the Most High, thy habitation;

There shall no evil befall thee, neither shall any plague come nigh thy dwelling. For he shall give his angels charge over thee, to keep thee in all thy ways. They shall bear thee up in their hands, lest thou dash thy foot against a stone. Thou shalt tread upon the lion and adder: the young lion and the dragon shalt thou trample under feet. Because he hath set his love upon me, therefore will I deliver him: I will set him on high, because he hath known my name. He shall call upon me, and I will answer him: I will be with him in trouble; I will deliver him, and honor him. With long life will I satisfy him, and shew him my salvation.

Prayer

Lord, help us dwell in Your secret place, and may our dance show that we live there.

Call To Action

- Dwelling: Meditate extra long in the presence of the Lord this week.

- Secret Place: Establish a "Prayer Closet" if you do not have one already.

- Remember: Recall some of God's fulfilled promises to you and reinforce your faith.

Pierre Rock

June 11

JUST IMAGINE

For the weapons of our warfare are not carnal, but mighty through God to the pulling down of strong holds; Casting down imaginations, and every high thing that exalteth itself against the knowledge of God, and bringing into captivity every thought to the obedience of Christ; 2 Corinthians 10:4-5

Just imagine…that we do not need to fight a physical war against the enemy of our souls.

Just imagine…that our warfare weapons are not carnal.

Just imagine…that our weapons are mighty through God.

Just imagine…that our weapons pull down strongholds.

Just imagine…that our weapons cast down imaginations.

Just imagine…that our weapons cast down every high thing that exalts itself against the knowledge of God.

Just imagine…that our weapons capture thoughts and make them obedient to Christ.

Just imagine…but we don't have to. We have all of the above in our repertoire when we engage God and His Word in our lifestyle, prayers, praise and worship…imagine that.

Prayer

May we know today that our warfare weapons are not of this world. They are more accessible and powerful than we may imagine.

Call To Action

Let the imagination of your heart be just and aligned with God's Word.

Pierre Rock

June 12

MAN OF WAR

The LORD is a man of war, the LORD is his name. Exodus 15:3

This verse excites me and it's comforting. This scripture comes from the chapter where the Israelites have been delivered from Pharaoh's rule, having been cast into the sea. Now imagine the things that happened before the deliverance came: slavery, suffering, and beatings. God was not asleep. He knew a time was coming when He would raise a man for this task, and raise him, He did. He sent plagues and killed the firstborns of each family that was not with the Israelites. He allowed death to pass over them because they covered their doorposts with blood, and he parted the Red Sea. He showed them who was boss and one not to be played with. Hallelujah! Thank you, Lord.

God will step in and do the same for us because we are His. Shout if you must, dance because you should and break those shackles free. There were times I had to war dance, stomping my feet, swiping my hands in the atmosphere wildly but purposefully, pulling down strongholds, and fighting for breakthroughs. I felt like I was in a physical fight afterward, but it was worth it. I declare even now that our Pharaohs shall die.

Prayer

Hallelujah. Thank You for Your protection and Your fight for me. I pray that I will rest in that knowledge and pass it on to others. Show me how to fight for Your people when needed, and help me not to be afraid when that time comes. Continue to cover me in Your blood. I thank You for the fire of protection around me, my family and my friends. Amen.

Call To Action

Repeat after me, "Intercession shall be upon my lips because my God is also a man of war and because I am my Father's child. I have hands and feet of iron and my warrior God with me".

Orissa Fitzpatrick

June 13

REALITY CHECK

Be self controlled and alert. Your enemy the devil prowls around like a roaring lion looking for someone to devour. Resist him, standing firm in faith. 1 Peter 5: 8-9

Satan is real. Demonic forces are real. There are things, plans and devices set up in the spirit realm that want to kill you so badly that they are relentless. Whether you acknowledge them or don't take them seriously is up to you, but if you understood the reality of what goes on behind the scenes where your life is concerned, you would make sure you are girded up.

Ignoring this fact is like knowing your car brakes are cut, but you still get in the car and drive. It's like knowing someone has given you poison, yet you consume it willingly. As dancers, we must understand this because when turmoil is going on in the church or with individuals, we have to go in there and command those situations to stop. Break out in a praise dance or fight, sending up a shout of victory. We must be alert and sensitive to the changes happening in the spiritual realm. We may miss it sometimes but don't be counted out when the time comes. You can still play a part. There is a saying that I hear, "The devil has a job to do, but so do you". Be alert!

Prayer

Ignite a fire within me, Lord. Help me not to sit back and let the enemy have control over my life. I embrace Your strength, wisdom and knowledge. Cover me in Your blood. In Jesus' name, Amen.

Call To Action

Repeat after me, "I will not become a statistic for the enemy of my soul. Open my eyes and heart daily, Lord, to see what I must do".

Orissa Fitzpatrick

June 14

THE DEMOLISHER

We demolish arguments and every pretension that sets itself up against the knowledge of God, and we take captive every thought to make it obedient to Christ. 2 Corinthians 10:5

The worst battles are those in your mind. Your thoughts can keep you captive. As a dancer, you often hear yourself saying, "I can't do this move. I will look bad doing it, or I will forget this move". There were times I had to depend on God and not on my own strength and speak to myself to reverse these negative thoughts. As the battle rages in your mind, we must take every thought captive by replacing the negative thoughts with God's Word. You could even use a song. I have done this many times, and it works.

There were times when I was part of a dance piece and kept forgetting my choreography. My mind told me I could not get it done, so I would stop and pray and ask God for help. I would then begin to speak to myself and say that I can do all things through Christ who strengthens me, Philippians 4:13. Whatever the enemy may say to us, we know we have a God that enables us, so let us demolish those strongholds that keep us captive. God truly gives us the ability to accomplish anything.

Prayer

Lord, I destroy every proud obstacle that keeps me from knowing You, and I take every negative thought captive to obey Jesus Christ.

Call To Action

Become aware of the negative thoughts that come into your mind. When this happens, find a scripture verse that counteracts the very thought.

*** Maxine Butcher***

June 15

FIVE STONES AND A SLING

Let no one lose heart on account of this Philistine, Your servant will go and fight him. 1 Samuel 17:32

Warfare dance can be draining on the body, so you must know God's Word, not just the movements. Strong knowledge of God's Word backed up with faith empowers your movements and gives you the security of knowing God will fight for you.

Flags were always my weapons of choice to do warfare dance. I danced, knowing that the power was not in the flags but in the Holy Spirit, enabling me to use the flags as an instrument of warfare.

There is a time for everything under the sun (Ecclesiastes 3:1-8). We need to know when it is time to fight and when to choose the right weapon. David was a small boy up against a giant, but David knew His God would fight for him. When we know the greater one lives inside us, we can stay in the battle "for the battle is not ours, it's the Lords", 2 Chronicles 20:15. A sling, a stone and faith defeated a giant.

Prayer

Lord, help me to know when to fight and not give up. Please give me the faith to believe in Your power to deliver.

Call To Action

Memorize Ephesians 6:11-12, 14-17 and put on the full armor of God, that you may be able to stand against the wiles of the devil:

For we wrestle not against flesh and blood, but against principalities, against powers, against rulers of the darkness of this world, against spiritual wickedness in high places.

Stand therefore having girded your waist with truth, having put on the breastplate of righteousness, and having shod your feet with the preparation of the gospel of peace; above all, taking the shield of faith with which, you will be able to quench all the fiery darts of the wicked one. And take the helmet of salvation, and the sword of the Spirit, which is the word of God.

Maxine Butcher

the Spirit, which is the word of God.

Maxine Butcher

June 16

THE WARFARE IN YOUR PRAISE

As they began to sing and praise, the Lord set ambushes against the men of Ammon and Moab and Mount Seir who were invading Judah, and they were defeated.
2 Chronicles 20:22

If you're not excited just reading this account of King Jehoshaphat going into battle, I encourage you to get excited. King Jehoshaphat put his situation before the Lord, and the Lord laid out a strategy for him. God will do the same for you. Sometimes, winning the battle is all about our praise. The enemy often tries to come against you, your family, your job, your mind, your possessions, and your physical body. As a dance minister, get up and start to praise and see your victory through Jesus. Dance your way through situations that try to defeat you. Dance on the head of the enemy and crush the situations that come against you. Fight on behalf of yourself, your ministry and your church. Do not ever underestimate the power of your praise.

Prayer

Father, I thank You for giving me this weapon of praise that I can use to defeat the enemy when he tries to attack me. Today, I establish my praise as my weapon of war, and I put on my garment of praise and dance over the head of the enemy. Every situation will be defeated with the help of the Lord. As I dance, oh, Lord, I declare that You will establish ambushes for the enemy on my behalf, and the enemy shall be defeated in Jesus' name, Amen. (Now do that Victory dance.)

Call To Action

If you have not spent any of your prayer or devotion time in praise or dancing before the Lord concerning the situations in your life, this day, I encourage you to do just that. Take out this weapon and see the Lord come through for you as He did for King Jehoshaphat.

Laina Jacob

June 17

BATTLE READY, ALWAYS!

Praise be to the Lord my Rock, who trains my hands for war, my fingers for battle.
Psalm 144:1

Listen, the one thing I learned early in dance ministry is that you need to be fit, spiritually and physically. Why? Because when God is ready to push you into a prophetic or intercessory dance for the people of God, if you are not ready, you can get weary in the battle. Dance ministers are called to change atmospheres and root out demonic spirits. When God starts to work through you to heal and set His people free, you want to be ready. You know that it could be anytime and anywhere, so you need to be ready. Spiritual awareness and discernment are necessary, but being a trained soldier is key. You have to understand the enemy's devices and plans. You have to be able to hear from God about His strategy and then execute it. People are depending on you, so stay battle-ready.

Prayer

Lord, teach me how to fight. Train my hands and feet so that I may be an instrument that You can use for the deliverance of Your people. Help me, Lord, to never go into battle without You. Help me to listen and move according to your direction. Thank You, God, for the assurance that victory is guaranteed with You on my side. In Jesus' name, Amen.

Call To Action

Ask God to show you the areas in your life that may trip you up if there is a spiritual war. Commit to working on strengthening yourself in these areas.

Laina Jacob

June 18

PUT ON YOUR FULL ARMOR

Put on the full armor of God, so that you can take your stand against the devil's schemes. Ephesians 6:11

God has given us our daily robe to wear. He did not provide us with a part of it, but He, in His infinite wisdom, gave us the full dress code. God has done this so that we can stand against the enemy's devices. Soldiers all over the world prepare themselves for war; they ensure that everything they need to go to war is ready and in place. The enemy can attack at any moment, expected or unexpected, so being alert is crucial.

As Christians, we need to be spiritually ready by putting on the full armor of God. Let us make sure that every part of the armor is on. We can ask ourselves the following questions:

1. Belt of Truth – Are we always living in honesty and speaking the truth?

2. Breastplate of Righteousness – Are we living purely?

3. Gospel of Peace – Do we believe that God will help us get through all situations that come our way in as peaceful a manner as possible?

4. Shield of Faith – Do we believe that we can get over any mountain that comes our way with God's help?

5. Helmet of Salvation – Are we asking God to renew our minds as the battle starts with the mind?

6. Sword of the Spirit – Do we read His Word often for guidance?

Arming ourselves daily is vital; it is not a one-time task. It is easy to slip up, so we need to constantly be prepared.

Prayer

Heavenly Father, thank You for being there, ready to dress us with Your armor. We ask You to forgive us for the times when we have not kept on the full armor. Help us to make it a habit to dress in Your armor daily. Amen.

Call To Action

Let us ask God to dress us daily with His full armor. The Holy Spirit will guide and empower us.

Julie Greene

June 19

OPEN OUR EYES

For though we live in the world, we do not wage war as the world does.
2 Corinthians 10:4

Yes, we live in this physical world, and it is very easy to operate in the physical and neglect the spiritual. The Word reminds us that we were born in sin and shaped in iniquity. Jesus died for our sins, so He has already paved our way in the spiritual battle. Our duty is to be obedient and faithful to God.

The spiritual realm is so real. There is a battle going on every second between good and evil. It is very easy not to focus on the spiritual realm since it is not as visible as our physical realm, but angels and demons impact how we live. We have the ultimate weapon in Jesus Christ to win. In these last days, we cannot afford to be blinded by this battle. We can only fight in this realm with the power of the Holy Spirit. Since we cannot see with our natural eyes, we can ask God to give us spiritual eyes. We can pray to God for insight; His Word will also show us what to do.

Our minds are a virtual background when it comes to warfare, for it is in the mind where Satan plants thoughts contrary to the Word of God. Romans 2:12 reminds us, "Do not conform to the pattern of this world but be transformed by the renewing of your mind." This needs to be a daily habit, as the devil never sleeps. We need to always be spiritually alert.

Prayer

Father, cover and flood our minds only with Your Word and Your promises. Renew our minds daily. Thank You for opening our spiritual eyes and keeping them open so we can be spiritually alert. Amen.

Call To Action

Let us dive into the Word of God every minute we get, as this is our guide to win this battle.

Julie Greene

June 20

THE BATTLE IS THE LORD'S – NO RETREAT, NO SURRENDER

Put on the whole armor of God, that you may be able to stand against the wiles of the devil. For we do not wrestle against flesh and blood, but against principalities, against powers, against the rulers of the darkness of this age, against spiritual hosts of wickedness in the heavenly places. Therefore take up the whole armor of God, that you may be able to withstand in the evil day, and having done all, to stand.
Ephesians 6:11-13

Isn't it amazing how David went out to fight against Goliath wearing no armor? In contrast, Goliath was there in his own strength, dressed in full armor and bearing his sword and spear. David acknowledged that the battle was not his but God's, so God would do the fighting for him. Just as he did with David, God has provided spiritual armor for us to resist Satan's attacks when they come.

Belt (waist) Truth – Allows us to use the truth of God's Word against Satan's lies;

Breastplate (heart) Righteousness – Ensures God's approval;

Shoes (feet) Readiness to spread the gospel of peace – Gives us the motivation to continue;

Shield (faith) Vision– Gives us the ability to look beyond what we can see;

Helmet (head) Salvation – Protects our minds from doubting God's saving work;

Sword (the spirit) The Word of God – Our only weapon of offense;

And finally, Prayer.

As we put on the full armor, stand firm and begin to declare God's Word with authority. Satan will flee from us. Let us make sure that when the enemy comes, he can find nothing in us with which to condemn us.

Prayer

Lord God, we declare that any weapon that is formed against us is rendered impotent, for we are more than conquerors through Jesus. Build us up, Lord, in our faith so we do not falter and can do Your calling. In Jesus' name, we pray. Amen.

Call To Action

- Pray God's Word with passion and stand on His Word.

- Memorize God's Word to silence the enemy.

Gurlain Applewhaite

June 21

MAKING WAR IN THE HEAVENLIES

For the weapons of our warfare are not carnal, but mighty through God for pulling down strongholds, casting down arguments and every high thing that exalts itself against the knowledge of God, bringing every thought into captivity to the obedience of Christ. 2 Corinthians 10:4-5

In the natural world, soldiers in the army use weaponry such as guns, grenades and bombs. However, this war in which we are engaged is a supernatural war. Therefore, it requires spiritual weapons of God that can effectively dismantle Satan's strongholds. A spiritual stronghold is a way of thinking which dominates our behavior. One of the most effective methods of dismantling the devil's strongholds is through prayer.

From the moment a person decides to give their life to God, Satan starts to strategize to get them out of the will of God. As Christians, we are at war with the devil. He is against God and does not want to see us succeed in this life, so he fights us at every opportunity. Therefore, the war starts from the moment we enlist in this army of God.

The enemy attacks us in our thought lives. He does not want us to be united, so he allows seeds of discord to be sown through misunderstandings that set our hearts against our fellow ministers. When that happens, it is impossible to minister under the anointing of God and in unison with each other.

Prayer

Lord God, thank You for equipping us with the weapons we need to take every negative thought captive and bring it to the obedience of Jesus Christ. In Jesus' name, we pray. Amen.

Call To Action

- Release the areas in your life that you have not yet submitted to God.

- Study the Word pertaining to that area of your life where there is a stronghold.

- Counteract each lie of Satan with the truth of God's Word.

Gurlain Applewhaite

June 22

OLLY, OLLY, OXEN FREE

No temptation has overtaken you except what is common to mankind. And God is faithful; he will not let you be tempted beyond what you can bear. But when you are tempted, he will also provide a way out so that you can endure it.
1 Corinthians 10:13

'Olly olly oxen free' is an expression used most commonly in children's games, like hide and seek, which generally indicates that people who are hiding can safely come out into the open without fear or penalty.

Oftentimes in life, we experience trials and tribulations that make us want to hide, disappear and lay low until the dust settles and everything seems alright again. While our problems seem to surround and follow us, we play hide and seek with them. However, this is a call to come out and stop hiding! God will never give us more than we can bear. The truth is that God gives us these weights to lift in order to make us stronger, more resilient and, most importantly, for us to lean on and rely on Him. We can't fulfill God's plans for us if we hide.

We, as ministers, need to step out and trust that God will protect us from every attack. We must use our dance as a weapon against the enemy: our hands as swords that cut the enemy, our feet to trample the enemy's head, and our bodies as a testament to our unwillingness to fail, hide and give up. We know that God has our backs.

Prayer

Dear God, I pray today that even as we face adversity and trials, we will not hide and we will not back down. Instead, we will lift our eyes to You and stand firm with our feet planted in the promise that You will not give us more than we can bear. In Jesus' name. Amen.

Call To Action

I challenge you to face your trials head-on and trust God to provide you with a way through.

Gabrielle Blackett

June 23

BREAK FREE
(POEM)

So if the Son sets you free, you will be free indeed. John 8:36

Break Free from the bonds that so easily entrap us,

From the things that seem to make us mysterious.

We know that having Jesus is a plus and not a minus,

Let us dance like we are painting with a brush,

The picture of God's forgiveness of us.

Break Free from the fear within our souls

And embrace that Jesus has made us whole.

Dance to the beauty of the Creator that frees our souls.

So, express your art and

BREAK FREE, BREAK FREE

Prayer

God, You help us to break free from all sins. As Your children, may we know that You are the only one that breaks yokes and loosens the chains that bind us. We thank you for freeing us from the pit of hell, in Jesus' Name. Amen.

Call To Action

Take 5 minutes out of your day to remember what God has done in your life and thank Him for breaking you free from sin.

Eslyn Taylor

June 24

GOD'S FIGHT

Do not fear them, for the Lord your God is the one fighting for you.
Deuteronomy 3:22

What a powerful verse that is so relevant today. God is telling us not to fear those people, things or situations that usually cause us to be afraid, remembering that the Lord our God is the one who is fighting for us. Jesus said that the battle is not ours; it's the Lord's.

I did not always feel this confident as a dancer. Actually, I was always fearful that I would mess up. This fear came from a place of wanting to be perfect and not fail. But what is fear? Fear is defined as "A feeling of anxiety and agitation caused by the presence or nearness of danger, evil, pain, etc.; timidity; dread; terror; fright; apprehension".

When I read that definition, I had to take a step back. Was I fearful of God? As I began to think of where my fear was coming from, I realized that the devil was the one fuelling my fear. I needed to believe God had already fought against my fear by dying on the cross. As I pray and delve into His work, believing what He has done for me, my fear starts to disappear.

Now, every time I am to minister in dance, I do get a little fearful but I am assured that God is fighting that battle for me. As you go about your daily life, remember that no matter the situation that causes you to fear, God is right there fighting that fear with you.

Prayer

Heavenly Father, thank You for Your Word that assures us that You are fighting for us. We, as your children, have nothing to fear. So, as we dance, we will not fear those butterflies we get in our stomachs, but we will know that it's Your presence drawing us to You. May we be blessed in Jesus' name. Amen

Call To Action

Every time your fear comes, just ask the Lord to show you where that fear originates. Study the word and meditate on it. Resist the fear (devil), and it (he) will flee.

Eslyn Taylor

June 25

SPIRITUAL WARFARE

Casting down imaginations, and every high thing that exalteth itself against the knowledge of God, and bringing into captivity every thought to the obedience of Christ. 2 Corinthians 10:5

Stop...wanting it to just...Stop! Why is this happening to me? God, where are you? You said you'll always protect me. I'm putting my trust in you, believing that I'm righteous.

Destructive thoughts are still racing through my mind. It seems like the devil isn't fleeing. It seems like the past isn't really gone. Doubt seeping into my mind: you're not really saved, if He really was for you, then why does life seem to be against you? You can't get that done. You're not good enough; remember what happened last time? And the time before? And the time before that?

And just before another accusing thought enters my mind, the Holy Spirit alerts me that this is spiritual warfare. Now, knowing that the thoughts are from the enemy, specific verses come racing through my mind: Philippians 4:6-8, Psalms 23, Isaiah 12:2, Isaiah 41:13, Ephesians 6:13, along with many others and suddenly His presence is felt. My mind is at peace. He restoreth my soul.

Prayer

Dear God, Thank You for being our strength in times of trouble, distress and temptation. Thank You for always answering when we call. Help us to know that You'll never leave us or forsake us; You'll forever be by our side and will never give us more than we can bear. Help us to remember to come to You even in the small things. Help us to keep our armor on. We know that the enemy is always looking to see who he can devour. We pray that You'll always give us the strength to defeat the enemy and that You'll remind us that You have already defeated him. In Jesus' name, Amen.

Call To Action

When we read our Bible and pray daily, we're feeding our spirit, but when we constantly disobey God, that is when we feed our flesh. I know it may be hard, but I encourage you to say no to your flesh and no to the enemy's temptations. Remember, God is our strength and He will give us the strength to choose the Spirit.

Danielle Harewood

June 26

WAR AGAINST LEADERS

Everyone must submit to governing authorities. For all authority comes from God, and those in positions of authority have been placed there by God. Romans 13:1

Satan was thrown out of heaven because he waged war against God. What was he thinking? How could he think it wise to take on this mindset when God has given him more than enough? He covets the power and authority of his creator. We as humans also try to step into positions that belong to others without even considering what we are up against. When we run into God's face, expect to be held accountable for our actions.

When we war against leadership, we fall short of the purpose God has for us. We tend to think we deserve more and lose sight of the vision. We become fleshy, and our motives begin to cloud our judgement of who we really are. Authority is there to bring order, and when we seek to fight against authority, it causes a war between the flesh and the spirit. As a believer, you must consider your ways because the Word says that everything we do must bring honor and glory to our Heavenly Father.

As ministers of dance, we must not seek to be in a position that God has not called us to be in. We must remain humble and trust God's perfect plan for our lives and the authority He has placed over us. Our dance should be one filled with holiness and not filled with greed, for we are God's chosen vessels.

Prayer

Lord, help us never to seek our own agenda as we sit under the authority You have placed above us, in Jesus' name, Amen.

Call To Action

- Never covet what doesn't belong to you.

- Wait until God promotes you.

- Trust the authority over you.

Rhonda. A. Babb

June 27

SPIRITUAL WARFARE AGAINST US

But the prince of the kingdom of Persia withstood me one and twenty days: but, lo, Michael, one of the chief princes, came to help me; and I remained there with the kings of Persia. Daniel 10:13

There is not only war on the earth but in heaven as well. If we read Daniel chapter 3, it says that Michael the archangel had to battle with the King of Persia in order for Daniel to receive his answered prayer. There are times when we are going through spiritual warfare and have no idea why the answer to our own prayer is taking so long, and we blame God. God is not the problem; it's the enemy who seeks to fight against us.

In heavenly places, there are spirits in operation against what God has ordained for us, but we know, "When God is for us, who can be against us?" according to Romans 8:31. There is an enemy fighting to stop our answered prayers, our children, our marriages and our families from fulfilling their purpose and destiny, but we have a God who fights for us when we call on Him because 2 Chronicles 20:15 says the battle is not ours but the Lord's.

It is a given that we have to fight against principalities and powers in high places. Not only is prayer a weapon for war but our worship can also be used to fight our spiritual battles. As dance ministers, we know the enemy hates worship, but when we worship, strongholds are broken, healing takes place, and people are delivered from bondage. We have been spiritually equipped by the commander in Heaven, our God; He has given us the same power that raised Jesus from the dead. He has also given us power to trample over serpents and scorpions, so never forget God has already given us victory over the enemy, for no battle is too hard for God to win.

Prayer

Heavenly Father, You are the highest commander on the earth and in heaven. May we always know that You are standing by, waiting to represent us in Jesus' name. Amen.

Call To Action

- Remember that prayer and worship are your spiritual weapons.

- Do not blame God.

- Remember, God is the commander.

Rhonda. A. Babb

June 28

W'S - WINNING THE WORLDLY WAR WITHIN

For what shall it profit a man, if he shall gain the whole world, and lose his own soul? Mark 8: 36

It is war! A tempestuous tug-of-war. There is a fierce inner battle that goes on between flesh and spirit. The world in which we live is full of opinions, beliefs and temptations meant to lure us away from God. These include the songs we dance and listen to, the movies we watch, the books we read, the videos and reels we absorb on social media, and even the people we interact with can influence us to live sinfully and selfishly. Power, notoriety, status, money, illegal drug usage, sexual immorality, overeating, or creating our own standards of beauty are idolized. On the surface, these things may seem agreeable, but earthly gains are temporary and can come at a costly price.

Our soul is the most precious thing we own. It is eternal! It survives the death of the body. To trade it for worldly things that will fade away is a grave mistake. The world will always try to influence us. The enemy will also prowl around like a roaring lion looking to devour our souls. The battles within us and around us will come. When they do, though, we shall resist our sinful desires and put on all of God's armor in order to triumph by the power of the Holy Spirit. Our focus will be on loving God more than we love the world. God has promised people who love Him the Victor's Crown, the crown of eternal life.

Prayer

Heavenly Father, I give thanks for Your world, created by You for us. Thank You for the many blessings we have received according to Your will and divine right. Help us to be steadfast when worldly temptations come. Keep our spiritual eyes focused on serving You. Give us daily reminders that the things of this world are temporary and Your promise of eternal life is true.

Call To Action

When the war within comes, let Exodus 20 speak:

You shall have no other gods before me,

I am the creator of heaven and earth,

I have made everything unique.

No images shall you make and bow down,

If you want to wear the Victor's Crown.

Remember to keep the Sabbath Day Holy,

I expect you, my child, to always give me the glory.

Honor your father and mother in everything you say and do,

This is my commandment, this is what I request of you.

Don't forget you shall always tell the truth,

Lies and false stories simply will not do!

You shall not call my name in vain,

My child if you do, I will surely cause you pain.

You shall not kill, covet, commit adultery or steal

You were created to love, to praise and to worship, That's the deal!

Akia Brathwaite

June 29

DEMOLISH STRONGHOLDS, ARGUMENTS & PRETENSION

The weapons we fight with are not the weapons of the world. On the contrary, they have divine power to demolish strongholds. We demolish arguments and every pretension that sets itself up against the knowledge of God, and we take captive every thought to make it obedient to Christ. 2 Corinthians 10:4-5

The Apostle Paul, in the book of 2 Corinthians, shares truths about the weapons of the believer. The weapons are not of the world; they have the power to demolish strongholds. The interesting thing about this passage is that the believer also has a part to play. The weapons don't just operate by themselves. Paul encourages us to demolish arguments and every pretension that sets itself up against the knowledge of God and take captive every thought to make it obedient to Christ.

Every dancer then must ask themselves: what thoughts do I entertain? What arguments do I have? What pretensions am I allowing? Oftentimes, the warfare we experience is a battle of the mind, in the realm of the spirit. God wants his children to fight in the spirit because He has given us His Spirit.

We pray according to His word and His will. We rebuke, reject and speak against those things that are not of God. Pretension speaks of covering the truth, presenting a false idea or impression. It involves pride and deception. Christ does not want us to be deceived, and therefore, we must test the spirits. Not everyone nor everything that we see or hear is of God.

I encourage you to be genuine, have the right motives, be spiritually minded, pray without ceasing, exercise faith in God, and trust and obey God's instruction to you.

Prayer

Dear Lord, help me to fight using weapons according to Your spirit and not those of this world. Train my fingers for battle and my hands for war so that every weapon formed against me will not prosper in Jesus' name. Amen.

Call To Action

Today, I encourage you to have your loins girt with truth (belt of truth), have on the breastplate of righteousness, shoes with the preparation of the gospel of peace, the shield of faith, the helmet of salvation, and the sword of the spirit which is the Word of God. Resist the devil.

Sobrina Forde

June 30

WARRIOR'S TRIUMPH

Finally, be strong in the Lord and in his mighty power. Put on the full armor of God, so that you can take your stand against the devil's schemes. For our struggle is not against flesh and blood, but against the rulers, against the authorities, against the powers of this dark world and against the spiritual forces of evil in the heavenly realms. Ephesians 6:10-12

"Warfare" refers to the spiritual conflicts and difficulties that people face when met with life's challenges, temptations, and sufferings. This concept is predicated on the belief that there is a spiritual dimension containing both good and evil. Throughout the Bible, the combat metaphor is used frequently to depict the ongoing conflict between the forces of darkness headed by the adversary (Satan) and the forces of light led by God.

Warfare dance is a powerful expression of spiritual battle, overcoming challenges, and celebrating triumph in Christ. Is it possible for our dancers to go to war? Yes, but we must understand our dance in the context of spiritual combat in the Biblical sense (being obedient/ living by God's Word, submitting to God, rejecting the adversary, and walking in the Spirit).

As Psalm 149:3 says, "Let them praise his name with dancing and make music to him with timbrel and harp." Begin your day by acknowledging that the challenges we encounter are not just our own. Read and consider 2 Chronicles 20:15, in which God promises His people victory. Spend some time in prayer, submitting your problems to God and seeking His guidance.

Pause to mentally visualize putting on each piece of the armor described in Ephesians 6:13-17.

Prayer

I approach Your throne of grace with reverence and humility. I understand that our battle is not against flesh and blood, but against spiritual forces of evil that seek to block Your Kingdom's goals. Today, I take up the power You have bestowed upon me via the shed blood of Jesus Christ, and I put on all of Your spiritual armor.

Call To Action

The fight may be difficult, but we are not alone, troops of light. Allow the Holy Spirit to guide you and Christ's love to empower you. Get up, put on your armor, pray constantly, renew your thoughts, stand firm, and declare your victory in Christ. As you fight for God's glory and the advancement of His kingdom, may the light of Christ shine brilliantly through you. Amen.

Alicia Olton

July 1

FAITH OVER FEAR

"Do not worry about your life, what you will eat; or about your body, what you will wear. Life is more than food, and the body more than clothes. Consider the ravens: They do not sow or reap, they have no storeroom or barn, yet God feeds them. And how much more valuable you are than birds! Who of you by worrying can add a single hour to his life? Since you cannot do this very little thing, why do you worry about the rest?" Luke 12:22-26

Unfortunately, it can be easy to give into fear in today's world. We are often so used to living in fear that it becomes our new normal. However, it is important to realize that this can negatively impact our relationship with Christ. It is natural to feel fear, but when we let it consume us, we can be held back from doing the things God has called us to do.

When it comes to overcoming fear, a lot can be learned from the story of David and Goliath in the Bible. Goliath was a Philistine giant who was over nine feet tall. He would mock the Israelites and challenge them to fight, knowing they were terrified of him. However, a young teenager named David was not afraid to stand up to Goliath. You probably know how the story goes, but David conquered Goliath by using only a rock, a sling and, most importantly, God's strength. Before going into battle, David asked the Lord to be with him and give him the strength to complete the task.

What set David apart from the rest of the Israelites was his confidence in Christ. Despite being one of the smallest and youngest members, he had the greatest amount of confidence in what could be done with Christ on his side. So, how can we apply this story to our own lives? While we may not face a giant in our lifetime, we can do exactly what David did when we face trials that cause us to be filled with fear. Believe, have faith.

Prayer

Dear God, we come before You to lay our panic and anxiety at Your feet. When our fears and worries crush us, remind us of Your power and Your grace. Fill us with Your peace as we trust in You and You alone.

Call To Action

Whenever fear grows within you, picture David and Goliath and remember with the help of God, anything can be overcome.

Danae Niles

July 2

FEAR STEALS

And he was in the hinder part of the ship, asleep on a pillow: and they awake him and say unto him, Master, carest thou not that we perish? And he arose, and rebuked the wind, and said unto the sea, Peace, be still. And the wind ceased, and there was a great calm. And he said unto them, Why are ye so fearful? How is it that ye have no faith? And they feared exceedingly and said to one another, What manner of man is this, that even the wind and the sea obey him? Mark 4:38-41

One thing I know for sure is that fear steals. It steals your joy, your peace, your everything. What are we supposed to do when fear holds us and stops us from physically moving or speaking? It is a horrible feeling. I was once in that position and I never want to be in it again. So, I prayed and prayed, "God, help me not to fear. Remove any fears that I have about what is in your will for my life". But getting rid of fear doesn't happen overnight; you have to work at it.

I first had to put my trust in God, not only some of it but all of it. Some circumstances in life have us so afraid, even situations that haven't happened yet that we think might happen or we fear might happen in the future. When you put your trust in God, He will give you the peace that passes all understanding, no matter the circumstance.

Prayer

Dear God, let us remember to turn to You when we feel fear trying to creep in. We know that the enemy tries to control us sometimes with fear, but You said in Your word that You did not give us the spirit of fear, but of love, power, and a sound mind, in Jesus' name. Amen.

Call To Action

Everyone is afraid sometimes. But if we run to God, knowing that He is always in the boat with us, He will give us the strength and wisdom we need. He will always give us peace during the storm.

Danielle Harewood

July 3

FEARING GOD, NOT FEARING MAN

And Saul said unto Samuel, I have sinned: for I have transgressed the commandment of the LORD, and thy words: because I feared the people, and obeyed their voice. 1 Samuel 15:24

Many people struggle with fear. Fear of failure, fear of success, fear of insects, and the list goes on. Some people specifically fear others and what they might say or think about them. This type of fear can cause us to be stuck when we should be growing in the will of God. In this verse, we see Saul realize his mistake: he feared people instead of God.

Earlier in the chapter, we see that even though the people sacrificed the best of the sheep and the oxen to God, Saul's disobedience caused God to tear the kingdom of Israel from him that day and give it to his neighbor. Saul stopped growing in the will of God.

When we completely put our trust in God, our fears of what others might think or say about us will no longer be there. Let's ask God to help us not to fear others.

Prayer

Dear heavenly Father, help us fully trust and obey You, for we know that fear will be canceled from our lives when we fully commit to trusting and obeying You. I pray that You will release us from the fear of what others might say and think about us. May we want to please You more than we fear people and situations, in Jesus' name. Amen.

Call To Action

I encourage you to tell God about your fears and give them entirely to him. No matter your situation, you have a God who is all-powerful and loves you. Let us always remember that through him, we can live a fearless and victorious life.

Danielle Harewood

YOU ARE WITH ME

Even though I walk through the valley of the shadow of death, I will fear no evil, for you are with me; your rod and your staff, they comfort me. Psalm 23:4

Everyone knows this famous and beloved Psalm of David. Because David was a Shepherd, he likened God to a shepherd and us, God's people, to sheep. One might not want to be compared to a sheep, but think about all the things a shepherd does for his sheep. Like the Shepherd, God provides and cares for us; He gives us peace, provision, protection, and sometimes correction. Compared to the sheep, we are unable to defend ourselves, and without a shepherd, we are easy prey to evil. We sometimes even wander off, get lost or go astray. Shepherds have to put their lives at risk to rescue their sheep. They have to use the rod and staff for protection and correction, to ward off attacks from predators and to prod their sheep to bring them back to safety when they wander off. Isn't this how God is to His people? He will leave the 99 to go looking for that one lost soul.

As dancers in a group, we have leaders to help, guide and even correct us. When our lives are not what they should be, it is reflected in our dance. When we find ourselves in that valley, we must know and trust that God cares and will protect and guide us if we are willing. Even when we are going through difficult times in our lives, we need not be afraid because God is right there walking with us through that valley.

Prayer

Father God, thank You for Your presence that is always with me, even when I fail. Thank You for Your rod of correction and Your staff of comfort. As we face our fears, let us be mindful that You are with us. In Jesus' name. Amen.

Call To Action

Face your fears head-on, knowing that God is with you every step of the way.

Eslyn Taylor

COMMANDED TO BE FEARLESS

Have I not commanded you? Be strong and courageous. Do not be terrified; do not be discouraged, for the Lord your God will be with you wherever you go.
Joshua 1:9

The above verse is considered the verse of encouragement in the Bible. God knew that as a leader, Joshua would face many challenges from the people. So, Joshua had to be a fearless leader. This verse is not just for Joshua but for you and me. There are times in our lives when we are distressed and fearful of our present and our future. God commands us as believers to be strong and courageous, not just physically but spiritually, too. Do not be afraid of the challenges that we face or be discouraged by the negative words or news that we hear because God will be everywhere we go.

I see dance as an act where God commands us to be fearless. As a ministry, we are sometimes asked to minister for a particular event, and it may be a rally against homosexuality or just spreading the Gospel through dance. Dancing can even be considered going to war. So, when we are on that stage, every foot stomp or raised hand must be strong, and if the music doesn't play properly, we must not be discouraged. We know that God is with us.

Prayer

Thank You, God, that You have commanded me to be fearless. Thank You for Your encouragement through Your Word. I will not be terrified or discouraged, but I will stand on the promise that You are with me wherever I go. Continue to be the source of my strength as we war against the enemy. In Jesus' name. Amen.

Call To Action

Be an encouragement in someone's life today. Reassure them that God is right there with them.

Eslyn Taylor

FEAR NO EVIL

The Lord is my light and my salvation—whom shall I fear? The Lord is the stronghold of my life—of whom shall I be afraid? Psalm 27:1

Do you have a pattern of being fearful? Unfortunately, the truth is that it can be incredibly easy to become overrun and overwhelmed by fear in today's society. It seems like everywhere you turn, there's a new problem, a threat, whether big or small, to our lives and peace of mind. Oftentimes, we become so used to living in fear that, before we know it, it becomes our new reality. However, it is crucial to understand that this can negatively affect our relationship with Jesus.

We are human, and it is natural to feel fear, but when we let it consume us, we can be held back from doing the things God has called us to do. Our ministry is attacked whenever we go through a season of fearfulness, which is why we must fight that fear. When we are not confident in Christ because of our fear, we don't know who will be affected by our inability to walk in alignment with God's purpose for us. We must fight our fear and stand firm in our purpose because God has our backs. With God on our side, we have nothing to fear.

Prayer

Dear Lord, I place my worries and anxiety at Your feet. I ask for forgiveness for all the times I have taken my worries everywhere except to You. I know You hear me, Lord, when I struggle with my fear. You care about what is going on in my life, and I know that You will do what is best for me. I know that You will remove all fear from my life, and I depend on You. In the end, may all honor and glory go to You. Amen.

Call To Action

Consider where the Lord has brought you from and where you are now. Think about all that you have survived and thank the Lord for it.

Gabrielle Blackett

July 7

FIGHT OR FLIGHT

Even though I walk through the valley of the shadow of death, I will fear no evil, for you are with me; your rod and your staff, they comfort me. Psalm 23:4

How many of us have experienced fear at some point in our lives? All of us, right? We've experienced the fear of getting a bad grade, getting in trouble at work, and forgetting the choreography on stage. We are no strangers to fear. Feeling fear is not the problem because it is a normal human emotion. It is when we give into fear that we need to take a moment to remember who has dominion over our emotions, and that is Jesus. We need to ask Jesus to remove all fear from our lives because fear is a hindrance.

Dance is such a vulnerable expression because we are telling stories that have been experienced by ourselves and those around us. This means that if we are struggling with fear, those around us will be able to see it. Not only is this a distraction from God's purpose, but it hinders us from ministering to the best of our ability. Neither of these things is good. We don't want to be a part of anything that blocks the purpose of God from being shown fully. So, we must attack fear head-on and fight the fear that seeks to blind us.

Prayer

Our most heavenly and gracious Father, I pray that You will remove any evidence of fear in my life. Destroy all roots of fear. Any fruit that has come forth from the fear tree, may it shrivel up and die. I declare that fear has no place in my life, in Your mighty name. Amen.

Call To Action

Take authority over your circumstances, leaning on the knowledge that God walks with you daily, keeping you safe. Do not be afraid.

Gabrielle Blackett

July 8

UNDER THE SHADOW OF THE ALMIGHTY

The Lord is my Light and my Salvation; whom shall I fear? The Lord is the Strength of my life; of whom shall I be afraid? Psalm 27:1-2

Throughout the scriptures, God has repeatedly told us that we should not fear. He knows that in our human nature, we tend to take our eyes off Him and focus on the Goliath before us. When we focus on the giant, we are saying to God that we don't trust Him to take over and fight on our behalf.

King David had to flee from King Saul on several occasions, but his trust and confidence in God did not wane. He knew who his God was and placed his life in His hands. In Psalm 18:1-3, he also referred to God as his rock, fortress and high tower. Just as David was protected, God is also watching over us and protecting us from the snare of the devil.

All of us have encountered fear at some time in our lives but be assured that God is with us even though we may not feel His presence or we may not hear His voice. It is natural for a dancer to experience a fear of ministering for the first time. Even some well-seasoned dancers confess that they experience "butterflies" each time they face a congregation. Let us always remember that we do not go out to minister in our own strength or power but in the power of the One whom we are worshipping.

Prayer

Heavenly Father, we thank You for the assurance that we can trust You to watch over and protect us from all harm and danger. Help us always keep our eyes fixed on You and acknowledge You as Lord over our lives. In Jesus' name, we pray. Amen.

Call To Action

- Refuse to be anxious or worry about anything.

- Turn over every care and concern to God.

- Trust in the Lord with all of your heart.

Gurlain Applewhaite

July 9

FAITH OR FEAR… YOUR CHOICE

You are of God, little children and have overcome them, because He who is in you is greater than he who is in the world. 1 John 4:4

When we see the amount of evil which goes on and often goes unpunished, it can cause the strongest of us to cower and not want to confront what is ahead. But there's no need to fear; the same Spirit who raised Jesus from the dead is in us, so we do not fight in our own strength. God is fighting for us and victory is sure. We are on a winning team!

The spirit of fear can take hold of us and hinder our ministry unless we nip it in the bud. Satan only needs a foothold to gain entrance into our ministry. Each minister is different; some may be shy, while others may be bold and outgoing. Therefore, each dancer must move together as one unit in boldness, for the strength of a chain is its weakest link. Those who are timid in the group can feed off the strength of the more courageous, though ultimately, the strength comes from God.

Dancers should be cognizant that God is working behind the scenes on our behalf, and whilst we may not be venturing out as strong as we ought to be, God sees our potential and is waiting for us to catch up. Whichever belief we give more attention to is the one that will rule our lives. So, will you give more attention to faith or fear? The Word of God must renew each dancer's mind so that we can speak and act with authority.

Prayer

Lord Jesus, You said that You would not leave us alone, and You would send the Holy Spirit, the Comforter, to be with us. We don't have to be crushed or paralyzed by fear of the unknown or anxiety. Instead, we can break the chain of fear over our lives and declare that who the Son sets free is free indeed. In Jesus' name, we pray. Amen.

Call To Action

- Pray for God to calm your heart and guide you through each day.

- Invite God's presence in your midst.

- Pray that God's angels go before you to prepare the way before you minister.

Gurlain Applewhaite

July 10

NO LONGER A SLAVE TO FEAR

For God has not given us a spirit of fear, but of power and of love and of a sound mind. 2 Timothy 1:7

God has not given us a spirit of fear, so where did it originate? God is a God of peace; where there is no peace, there is torment. It only takes one small lie to be planted in our minds, and as soon as we accept it, it gains a foothold. We know that Satan is the father of lies. His role is to keep God's people in torment so that they don't fulfill their purpose on earth.

We are told to reject every thought that Satan drops into our minds before it takes root, but we don't stop there. We turn our eyes toward Jesus, the Prince of Peace. That is why it is important that we spend time in the Word, so we are able to refute the lies of the enemy. The spirit of fear is a demonic spirit which seeks to take over our thought life and prevent us from achieving all that God has for us.

If negative thoughts enter our minds every time we step out to minister, causing us to doubt our ability, we should know right away that they do not originate from our Heavenly Father. Thoughts such as "You are too old. What do you think you are doing?" and "Look how people look at you and laugh" can become repetitive and prevent us from entering into worship wholeheartedly. We must remember that our bodies are the temple of the Holy Spirit. We carry the very Spirit of God in us.

Prayer

Lord Jesus, in moments when doubt and negative thoughts flow into our minds, help us discern their origin. We reject every lie that the enemy tries to sow, knowing that he seeks to hinder us from fulfilling Your purpose for our lives. May our thoughts align with Your truth, empowering us to minister without doubt. In Jesus' name. Amen.

Call To Action

- Confront the very thing of which we are afraid.

- Speak the Word over your circumstances.

- Focus on the love of God to counteract every attack of Satan.

Gurlain Applewhaite

CHOOSE CALMNESS & CONFIDENCE

So do not fear, for I am with you; do not be dismayed, for I am your God. I will strengthen you and help you; I will uphold you with my righteous right hand.
Isaiah 41:10

It is normal to feel uneasy about the unknown, for only God himself knows the unknown. Earlier in this chapter, God spoke to Isaiah to give His people a sense of comfort because they had been facing adversity for many years. We, too, can ask God to provide us with comfort when we face our hard times.

One may describe fear as the unpleasant feeling you have when you think you are in danger. The opposite of fear is calmness or confidence. God knows we will encounter fear, so He reassures us that He is with us and encourages us not to be fearful. We have the power of the Holy Spirit to fight off this feeling of fear and worry. We can ask God to give us a spirit of calmness and confidence when this negative feeling arises.

Our adversity may not be to the extent of what the Israelites faced in the book of Isaiah, but whatever situations we face today, just know that with God by our side, we can overcome any fear.

Prayer

Jesus, we call on Your Name. Help us always put our trust in You. When the feeling of fear steps in, we thank You in advance for being there to help us overcome it. Give us the spirit of calmness and confidence that only comes from You. Thank You, Father. In Jesus' Name, Amen.

Call To Action

Let us take courage and rely on God to strengthen us when situations arise that will lead us to be fearful.

Julie Greene

July 12

FEAR, WHAT FEAR?

The Lord is with me; I will not be afraid. What can mere mortals do to me?
Psalms 118:6

As a dancer, you're familiar with that feeling you experience when you are just about to go on stage. Sometimes, you actually get on stage, and the eyes steering back at you are so piercing that you can forget all your preparation. Thank God for muscle memory because if you had to depend on your brain, you would freeze right there on the stage.

I do not think you ever completely get rid of those jitters, but certainly, when you are aware of who you represent and what He can do through you, the realization that you are never alone knocks that fear right out of you. You become so focused on being a vessel for God, showing love for His people and embracing His promise to fight on their behalf that you know the enemy has no chance. You become so focused on that one person that God placed on your spirit that there is no way, with the Lord beside you, that you would let faces distract you to the point that you are paralyzed by fear.

When you have to minister on the highways and byways, you are going into the enemy's camp, and the enemy will use people to do all kinds of things to distract you. You must come spiritually prepared and geared up for battle. Ask the Victor of every battle to show up with you, and "Fear gone one time! It's just ministry!"

Prayer

Father Lord, we are so thankful that when we call on You, You are always there to back us up. We discount the power of Fear over our lives, and we replace it with the knowledge that when we do Your will, You are always with us. We declare the spirit of fear broken over our lives. May we live in victory through You, in Jesus' name. Amen.

Call To Action

When you feel fearful in a situation, say this: "Lord, You promised to be with me. I am going as a representative of You, and I take the entire heaven's army with me as I step into this situation." Say it aloud. It works better.

Laina Jacob

July 13

WHAT ARE YOU AFRAID OF?

For God did not give us a spirit of fear but of power, love and a sound mind.
2 Timothy 1:7

In life, we have many fears. Even though I love to dance, I was always afraid to go on stage. I would get nervous, my feet would feel as if they were glued to the ground, and automatically, I would forget my moves. Those feelings stemmed from fear.

Fear can keep you from stepping out and doing great things. I learned to overcome fear as I danced more and faced the audience. It is true that fear is not from God. He has not given us a spirit of fear but of power, love, and a sound mind. I learned to conquer my fear and not to let it conquer me.

The more I went on stage and spoke the Word of God to myself, the more I knew I had a big God that would help me overcome. So, I would like to encourage you to believe that you can do all things through Christ and overcome fear. Say it with me: "God has not given me a spirit of fear. I have power, love and a sound mind!"

Prayer

Lord, today I step out in faith, believing that You are there for me. I am bold because of You. I am an overcomer.

Call To Action

Pinpoint something that you fear and face it.

Maxine Butcher

I AM AN OVERCOMER

Be strong and courageous, be careful to obey all the law my servant Moses gave you do not turn from it to the right or to the left. Joshua 1:7

These words to Joshua from God always encourage me. I found strength in these words many times when I was afraid. There was a time I was asked to dance with flags in a dance piece all by myself, but I was so afraid to do a solo piece, "On that stage, all by myself? No, no, no!"

The first thoughts that came to my mind were: "What if you fall? What if you mess up? What if you forget the move? Fear just had the best of me. I could hear it speaking, and fear kept giving me excuses not to dance.

My dance leader assured me I could do it, and I put away the "what ifs" that kept me from accomplishing this task. "What if" will take away your hope and your faith in God, "what if" will make you give up, and "what if" will make you lose confidence in yourself. "What if" is not from God. Remember, you can do all things through Christ who strengthens you. I did that solo and it was a great ministry. Many people were blessed by it. So, let's be strong in the Lord and have good courage like Joshua. You will never know whether you can do something unless you try!

Prayer

Dear God, I pray that You will break every spirit of fear in my life and replace it with faith.

Call To Action

Memorize Joshua 1:7 and apply it to circumstances when you feel fear rising.

Maxine Butcher

July 15

DELIVER ME

I sought the LORD, and he answered me; he delivered me from all my fears.
Psalm 34:5

Fear is a serious thing. It can cripple, make you feel oppressed and even cause anxiety, which can all impact your life so strongly that you forget to live and, as such, do not reach your true and full potential. Once you are mentally or emotionally tired, it also affects you physically. I am sure a lot of you can attest to this. I have personally experienced it, especially within the last couple of months and as recently as the past couple of weeks. But there is a God, Hallelujah.

I find all of Psalm 34 (which is also a song) to be so powerful. It has carried me through trying times. Learning to believe, trust and lean on the Word of God is life to the mind, body and soul. There is peace that comes with it.

I remember when I had to carry out a special solo ministry on a Sunday at church. My stomach was in knots, and my mind was replaying all the possibilities of what could go wrong. I even feared what others would think of it and how I would feel if the response wasn't what I wanted. One could say the thoughts and feelings were natural, and I would agree, but I had to push past them and carry out God's assignment for me. And let me tell you, it surely was a setup because the worship leader's songs (all about giving praise) aligned with the song I chose, *We Exist to Give You Praise*. There was God, even in this situation, letting me know He's got me.

Don't ever miss out on when God is talking to you. Yearn for it and depend on it. Will life always go the way you want it to? Of course not, but we must learn to adjust our thinking to His. I hope this blesses, delivers and transforms your mind to all God is.

Prayer

Father, You are a deliverer. I ask that You deliver me from all fear in my life so that I may live to the true and full potential You have called me to reach.

Call To Action

Write down the things you fear, pray about the list, and, if need be, seek help to overcome them. It will be worth it.

Orissa Fitzpatrick

Call To Action

Write down the things you fear, pray about the list, and, if need be, seek help to overcome them. It will be worth it.

July 16

FIGHTING FEAR LESS*

Ye shall not fear them: for the LORD your God he shall fight for you.
Deuteronomy 3:22

I nah go fear, no matter what de enemy wan throw my way

Jehovah God will be there

He fights for me O yeahh

I nah go fear, nah wrestle against flesh and blood no sir

Tell wanna faith over fear

He will fight for you and I

Listen me, God ah we warrior we tell yah that long time

White flag ah no fi we, wrong sign

God still in charge in ah quarantine

Still ah win the battles in church or online…

- DJ Nicholas ft. Positive *Faith Over Fear*

We fight *fearless* when we are fighting *fear less*. We are not to fear because the Lord our God is fighting for us. One of the enemy's main warfare tactics is to make us focus on the wrong target or the wrong enemy. We are not fighting a physical battle, "nah wrestle against flesh and blood no sir"…"for the weapons of our warfare are not carnal, but mighty through God to the pulling down of strongholds" (2 Corinthians 10:5). Therefore, we are encouraged to place our faith in God to fight for us. We must put faith over fear.

Remember, when fear comes calling, allow God to fight/answer for us through the Word, prayer, praise, and dance, "Ye shall not fear them: for the LORD your God shall fight for you" (Deuteronomy 3:22).

Prayer

Help us to continue placing faith over fear, and fighting fear less.

Call To Action

Practice faith over fear, fighting fear less and using your warfare weapons (the Word, prayer, praise, dance).

Pierre Rock

Incorporates Barbados Slang

July 17

LET'S FACE IT

Be not afraid of their faces: for I am with thee to deliver thee, saith the Lord.
Jeremiah 1:8

When I first started dancing, I remember someone telling me if I'm too afraid to look at people in the audience, I can look over their heads. This way, I look like I'm looking at them, but I'm not. I used this technique for many years because I was afraid to look at men in their faces. I was intimidated, and I didn't have the confidence. What or who are you afraid of facing? Think about the God we serve. Jesus reassures us that we need not be afraid. He does not only send us, He goes with us. Let's have some God-confidence. There's no one we should feel intimidated by. Our confidence is in the One who equips us.

I thank God that I am now bold and fearless enough to look straight at someone in the audience when I dance and connect with them. This didn't happen overnight, but it came with an understanding of who I am, having God-confidence and recognizing that a child of God need not be intimidated. In the words of John Yarde in his song *Not Afraid*: "Who shall I fear, Who shall I be afraid, cause God is with me I know it's okay. Who shall I fear? No one. Shall I be afraid? No one."

Prayer

Lord, give me a bold spirit and accelerate my growth in becoming more God-confident. When I feel afraid or intimidated, please remind me of Your Word. Remind me that You are with me and I need not be afraid. Help me to face and conquer every fear, so that I may move forward unhindered and boldly. In the mighty name of Jesus, Amen.

Call To Action

Challenge yourself to make small steps towards facing your fears. You may not feel ready to face that fear head-on as yet, but you can make small steps in that direction.

Rheanne Rock

July 18

DO IT AFRAID

For I, the Lord your God, hold your right hand; it is I who say to you 'Fear not, I am the one who helps you.' Isaiah 41:13
When I am afraid I put my trust in you. Psalm 56:3

I once read a quote that said, "Sometimes the fear won't go away and you'll just have to do it afraid". This quote may seem contradictory, but stay with me. We have all experienced fear at some point in our lives or have something we are afraid of. But until we truly get over the fear, should we stay stuck and let it stop us from doing what we need to? No. Do it afraid. God knows our fears, and He's right there walking beside us, whispering, "Fear not". Don't wait for the fear to go away for you to move; do it anyway. Start that ministry group, do that solo, write that book, start that business idea, pursue that program of study, and speak the word God has given you. Do it, even if you are afraid.

The Bible says to us that we need not be afraid. Fear is a real experience, and until we reach that point of deliverance from fear, we must go on. Don't stay stuck waiting for the fear to go. After all, you may only realize the fear is gone when you move. God is not surprised or caught off guard by our fear. He's a loving God who gently says, "Come my daughter, come my son. I know you're afraid, but you got this. I'm right here holding your hand. Just trust me."

Prayer

Lord, help me to step out even when I'm afraid. I thank You for staying by my side as I walk through and past every fear. I look forward to the testimony I will have of how I overcame fear.

Call To Action

- Write a list of things you want to do, but fear has stopped you from pursuing.

- Start tackling something on this list, and when you feel like walking away because of fear, do it anyway.

- Keep track of your list, and as you tackle things on your list, record your progress.

Rheanne Rock

July 19

TRUST IN GOD

When I am afraid, I put my trust in you. Psalms 56:3

To me, this verse means that there is no reason I should be afraid because I can always trust in our Father. For example, for us children, there are many situations we may be fearful of:

1. Some of us are afraid of the dark at night when it is time to go to sleep and our parents turn off all the lights.

2. At times, we may be afraid of heights, like when we are on a roller coaster, and it goes up really high. The thought that we may fall over or that the ride may stop working while we are on it scares us.

3. Some of us get bullied at school and are afraid of the person being mean to us.

4. There are times when we feel alone. When someone gets lost in a store, fear may take over them.

5. When you visit a friend's house, their dog gets all excited. When that dog jumps on you, that could make you feel fearful.

6. Sometimes, at night, you hear scary sounds and wonder what or who it is.

7. There are so many reasons we children get afraid, but no matter where you are, I want you to know God is always with you. So, you don't need to be afraid.

Prayer

Dear Lord, as You helped me to overcome fear, please help others get over their fears. Help them to know that they can always trust You, and there is no need to be afraid. Help them to be brave and bold in Jesus' name. Amen.

Call To Action

Everyone has experienced and is experiencing fear of some kind. Go up to that fear and say, "I am a child of God. You will not scare me because I put my trust in God."

Rhema-Jae Greene

FEAR ENDS TODAY

Don't be afraid, for I am with you. Don't be discouraged, for I am your God. I will strengthen you and help you. I will hold you up with my victorious right hand.
Isaiah 41:10

Within this passage, we can see there are two emotions taking place: fear and discouragement. God knows that these can sometimes stop us from achieving things within our lives, so God is very clear that He is here with us.

Emotions are reactions caused by something that affects our mood in a particular situation. I remember one day, I was in a place of doubt and fear, and I asked myself, "But what if I am wrong? Then, what do I do?" Fear made me limit myself into thinking I could be wrong about what I heard, but when there is a little mustard seed of faith in you, fear becomes silence, and your thoughts become, "But what if I am right?" Then you would have been obedient to your Abba Father.

Fear becomes like a chain on a dog which limits his movement, and he can decide if he will wait on his owner or break free. It's time to decide how far you want to go or if you want to remain restricted from finding your purpose. If, by chance, discouragement clouds your vision, know that God is there to help if you call upon Him. So, will you remain in fear or move by faith into what God is calling you to do today? You decide. All it takes is the first step.

Prayer

God, please help me if I am too fearful to move forward in my calling. I pray that as I reach out, Your hand will help me break free, even now, in the mighty name of Jesus. Amen.

Call To Action

- Keep in mind that a little faith is all you need.

- Know that it is time to break free.

- Remember that your fear is just an emotion.

Rhonda .A. Babb

July 21

STEP, LEAP, JUMP!

I will lift up mine eyes unto the hills, from whence cometh my help. Psalm 121:1

Beginning a new journey is scary. Let's face it, the unknown is downright terrifying, especially when navigating the unknown in front of a crowd. If we give it too much thought, we will back out of it and not do it, but there is too much excitement knowing that what you are about to do will bring honor and glory to the Most High. Fear is an emotion we must push past to get the result that will bring healing, deliverance and salvation to the lost. If we live in a posture of fear, backing into a corner, crouched down into a ball, time is wasted, and it will take us even longer to get the desired outcome.

Our help comes from the Lord; if only we would look up to be strengthened and look inside to be empowered. Nothing great comes easy, and we need to use that feeling of fear to propel us as we enter the unknown. Fear is a weapon used often by our adversary, which stunts our spiritual growth and keeps us in a child-like state of uncertainty. It puts us at the back of the line to be used by God.

You can do all things through Christ, who strengthens you from within. God has called you for such a time as this; His Kingdom business must come first. Kill the flesh and let the Holy Spirit take over. Resist the devil and he shall flee. His false evidence appearing real is just that – false. Our God is bigger, and He is calling you to release that fear unto Him and step, leap, jump.

Prayer

Lord, we glorify and exalt Your name. Your name is above fear and timidity. Help us to be bold and tenacious for Your kingdom so that Your name will be honored and praised. In Jesus' name, Amen.

Call To Action

Step out in faith, leap into the unknown and jump into the arms of God. He'll catch you.

Sandra Britton

July 22

CALLING FOR BACK-UP

For God hath not given us the spirit of fear, but of power, and of love, and of a sound mind. 2 Timothy 1:7

Ahh! It's time. The big day is here, and after all the pep talks, we must do what we've been called to do. Putting our faces like flint, there is no turning back. And boy, our adversary must be shaking in his boots! It's now time to jump. It's our first time ministering, and these jitters are real, but we are bursting with excitement. Garments pristine, instruments sharp, we're ready for this battle. Our "fears" won't keep us from pleasing the Father. Prayed up, anointed and ready, En-Garde!

Preparing for any ministry is no easy feat, and bringing your fears under control, knowing that the Kingdom is waiting for souls to be reborn, is a process. Still, it's a very rewarding process, especially for the Kingdom. Our ministry is a tool that, when used wisely, can shake the kingdom of darkness, so we must press towards the mark for the high calling in Christ Jesus. There are many ways we can defeat the enemy, and one sure way to diminish our fear is to build our spirit; this is accomplished not only through our physical efforts but also with the help of the Holy Spirit. He is very much aware of what we are capable of. It's only us that seem unsure of what we can do when we put everything in God's hands.

Our arsenal of weaponry is always at our disposal and within arm's reach. God did not give us a spirit of fear but of power, love and a sound mind, and we have the power to speak life and death. So, call on His power and sound mind when fear wants to step in. It can only come in if we allow it, and if it does, it will only stay if we feed it. Constant communication with the Father can give us confidence, knowing that He has our backs. His words clearly state that He will never leave us nor forsake us.

Our fears can keep us from accomplishing so much God has for us to do in our lives. If we let fear win, what will be our excuse when we face Him on the day of judgement? Will we play the "blame game"? Fight your fear with faith, for your accolades are not for this life but for the time of judgement when we might hear, "Well done, my good and faithful servant."

Prayer

Lord, we know all we have to do is ask. We call in a sound mind when fear grips us, and we thank You for Your Word that keeps us, in Jesus' name, Amen.

Call To Action

Do not dwell on the thoughts of fear when they come. Find a scripture to use as your weapon when fear tries to grip you.

Sandra Britton

July 23

PEACE

Peace I leave with you, my peace I give unto you: not as the world giveth, give I unto you. Let not your heart be troubled, neither let it be afraid. John 14:27

When we think of fear or anxiety, thoughts of being unsteady come to mind. In life, when you have important things to accomplish, sometimes nerves creep up on you and stunt your confidence. You might be preparing for this new hurdle in your life for months, weeks or even days. But, when the day actually arrives, the devil may try to put negative thoughts in your mind, such as: "You can't do it, you will fail," and "Why even try?" If you let these stunting words feed your mind, you may start to believe them. But did you know that the Lord brings us peace? Jesus encourages us not to be afraid because we can always find peace and confidence in Him. We must remember that we can do whatever we set our minds to and live courageously.

Prayer

Heavenly Father, I pray that in times of trial and angst, we will remember that You have given us peace. Therefore, we won't be fearful of the circumstances but will continue to move forward in confidence and faith in You. Amen.

Call To Action

Commit to strengthening these aspects of your life:

Daily bread - It is important to get your daily dose of God. It's your one-on-one time with Him when you can just have a conversation about what's going on in your life. It is also when you can ask Him to grant you peace and courage.

Daily affirmations - These are crucial to boosting one's confidence.

Positive mindset - Think positively; your attitude determines your altitude.

Faith - Trust that the Lord has your back. He won't burden you with anything He knows you can't overcome.

Halal Teens

July 24

DON'T WORRY — GOD'S GOT YOU

Even though I walk through the valley of death, I will fear no evil for you are with me your rod and your staff they comfort me. Psalm 23:4

Fear sometimes causes us to be paralyzed. When I was preparing for my Common Entrance Examination, I became very fearful and anxious about not being able to pass for the best school. As time drew nearer, I still felt unprepared, like I did not learn enough during online school. Whenever I felt anxious, my mom reminded me I should be anxious for nothing. Philippians 4:6 says, "Be anxious for nothing, but in everything by prayer and supplication, with thanksgiving, let your requests be made known to God."

I realized that God's got me in every situation, and I do not need to fear anything because He is always there to comfort me. Whenever fear tries to take over, I fight back by praying to God to help me overcome my fears. Sometimes, when I have to dance, I get fearful that I may mess up, but praying and asking God for his guidance always helps.

Prayer

Thank You, Lord, that You are the reason I do not have to live with the spirit of fear. Help me through all of my days and teach me not to worry. In Jesus' name, I pray, Amen.

Call To Action

Write out your favorite Bible verse about fear, stick it on your bedroom wall, and whenever you are afraid, repeat it over and over until you feel better.

Trinitee Angus

July 25

WHOM SHALL I FEAR?

The Lord is my light and my salvation, whom shall, I fear? The Lord is the stronghold of my life, of whom shall I be afraid? Psalm 27:1

Struggling with fear is not easy. Trust me, I know. As someone who struggled and is still struggling with fear, it can really consume you. I used to pray to God every day to help me get over this spirit of fear, and He placed this scripture in my head. Since then, it has been a staple in my life, and I hope after reading this devotion, it can also be a staple in yours. This Bible verse is self-explanatory and needs no real introduction, but I know we can dig deeper.

God is saying here, "I am your light and your salvation. Who shall you fear? I am the stronghold of your life. Who shall you be afraid of?" Really and truly, with God as a "backative," you do not need anybody else to fight your battles. God did not give us a spirit of fear, so why are we afraid to step out of our comfort zones, why are we afraid to speak in front of large crowds, and why are we afraid to spread the Gospel of Jesus Christ? Saying it is one thing but believing it is another. You cannot say this verse without meaning, believing, or living it. Otherwise, you will never be able to move on from where you are.

As Christians, we cannot live our lives in fear of tomorrow, in fear of how people will see us, in fear of anybody's opinion on how we live this life. As a younger Christian growing up in the dance ministry, whenever we had to do a special ministry, I would always hide in the back, hoping not to be seen or called to the front, but boy, did God test me! Not only did I get called from the back, but I got my first-ever solo. I was terrified, but when the day came, I did my solo, and I didn't just dance, I ministered. From then on, anybody could have called me to the front, and I would have jumped at the opportunity. You think God doesn't see, but He does, and He will test you to see if you're ready to take the step you fear most. The question is, will you be ready?

Prayer

Dear Heavenly Father, I pray that You remove the spirit of fear from our lives. Remind us, oh God, that You are always with us. Fill us with Your peace and grace. Help us to stand tall against our fears; help us to be bold and courageous in You so that whenever we have to face our fears, we will be ready. In Jesus' Name. Amen.

Call To Action

Always remember to pray about your fears and ask God to help you overcome them. Keep reading scriptures on fighting your fears and let God do the rest.

Zariah Watson

July 26

NAKED *(POEM)*

I sought the Lord, and he answered me and delivered me from all my fears. Those who look to him are radiant, and their faces shall never be ashamed. Psalm 34:4-5

Is it visible

Or is it just all in my head?

No

You see it, don't you?

My vulnerability, my soul not being good enough,

Feeling judged

Do I look tainted to you?

Do I look undeserving of allowing the naked soles of my feet to become one with this stage?

In front of all these people

His people

Somehow I believe they see the imperfections in me

And oh, how it scares me

It terrifies me

But maybe it's not that it's supposed to

Maybe it's just necessary

For them to see

Maybe He wants it to be seen

That this raw emotion

Isn't manufactured

That the pain and loss and hurt I show you through my movements

Is allowing myself to become transparent with you

Letting go

Letting you in to understand that I'm fighting too

I'm fighting this same war up on this stage

I have allowed this fear of being unworthy to consume me

And me making that first movement, taking that first breath

Is me taking it back

Fighting back!

Zenaida R. Mayers

July 27

AZIEL - "GOD IS MY STRENGTH" *(POEM)*

I have told you these things, so that in me you may have peace. In this world you will have trouble. But take heart I have overcome the world. John 16:33

Fear is feeling unsafe

It's the thought of losing someone special to you

It's messing up choreography you practiced day in and day out

It's something you're afraid of

It's something you're unsure of

Or maybe it's even a reaction to something that feels dangerous

That feeling you get when your palms become sweaty

When you play with each individual finger

When your heart suddenly sinks

Or beats rapidly through your chest

That distasteful feeling you get when you dread what's to come

The unexplainable

The unthinkable

The unimaginable

And at that moment, when everything slows down, there's that spark

A switch that goes off

A voice you suddenly hear

A burst of braveness

A wave of courage

At that moment you wonder where

Or who gave you the strength

The strength to keep going

To persevere

To take that leap

Suddenly you laugh to yourself

How you couldn't have realized sooner that you're not alone

Or have you forgotten that he said

He will never leave you or forsake you

For one split second, you forgot about what He has promised you.

Zenaida R. Mayers

July 28

STEP OUT OF YOUR COMFORT ZONE

Have not I commanded thee? Be strong and of a good courage; be not afraid, neither be thou dismayed: for the Lord thy God is with thee whithersoever thou goest. Joshua 1:9

I know stepping out of your comfort zone can be very difficult. Take it from me because I am currently in a battle with myself on whether I should step out and step up or stay in the background until I feel comfortable doing so. Sometimes, you may feel like you're not good enough to step out, so you start to compare yourself to others, trying to make yourself small or digestive for the people around you, but that stops today.

I have a message for people like me, and I have two words for you: "Do it". Whatever it is that you may be battling within your mind and heart or even within your spirit, if God wills it, do it. Whatever it is that the Lord has asked you to do, but you are afraid of what people will think, do it. You may be afraid you will never be good enough, but I came here to say enough is enough. Has God not commanded you to be strong and courageous? Hasn't God shown you that He will be with you wherever you go and in whatever you put your mind and hands to do that pleases Him?

In writing this, I, too, have also come to the realization that when God says move, we must move. Don't question it, don't question yourself, don't even ask why me because God moved you from where you may have wanted to be to a place where He needed you to be. So, to my sisters and brothers out there who are still in that box called a "comfort zone". It's time to move. It's time to step out.

Prayer

Dear Heavenly Father, I pray that whoever reads this and is still in a comfort zone stage will get uncomfortable in it. May they move to Your will and to Your plans for their life, in Jesus' Name, Amen.

Call To Action

Step up and step out!

Zariah Watson

July 29

FEAR NOT, GOD IS HERE

The Lord is my light and my salvation—whom shall I fear? The Lord is the stronghold of my life—of whom shall I be afraid? Psalm 27:1

Fear is an emotion that every human has experienced before in their life; no one is exempted from this natural phenomenon. Some people are afraid of heights, spiders, public speaking, the ocean and dogs, and sometimes their fears are debilitating, meaning that it cripples them for the moment that they are exposed to their fears. While it is natural to experience fear, we should not allow it to cripple us because it limits our functions as human beings and can even hinder us from being used by God to help others.

You may be thinking, "How does my fear hinder God from using me to help others?" When fear cripples us and makes us retreat or hide, it makes it harder for us, as dance ministers, to effectively spread His messages. We don't know exactly what will happen when God's messages aren't spread, but we do know that whoever that message was for wouldn't receive it. Don't doubt your part in God's plans because someone might be depending on you. Fear can show up as insecurity, unwillingness to help, or even a bad attitude; it really requires us to self-reflect on why we may be feeling a particular way.

Prayer

Lord, I thank You for the assurance that You are my light and my salvation, the stronghold of my life. It is because of this assurance that I will not be afraid of anything that threatens to break me or intimidate me. Instead, I will look to the hills from which my help comes and take authority over every fear that stops me from fulfilling my purpose in life. I pray that even in the moments when I may feel fear, I will draw closer to You and remember the words of Psalm 21:1. Amen.

Call To Action

Look one fear in the face this week and conquer it with the help of God. Find your courage in the Word of God, and let this Bible verse lead the way for your triumph.

Gabrielle Blackett

July 30

YOU'RE GOING TO BE ALRIGHT

I cried out to him with my mouth; his praise was on my tongue. Psalm 66:17

I want to start this devotion by stating: His grace is sufficient, so lean not unto your own understanding. Even as I am writing this, I am facing a situation where I am fighting fear. You may be, too, or can think of a time when you experienced it. My friend, it's going to be alright. How do I know? Because the God I serve is awesome, and He is bigger than fear, so much bigger.

The author of Psalms is writing from a place of thanksgiving because the Lord had brought the Israelites from Egypt into the promised land. They went through so much, but God made a way in every situation they faced; even when they did wrong against Him, He was merciful. What promise has the Lord made to you? Hold on to that and believe it.

I want to declare to you right now that you shall be overcome by the blood of the Lamb and the word of your testimony. Don't let fear create a false identity for you. I found myself retreating into fear and not sleeping well, but the one who sees is merciful, He is faithful, and He comes through every time. My friend, you are going to be alright.

Prayer

Father, You are such a good Father. You take care of me and I bless Your name for that. Even as fear wants to consume me, I rebuke it in the mighty name of Jesus. It shall no longer hold me, and I am no longer bound to it. I am walking in the freedom that You have given to me. In Jesus name, Amen.

Call To Action

Declare over your life: "No weapon formed against me shall prosper. In Him, I live, and move, and have my being. I have the mind of Christ, and fear shall no longer have a hold of me".

Orissa Fitzpatrick

July 31

FEAR NOT!

Fear not, for I am with you. Isaiah 41:10

Fear is caused by anxiety from someone or something. Sometimes, when people say they fear God, they do not always mean they are scared of Him. They mean that they respect or submit to God. When we go to dance in front of a big crowd, we may be afraid. God is telling us to fear no more, for He is with us. My encouragement to you is, whenever you feel afraid, repeat this Psalm, "Yea, though I walk through the valley of the shadow of death, I will fear no evil".

Fear is caused by Satan. He is trying not to let you live in God's purpose or plan for your life. I once had to dance in front of a crowd, and I was very scared, but a day later, God reassured me I did not need to be afraid.

In the Bible, the Israelites were fighting the Midianites; God used a man named Gideon to be the deliverer of the Israelites. Gideon was fearful and hesitant, so he asked God for signs to confirm what he was meant to do. He set God a task, "If the fleece is wet with dew in the morning but the ground around it is dry, then I would believe you". God gave Gideon the assurance he needed and he set off to fight with his army. They were victorious in the battle. This story teaches us some valuable lessons. There are two ways to respond to fear: drop your fear and run or face your fear and rise up. With God, we will always rise up.

Prayer

Lord, I pray that You help me to overcome my fear of… (*say what your fear is*). In Jesus' mighty name, I pray. Amen.

Call To Action

Draw or write what you are afraid of and pray over it.

Shaquonna Rock

August 1

UNDERSTANDING THE HEART OF PRAISE AND WORSHIP

I will give you thanks in the great assembly; among the throngs I will praise you.
Psalm 35:18

Before worshipping, it is important to understand why we worship and what the heart of worship truly is. To worship is to admire something or someone so deeply that your only response is extravagant love and incredible submission to that thing or person – that is what God desires of us. To know Him so well, to love Him so dearly and respect him so much, that our only response is to live in honor of Him every day in all that we do. Worship is a response to His love and His might.

It is imperative to point out that worship is not about us. Exalting God is not about what you can get out of it; it is about choosing to praise God and trust Him regardless of your circumstances because you know Him, and you know that He is sovereign, loving and always by your side. Worship is about praising God and giving to Him, not receiving. God has already given us life, His Son on the cross, grace and the promise of eternal life. When we find ourselves falling into worship for our own gain, we need to come back to the heart of worship.

Praise and worship are responses to the character of God that can be manifested in several ways. We can glorify God throughout our entire day. Worship can happen anywhere you are and in whatever you're doing, assuming it is not sinful or against God. When you are in a hearty posture of gratitude and reverence to God, you can use everything you do to praise Him. Worship through song is one of the most powerful ways to connect directly to God's love, compassion, power, and grace.

In worship, the walls we've placed between God and us get torn down, just as God tore the veil at the death of Christ. In worship, our hearts become soft, aware, and open to the glorious majesties of God's nearness. In praise and worship, God makes His nearness known to us and fills us anew with the power of His manifest presence.

Prayer

We lift our eyes to see Your glory. We open our hearts to receive Your love. We engage our minds to understand Your truths. We offer our songs to praise Your name. Lord, as we give You our lives, please take everything that we are, so that we may reveal Your blessings to the world. In Jesus' name, we pray, Amen.

Call To Action

Praise and worship can take many different forms, so as often as you can, read the Bible, pray and engage in gospel music as these are all forms of praise and worship.

Danae Niles

PRAISE HIM!

Shout for joy to the Lord, all the earth. Worship the Lord with gladness; come before him with joyful songs. Know that the Lord is God. It is he who made us and we are his; we are his people, the sheep of his pasture. Enter his gates with thanksgiving and his courts with praise; give thanks to him and praise his name. For the Lord is good his love endures forever; his faithfulness continues through all generations. Psalms 100:1-5

Feet dancing, hands raising

Tambourines sounding

The Spirit is moving

Loud shouts

Heart filled cries

The atmosphere is shifting

Intimately connecting

With the omnipotent one

Bowing in submission, and in awe

Burdens lifting

Chains breaking

Hearts being set free

Souls being set free

Focusing on the one who gave it all for me.

Prayer

Dear God, what a privilege it is to be able to worship and praise Your matchless name. I pray that we never take this privilege for granted. We know that some of our brothers and sisters in Christ around the world are not able to worship and praise Your name as freely as we do, so we thank You and bless Your name for this privilege. I pray that when we praise and worship You, we will be able to tune out everyone and everything that is hindering us and focus on You and Your presence. May we worship You for who You are and praise You for all You have done. May You create in us clean hearts and renew our spirits so that we can worship and praise You in spirit and in truth. In Jesus' name, Amen.

Call To Action

The feeling we get during and after we give praise and worship to our God, our Savior, and our everything is truly indescribable. As Christians, we always long to give our Creator all the praise and worship He deserves. So, if you are feeling down in your spirit, I encourage you to focus on what God has done for you. Focus on all that He is and all that He has promised you, and I'm sure you'll find a reason to worship Him and give Him all the honor and glory that is due to His matchless name.

Danielle Harewood

PRAISE JAM

Let them praise His name with dancing; Let them sing praises to Him with timbrel and lyre. Psalm 149:3

Wow! What a verse! This verse reminds me of David dancing before the Lord as the Ark of the Covenant was brought into Jerusalem. I can just imagine how free he felt. Can you think of a time when you felt so full of gratitude and love for God that you could not contain yourself, and you danced before the Lord? I believe that this verse tells us not to be shy about expressing ourselves but to praise God for what He has done for us. I know that some religions have issues with dancing in the church, but in this verse, God has given us the freedom to express our hearts when we have no words. He does not limit us to only dancing with our bodies, but we can praise Him with instruments.

We, as God's people, should not only use words to glorify Him but to praise His name with dancing, timbrel and lyre. I remember a time at church when the spirit of God led our Pastor to just have a worship session. We had a praise jam that Sunday morning, I can tell you. There were flags, cymbals and shofars. I felt the spirit of God just come and sit in our presence. People were literally drunk in the spirit, and I felt that praise jam continue in my spirit the whole week. Although we did not receive an actual word from God, it felt like He was telling us to be free and let go of all our worries and fears.

Prayer

Oh, how good and pleasant it is to be in your presence, Lord. Thank You for the freedom that You have given us to just praise You with dance and instruments. You have set us free from the bondage we were in. Thank You, Jesus, for your liberty.

Call To Action

Take time out to give God praise. Clap a cymbal or wave a flag. Just have your own little praise jam.

Eslyn Taylor

August 4

THE DANCE
(POEM)

You turn my mourning into dancing. Psalm 30:11

Do I point, flex, or turn?

Only to crash and burn.

But I continue in the dance,

Not knowing how I look,

Hoping and praying that I am doing everything by the book.

You know what?

That does not matter to me because I am showcasing what God has called me to be.

Dance is my worship and my praise.

So, I dance, I dance.

Prayer

Father, I dance because You have made me glad. You cause my heart to sing. May Your living water continue to flow in my life. Thank You, Abba Father, for the freedom to dance before You. May we not limit ourselves because of how we may look, but may we always want to praise You. We thank You for that liberty even now. In Jesus' name. Amen.

Call To Action

Put on your favorite song and dance before the Lord. Do not worry about if you are technically sound. Just dance.

Eslyn Taylor

August 5

(DON'T WAIT 'TIL YOU GET TO HEAVEN) PRAISE NOW!

Give thanks to the Lord, for he is good; his love endures forever.
1 Chronicles 16:34

Forever is a very long time, but that is just how long God has loved us and will continue to love us. Can you imagine that? No matter how many times we have fallen short, or have sinned and made mistakes, God still loves us and will forever love us. For this, we should thank Him. We should praise Him. We should have a praise party and we shouldn't wait until we get to heaven to do it. It is important that even now, we show God how appreciative we are of His forever-enduring love and that we don't take it for granted. His love endures forever; it is not like that of our friends or family. God's love for us is unconditional, which means that even when we sin, He doesn't love us any less; in fact, He forgives us and helps us move forward.

God's forever-enduring love comes with the promise of provision, kindness, help, blessings, miracles, goodness and mercy. How can we repay all that God has done for us? By praising Him while we receive all He has done. Our praise comes in the form of dancing, as we clap our hands and stomp our feet, every jump is seen as an act of praise, especially when our hearts are in the right place. Is your heart in the right place?

Prayer

Our Father in Heaven, we give thanks for the love that You have bestowed upon us. We pray for Your continued covering and strength to carry on as we try to live as You would have us. Even now, I ask that our hearts will be in the right place as we praise You for all Your blessings; this we ask in the name of Christ, our heavenly Father.

Call To Action

Use every day this week to thank the Lord for each thing listed: your family, your life, His provisions, your survival of trials and tribulations, His protection, your sound mind, and the conserving of your future.

Gabrielle Blackett

ACTS OF WORSHIP

Great is the Lord and most worthy of praise; his greatness no one can fathom.
Psalm 145:3

We can show acts of worship to God in different ways: following His commandments, being kind to others, praying, being thankful, utilizing our gifts to bring glory to His name and a myriad of other ways. It's important that we always take time out of our days to intentionally show these acts of worship, so they become natural to us. Once we become intentional in these acts, we won't even have to think about them in order to do them; they'll just become part of who we are. Being intentional is a way to show our commitment to God and His work in the world. But that's just one route.

We are given the opportunity to worship God unconditionally, the way He deserves. And while we can do it in ways like following His commandments and praying, we can also worship Him through our commitment to bring honor and glory to Him with our gift. We must maintain a posture of worship in our ministry so that as we dance, our hearts and acts of worship can be seen by those watching as well as God. We want to make sure that we are communicating with God through our ministry.

Prayer

Dear God, may my life be an act of worship. May everything I do bring honor and glory unto Your name. I thank You for all You have done for me, and I take this opportunity to show my appreciation. Amen.

Call To Action

Use your life this week as an act of worship. Let all of your actions be a reflection of God.

Gabrielle Blackett

August 7

HIS PRAISE SHALL CONTINUALLY BE IN MY MOUTH

From the rising of the sun unto the going down of the same the Lord's name is to be praised. Psalm 113:3

Is this even possible to be living in a state of constant, perpetual praise? No matter the circumstances, whether in good times or bad, in whatever form or fashion, the Lord's name is to be praised. David is our example of someone who was under constant threat of death, yet God was right there in the midst of it all. He made time for God and invited Him into his dire circumstances. He knew his God and His faithfulness towards him.

When we dance, we dance unto the Lord, and we should be carrying that spirit of joy. We should be testifying, "Lord, here we are in spite of our circumstances. You are a great God. We trust You to carry us through. We worship You in the beauty of holiness."

We do not know who is in the congregation going through a difficult time. As we minister in dance unto God, we also give a testimony to the congregation, "Do not despair. God will come through for you. Taste and see that the Lord is good. It doesn't matter what it looks like now, joy comes in the morning." Oh, glory, hallelujah! There's a song that symbolizes this constant praise and appreciation, "When I think about the Lord, how He saved me, how He raised me..."

Prayer

Heavenly Father, You alone deserve all the honor and the glory and the praise. Help us, Lord, to take our eyes off our situation and give You honor. With a grateful heart, we say thank You for Your hands over our lives individually and over our ministry. In Jesus' name, we pray. Amen.

Call To Action

- Seek to have an atmosphere of thanksgiving daily.

- Be intentional in your worship.

- Praise without ceasing.

Gurlain Applewhaite

Call To Action

- Seek to have an atmosphere of thanksgiving daily.

- Be intentional in your worship.

- Praise without ceasing.

August 8

KINGS AND PRIESTS OF PRAISE & WORSHIP

And have made us kings and priests to our God; and we shall reign on the earth.
Revelation 5:10

The priesthood is usually attributed to persons who have dedicated their lives in service to God and the church. We are familiar with the priests in the Old Testament, but a different concept of priesthood appears in the New Testament. Here, the scripture tells us that we have been made kings and priests unto God. Hallelujah! In the Old Testament, it was customary for the worshippers to lead the way when the armies went into battle, as they had an important role to play. Likewise, our role as dance ministers today is to usher in the presence of God. However, we can only be effective when we have spent time in His presence. An intimate relationship with God will be on display when we go out to minister. Our ultimate goal is that men and women see God in us and are drawn to repentance.

When we step out to minister, we should acknowledge that we are ambassadors for God. We are kings, priests and ambassadors of praise. But what does an ambassador do? We represent God as His administrators of His Kingdom on the earth. If Jesus is the King of Kings and we are also kings, then it means we have the same authority in Jesus' name.

Prayer

Heavenly Father, develop in us a passion for You, to crave You, to empty ourselves until all that remains is You, Lord. We commit ourselves to be Your representatives here on earth, to show forth Your praise throughout the earth as Your ambassadors of praise and worship. In Jesus' name, we pray. Amen.

Call To Action

- Strive to live a life of perpetual praise all day, every day.

- Be bold and boisterous in your praise.

- Step up in your praise life privately in order to make an impact publicly.

Gurlain Applewhaite

August 9

WITH ALL THAT I AM

After these things I looked, and behold, a great multitude which no one could number, of all nations, tribes, peoples, and tongues, standing before the throne and before the Lamb, clothed with white robes, with palm branches in their hands, and crying out with a loud voice saying, "Salvation belongs to our God who sits on the throne, and to the Lamb!" All the angels stood around the throne and the elders and the four living creatures, and fell on their faces before the throne and worshipped God. Revelation 7:9-11

What a glorious and magnificent sight it would be. It would be even more captivating than these times of celebration: Miriam in Exodus 15, where women were dancing in celebration, David dancing until his clothes fell off on the return of the Ark, the multitudes celebrating David's victories, the crowds with their palm branches celebrating Jesus' triumphant entry into Jerusalem, or our praise and worship in our own congregation. There is no comparison at all. This worship in Heaven is a blueprint of what praise and worship should be. As it is in Heaven, so should it be on the earth. What we do in terms of praise and worship here on earth is just a shadow of what Heaven will be like.

We create a celebratory atmosphere for God to show up by shouting, clapping and using various instruments of praise in our dance, such as tambourines, streamers, banners, flags and veils. Praise comes from our relationship with God. We kneel and lie prostrate in worship, humbling ourselves before a mighty God. Whatever we do, whichever form of praise and worship we take, we need to do it with our total being. If we shout unto God, we must shout our loudest. When we dance, we must do it with passion.

Prayer

Lord God, help us to please You in ways that bring You honor and glory. Let our mouths show forth Your praise, our bodies bow to You in reverence and let us praise You with all that is within us as we magnify Your Holy name. In Jesus' name, we pray. Amen.

Call To Action

- Praise God at the start of the day to usher in a good day.

- Practice worship and praise.

- Have a heart of thanksgiving which gives rise to praise.

Gurlain Applewhaite

Call To Action

- Praise God at the start of the day to usher in a good day.

- Practice worship and praise.

August 10

TAKE MY ENTIRE BEING

Therefore, I urge you, brothers and sisters, in view of God's mercy, to offer your bodies as a living sacrifice, holy and pleasing to God—this is your true and proper worship. Romans 12:1

Praise and worship are a lifestyle, and a lifestyle is the way in which a person lives. The Word of God encourages us to offer our bodies as a living sacrifice, holy and pleasing to God. Offering our bodies to God fully for His purpose is called sacrifice. Sacrifice is surrendering a possession as an offering to a deity. Our bodies are sinful in nature but thank God that we have been given a chance to be born again. It is difficult to give over our bodies to God because it means dying to the flesh. God knows how hard it would be for us to offer this sacrifice to Him. He wants us to be intentional with this offering. It calls for complete surrender of your body, your mind and your flesh to God. This sacrifice is now true worship.

As children of God, this is what God requires from us. Praise and worship are not only about raising our hands in the air, singing or dancing; that is just what people can see. What others never see is the sacrifice that is between you and God. We are here on this earth to live holy for Him. When it seems hard to do, our merciful God is willing and ready to help once we ask Him.

Prayer

Father, from today, we offer our entire beings to You. Forgive us for holding back and not doing so sooner. Thank You for giving us another chance. In Jesus' Name. Amen.

Call To Action

Let us be purposeful in our hearts to give over our entire being to our Maker. We can do it, and God will be pleased to receive this sacrifice.

Julie Greene

THE REAL WEAPON

As they began to sing and praise, the Lord set ambushes against the men of Ammon and Moab and Mount Seir who were invading Judah, and they were defeated.
2 Chronicles 20:22

It may seem strange that God would allow us to be in difficult situations and then expect that we would choose praise and worship as the weapon of choice for the fight. Almost always, it seems like prayer and intercession would be more effective in the battle as part of the arsenal of weapons He has given us. But, oh no! When it comes time to fight, the dance minister knows that this is the exact weapon for us to use to throw the enemy off and smash every plan he has. He is defeated in our praise. He is distracted by our praise. His plan has no chance when we praise. Listen! Praise, hear? Worship and see the walls of every troubling situation come down. Our God is able.

Prayer

God, You know what my sister or brother is going through. I know You care for them deeply. Give them the strength to praise despite their situation. In Jesus' Name, Amen.

Call To Action

Whatever the enemy has thrown at you in this season, if you have not tried it yet, throw some praise and worship at the situation and see God come through. See things change, I dare you.

Laina Jacob

IT IS FOR YOU

Lord, you are my God; I will exalt you and praise your name, for in perfect faithfulness you have done wonderful things, things planned long ago. Isaiah 25:1

As dance ministers, sometimes we get so caught up in our role on the team, in the ministry, on the stage, and on the date on the worship roster that we forget that praise and worship are not just to encourage other people; they are for us too. When was the last time you spent your devotion time with praise music? No one but you and God, and you got immersed in a dance with your Father? I mean to the point where you completely let go and let God. You forgot about time and location, and you were lost in God.

Imagine His goodness overwhelming you, His protection, provision and greatness becoming larger. Don't even get me started on His love. By this point, you cannot stop the flow of tears as your body, totally uncontrolled by you, moves to the music of heaven. Don't just dance because it is what you do. Dance because it is who you are. Dance with the ultimate dancer in the ultimate dance.

Prayer

God, I pray as Your dance ministers spend this kind of time with You, You will reveal Yourself to them in a different way, a new way. Build a great relationship with them and let them yearn for more of You. In Jesus' Name. Amen.

Call To Action

If you have not spent time dancing with God, just the two of you, find time this week. If it feels uncomfortable at first, play your favorite worship song and just go from there. Spend this time with God until it feels natural to dance in worship and praise unto Him.

Laina Jacob

August 13

MY DANCE

I will praise thee for I am fearfully and wonderfully made, marvelous are Thy works and that my soul knows well. Psalm 139:1

Praising and worshipping God is one of my favorite things to do. Whenever we are given a song to dance to that leaves us wanting to praise God, I would play the song repeatedly until I feel my heart express admiration for God. I would close my eyes and imagine myself dancing with Jesus doing the waltz. I'd begin to tell Him how much I love Him and give Him thanks for all His goodness towards me. Praise would just flow from my lips as I danced with the lover of my soul.

I remind myself that it's Him that has made me, it's Him that has given me the gift of dance, and it's Him that is worthy of praise. The Bible says, "We should praise Him in the dance" (Psalm 149:3) and "praise Him with timbrel and dancing" (Psalm 150:4). So yes, we can use our dance as a means of praise. Lord, I choose to dance as my way of praising You.

Prayer

I pray that my dance will always be part of my worship.

Call To Action

Find a praise song and simply dance before the Lord.

Maxine Butcher

August 14

OH, WHAT A DANCE!

David danced before the Lord with all his might and David was girded with a linen ephod. 2 Samuel 6:14-16

D - Do it! Praise God with the dance.

A - Admiration! Show it without words; use movement.

N - Now is the time to dance! The bridegroom in the Jewish culture is met with dancing just before the wedding. The bridegroom cometh!

C - Create an atmosphere for praise through dance.

E - Express your praise through dance.

David used his dance to express praise to God, and he danced unashamedly before God.

Prayer

Let my dance be a way to give You praise. May my whole body express love for You in Jesus' name, amen.

Call To Action

Find a song that expresses how you feel about God, then dance for Him.

Maxine Butcher

August 15

MOVE

Let everything that has breath praise the LORD. Praise the LORD. Psalm 150:6

If you've read this Psalm before, you may have noticed that it starts and ends with Praise the LORD. So, what's in between? Of all the six verses, verses 1-5 start with praising Him, while the 6th and last verse gives that double declaration, as you see in the above verse. What I also find interesting is that the last chapter in Psalms also speaks about praising God. See the pattern?

Most of the Psalms were written by David, who is known as a man after God's own heart. David went through so much: he did nonsense, repented, turned his heart back to God, praised until his clothes fell off, and worshipped the lover of his soul. The staple of David's life and his outlook was the God he served. God was moved not only by his heart and words but by his actions.

Everything begins in the heart, and what's inside the heart wants to be released, whether good or bad. We need to get to a place where the consistent pattern of our movement (life) is one where we walk in the freedom and declaration of praise and worship. I know we don't always feel like doing it, and we often like to wait for the feeling to come, but I advise you to do it despite feeling unmotivated. Sometimes motivation doesn't come first, but our actions prompt our motivation.

I acknowledge my gratitude, love, and indebtedness to God through praise and worship. I cannot count or measure the depth of my love for Him, but I also know it would never match the depth of His love for me. With this knowledge, I will always move for Him. I will praise the LORD.

Prayer

Heavenly Father, my heart inclines and reaches for Yours. In You, I live and move and have my being, and I know this to be true. Thank You for choosing me to be Yours. In Jesus' name, Amen.

Call To Action

Think of ways to express your praise and worship to God better and give Him thanks for being patient with you during the process.

Orissa Fitzpatrick

August 16

LOOSED

About midnight Paul and Silas were praying and singing hymns to God, and the other prisoners were listening to them. Acts 16:25

There are three things I'd like to point out in this verse: praying, singing and listening. Verse 26 continues: "Suddenly there was a great earthquake so that the foundations of the prison were shaken and immediately all the doors were opened, and everyone's chains were loosed." Hallelujah! That is definitely a praise break moment, one of many in this chapter. That's the power that praise and worship hold. They cause breakthroughs, miracles, shackles to fall off, and mindsets to be changed. They cause others to look and wonder about the God we serve and be encouraged.

I can recall many instances when we ministered, and God's presence was so tangible that things started to manifest in the room and in people's lives. That's the power of understanding missions that have people and situations assigned to them. Bondage and strongholds need to be broken; people need to be freed and saved.

You have it within you to do so through the Holy Spirit. You have it in you to break through for yourself on and off stage. When you have this knowledge, you recognize that it isn't just dancing anymore; it is ministry told through a story that says He who was and is and is to come showed up. It's a story that will cause people to run and jump because of who He is, to shout hallelujah, to bow down and worship and cry, "Holy, holy, holy is the Lord God Almighty, beautiful are you Lord, you are worthy to be praised and worshipped". Lord, most high, I am in your service.

Prayer

Father, I exalt You. You are precious and wonderful. Marvellous are Your works. Let springs of living water flow from my life and cause a change in the lives of others. In Jesus' name, Amen.

Call To Action

Commit to praying and asking God to show you the way in each mission assigned to you, so that others can see Christ through you.

Orissa Fitzpatrick

August 17

P-RAISE
(POEM)

And he shall live, and to him shall be given of the gold of Sheba: prayer also shall be made for him continually; and daily shall he be praised. Psalm 72:15

Prayer-raise

Passion-raise

Power-raise

Does your praise contain prayer, passion and power? Let's examine some ways to manifest this in Psalms 72:15 and 150:1-6 and raise our praise.

Praise ye the LORD. Praise God in his sanctuary: praise him in the firmament of his power.

Praise him for his mighty acts: praise him according to his excellent greatness.

Praise him with the sound of the trumpet: praise him with the psaltery and harp.

Praise him with the timbrel and dance: praise him with stringed instruments and organs.

Praise him upon the loud cymbals: praise him upon the high-sounding cymbals.

Let everything that hath breath praise the LORD. Praise ye the LORD. Psalm 150:1-6

Let us dance with the knowledge of what we can and are praising God for. Let us dance with the instruments suggested in Psalm 150 to enhance the passion we want to display for our God, remembering that dance is one of these instruments.

Prayer

May we live daily and continually with an attitude of prayer and praise as per

Psalms 72:15 and 150.

Call To Action

Practice raising your prayer, passion, and power in praise.

Pierre Rock

August 18

SPIRIT & TRUTH

But the hour cometh, and now is, when the true worshippers shall worship the Father in spirit and in truth: for the Father seeketh such to worship him. God is a Spirit: and they that worship him must worship him in spirit and in truth.
John 4:23-24

Let's meditate on these scriptures that give us insight into spirit and truth:

"Even the Spirit of truth; whom the world cannot receive, because it seeth him not, neither knoweth him: but ye know him; for he dwelleth with you, and shall be in you" (John 14:17).

"Howbeit when he, the Spirit of truth, is come, he will guide you into all truth: for he shall not speak of himself; but whatsoever he shall hear, that shall he speak: and he will shew you things to come" (John 16:13).

"For the fruit of the Spirit is in all goodness and righteousness and truth" (Ephesians 5:9).

"But we are bound to give thanks always to God for you, brethren beloved of the Lord, because God hath from the beginning chosen you to salvation through sanctification of the Spirit and belief of the truth" (2 Thessalonians 2:13).

"We are of God: he that knoweth God heareth us; he that is not of God heareth not us. Hereby know we the spirit of truth, and the spirit of error" (1 John 4:6).

"This is he that came by water and blood, even Jesus Christ; not by water only, but by water and blood. And it is the Spirit that beareth witness, because the Spirit is truth" (1 John 5:6).

To truly worship God, we must be connected to the Spirit of truth at all times. To do this, we must know God personally and the Spirit of truth must be dwelling within us. Worship is always associated with truth, and truth is always associated with the Spirit. Make a truthful assessment of your spirit and continue or get to spirit and truth worship.

Prayer

May we produce the fruit of the Spirit in all goodness, righteousness and truth.

Call To Action

Nurture your fruit of the Spirit this week or month (See Galatians 5:22-23).

Pierre Rock

August 19

WORTH IT

Give unto the LORD the glory due unto his name; worship the LORD in the beauty of holiness. Psalm 29:2

Give unto the LORD the glory due unto His name. Our worship involves giving God the Glory (Psalm 29:2). Our worship involves giving God our bodies (Romans 12:1). Our worship should be beautiful and glorious, "In that day shall the branch of the LORD be beautiful and glorious, and the fruit of the earth shall be excellent and comely for them that are escaped of Israel" (Isaiah 4:2). Our worship should be beautiful and holy. It should involve singing, blessing, declaring, praising (dancing), as well as honor, majesty, strength and offering to highlight some worship attributes found in Psalm 96:1-9. This Psalm speaks of worship in the splendour of Holiness, as seen in the extract below:

O sing unto the LORD a new song: sing unto the LORD, all the earth.

Sing unto the LORD, bless his name; shew forth his salvation from day to day.

Declare his glory among the heathen, his wonders among all people.

For the LORD is great, and greatly to be praised: he is to be feared above all gods.

For all the gods of the nations are idols: but the LORD made the heavens.

Honor and majesty are before him: strength and beauty are in his sanctuary.

Give unto the LORD, O ye kindreds of the people, give unto the LORD glory and strength.

Give unto the LORD the glory due unto his name: bring an offering, and come into his courts.

O worship the LORD in the beauty of holiness: fear before him, all the earth.

Let us always ensure that our gifts to God are worth it. Remember, we are to present our bodies as presents (gifts) to God, for He's worth it and our worship and dance should show it.

Prayer

Lord, help us to give You the glory due unto Your name.

Call To Action

Select - Choose some attributes (see Psalm 96) to express in your worship of God this month.

Give - Worship with your giving this week however you choose to express it.

Gift - Be the gift in someone's life today with your presence.

Pierre Rock

August 20

WORSHIPPERS FIRST

Lord, you are my God; I will exalt You and praise your name, for in perfect Faithfulness you have done wonderful things, things planned long ago. Isaiah 25:1

Praise and worship should come naturally for believers. We should not have to be begged, pleaded with or coerced into giving God what He deserves. As dancers, our worship is slightly different, as we should worship with our entire bodies extravagantly. But it is important to note that we are worshippers before we are dancers; whether we can no longer dance or we leave the dance ministry, we will remain worshippers, for God forever deserves our worship. Let us not neglect the fact that we cannot move away from choreography for extravagance; we are not performers. The choreography should be birthed out of our worship of God. Choreography should not be separate and distinct from our worship but rather understood as synchronised worship.

Let's look at these words and apply them to our worship, whether in our choreography, congregation or in our prayer and worship closet:

Halal - to be clear, to shine, to boast, show, rave, clamorously foolish in our praise to God.

Towdah - an extension of the hand in adoration, avowal, or acceptance.

Yadah - the extended hand, to throw out the hand, to worship with the extended hand.

Shabach - to address in a loud tone, to commend, to triumph, to exclaim, glory, shout.

Barak - to kneel down, bless God as an act of adoration.

Zamar - to touch the strings (used in instrumental worship).

Tehilla - to sing, to laud.

Prayer

Lord, let worship flow from me like a river that never runs dry. May I always be cognizant that my worship of You comes first, and my dance is not separate from my worship, but the two are beautifully intertwined. Amen.

Call To Action

Examine the words above and delve a little deeper into them. Research applicable scripture. Then apply, apply, apply the knowledge to make your worship unto God more extravagant and authentic.

Rheanne Rock

August 21

PRAISE AND WORSHIP AS LONG AS I LIVE

I will sing to the LORD as long as I live. I would praise my God to my last breath!
Psalm 146:2

God has called us, His children, to praise and worship Him. The Word of God reminds us that we need to worship and praise Him until we die. Many people do not understand the power of praise and worship. I feel free and very close to God when I worship and praise Him, and I know that good things are going to happen in my life. It makes God happy when we praise and worship Him. We should not be ashamed to do so. We should ignore the people who do not like us just because we praise and worship God.

I feel emotional in a positive way when I praise and worship. It brings tears to my eyes because He died on the cross for me. I feel free and that feeling overtakes me. I can use my entire body to show Him how much I love Him. This includes singing, praying, dancing, shouting praise, raising my hand and reading His Word.

Prayer

Dear Lord, I pray that we will always praise and worship You. We love You, and we will still praise and worship You no matter what people think about us. No matter where we are, we can still praise and worship You. At school, at home, in the church building or even online, we commit to praising and worshipping You. In Jesus' name. Amen.

Call To Action

I am challenging you to make praise and worship a part of your daily life. It does not matter if it is morning, afternoon, evening or night-time. God does not sleep, so it does not matter what time of the day you praise and worship.

Rhema-Jae Greene

August 22

WORSHIP IS A REQUIREMENT

Come, let us worship and bow down. Let us kneel before the Lord our maker.
Psalms 95:6

During my Christian life, I always heard that worship is a lifestyle, and I think that is so true. When you look at the trees, they are constantly in worship. Trees do not need music, but as the wind blows, they move to the melody and sound of the wind. Hmmm, it makes me wonder: if the trees can have that posture, why can't we as humans have that posture too?

God created us just like the trees, but if some of us have to worship at church for more than three hours, we start to become restless. Maybe if we see ourselves as trees, we will have a new mindset. Trees are humble, obedient and willing, and they allow the wind of God to take them where it chooses. Even during hurricane season, whenever the wind blows, the trees respond in reverence.

We, too, can respond in reverence to the Spirit of God and allow Him to take us wherever He chooses. We, too, can be just like a tree, willing to bow to God in worship, be obedient to God's voice, and be humble as God wants us to worship Him in spirit and truth, according to John 4:24. Trees are excellent leaders. Even as we think about dance or leading a dance, we too can flow with the sound of the music and the songs of the Holy Spirit living within us.

Prayer

God, today I want to worship even more than the trees; I want my worship to be true to You, and when I worship, it is in reverence to You, in Jesus' name. Amen.

Call To Action

- Live a lifestyle of worship.

- Go where the Spirit leads.

- Let your worship reverence God.

Rhonda. A. Babb

August 23

MY PRAISE POSTURE

My mouth is filled with Your praise and with Your glory all day long. Psalms 71:8

When I think about this verse, it reminds me of a fountain filled with water, and every time you turn it on, water comes out. Can you imagine your body being a reservoir of power with songs, hymns and glory that praise flows out to God every time you open your mouth? Isn't that amazing?

Imagine how many lives would change when you open your mouth. Imagine what you are representing on that stage when you dance – a reservoir of power. Your movement should flow like what is on the inside of you so that when it connects to someone's heart, they, too, would want to sing praises or even dance.

We can say that our hearts and mouths are connected because the Word of God says in Mathew 15:18, "But the words you speak come from the heart that's what defiles you." So, I believe that if we can fill our hearts with good words, songs and things of God, He will be pleased. We can freely open our mouths without fear, knowing what comes out will only be a sweet aroma to God.

Always remember that what you say or sing doesn't only go to one particular person; it also goes to God. So let us be careful with what comes from our mouths after today because our bodies are filled with a reservoir of praise and glory all day long.

Prayer

God, please help me make sure that the praises coming from my mouth to You please Your heart in Jesus' name. Amen.

Call To Action

- Be responsible for what leaves your mouth.

- Every day, fill your mouth with praise.

- Remember, your body represents a fountain full of praise.

Rhonda. A. Babb

August 24

NEVER-ENDING PRAISE!

Shout for joy to the LORD, all the earth. Worship the LORD with gladness; come before him with joyful songs. Know that the LORD is God. It is he who made us, and we are his; we are his people, the sheep of his pasture. Enter his gates with thanksgiving and his courts with praise; give thanks to him and praise his name. For the LORD is good and his love endures forever; his faithfulness continues through all generations. Psalm 100

Imagine how heaven will be when we get there. Wow! Praise galore. The angels, rejoicing, the saints who got there before us, praising, and I am even sure that God, three in one, will be tapping along to the music. Every spirit will be as one. There will be no time or space to bother about. We wouldn't be "self-conscious" about who is looking on. Carefree without abandon, pure, unadulterated worship, our inside (spirit man) will be outside singing praises to the Most High God, spirit to Spirit.

There are many ways to praise our almighty God: dancing, singing, and playing instruments. Just for His goodness of giving us life, we should praise Him with every fiber of our being. Oh, how good God is. His praise shall continually be in my mouth.

Even when it's tough, and you get angry or feel rejected, begin to talk to God and tell Him how you feel. He knows this life isn't easy, but praise be to God that we can use our weapon of praise to overcome those feelings. Our flesh has to obey what our spirit wants to do, and if there's one thing the spirit knows, it's how to praise the creator. Don't wait to get to heaven to begin to praise Him. Begin to praise Him today. Begin to praise Him now!

Prayer

Thank You, our Alpha and Omega, our bright and morning star, the lily of the valley. You are Holy, righteous, victorious, worthy, name above all names and more. We love You, Lord, in Jesus' name, Amen.

Call To Action

Praise Him in the morning. Praise Him in the noontime. Praise Him in your setting and your uprising. Praise Him in the good times and the bad. Don't wait until you get to Heaven!

Sandra Britton

HE'S WORTHY

Let them praise His name in the dance. Let them sing praises unto Him with Timbrel and Harp. Praise is to give glory to God in song, Worship and dance.
Psalm 149:3-4

Our God is worthy of our praise. You cannot worship and praise God deeper than your knowledge of Him. If you earnestly desire to grow in worship, you need to grow in knowing God better. Worshipping God is the expression of our love for Him through every moment and every struggle we face because He is God and deserves our every worship, adoration and praise. Regardless of what we go through, remember it's not by our strength or power that we overcome. In overcoming, praise and worship are the weapons used in thanking the Father for His grace, mercies and victories. Our God is faithful in honoring a contrite and repentant heart that worships through all difficulties.

As worship ministers, we are called to use our God-given talents and giftings to exalt the Lord while sending up our praises. By lifting clean hands and clean hearts and using dance, musical instruments, and other instruments of praise, we offer up clean, uncontaminated worship to the Most High. Throughout the Psalms (Psalm 95:6, Psalm 50:1-6), we are admonished to praise God while we worship because of His greatness and His mighty deeds to His saints.

Praise Him with your whole heart and strength. Praise Him while you worship and honor Him as Lord of our lives. Praise Him because He's worthy of our untainted praise. Dance is another form of worship, and we, the temples of God, are used to praise Him.

Prayer

Father, as Your ministers, teach us how we should focus on You as we worship. Enable us to connect to You, our True Vine, through Your Holy Spirit, who will teach us ways to glorify You as dance ministers for Your honor and glory. Amen!

Call To Action

- Make every effort to worship God in Spirit and truth.

- Seek out opportunities to express full worship to the Father.

- Learn the significance and the use of praise and worship instruments.

Timeless Ministers

August 26

A LIFE OF WORSHIP

Lord you are my God, I will exalt you and praise your name for in perfect faithfulness you have done wonderful things, things planned long ago. Isaiah 25:1

Let everything that has breath praise the Lord. There are so many ways to praise and worship God. We can worship Him by singing and playing a musical instrument or we can dance. I love to dance; I have always danced around in the house since I was very little, and this is how I praise and worship God to this day.

God also wants us to live our daily lives in praise and worship of Him. We can do this through simple things like being kind to each other, giving to the less fortunate and encouraging someone who might be feeling down.

Prayer

Thank You, Lord, for another day to praise and worship You. Thank You for being my good shepherd and for leading me to a place of peace. Help me, Lord, to worship You in spirit and in truth and let my life express the love that is only found in You.

Call To Action

Show God's love and kindness to everyone you meet. Find time daily to offer special praise and Worship to God.

Trinitee Angus

August 27

OUR WORSHIP IS OUR WEAPON

Submit yourselves to God. Resist the devil, and he will flee from you. James 4:7

Are you aware that praise and worship are our spiritual weapons against the darkness of the enemy? When we resist the enemy and submit totally unto God, the devil will flee from us. The devil has no authority over our lives, which God says in His word daily. God inhabits our praise; He inhabits our worship and fuels its authenticity. When we worship God with all our might and all our soul, the devil will have to flee, no questions asked, no "ifs," "ands," or "buts." Darkness can't linger where the light shines brightly.

God gave us ways we can worship. Our worship is our means of warfare on behalf of His Kingdom. God gave us mouths so we can destroy the darkness of the enemy. We hold so much power in our praise and worship that we do not even realize it. As dancers, we are gifted with dance, our own special type of praise and worship. Are you aware of how much damage we can do with our feet, our hands, our garments and our instruments? We have so many ways in which we can fight off the forces of darkness. It is time we start to use them.

Let us begin to stomp our feet. Let us begin to clap our hands. Let us begin to clothe ourselves with the garments made to do justice, and let us use our instruments, our flags and our symbols to begin to fight and cause some serious damage in the presence of the enemy. Let us begin to dance like David danced. We are worshipers; our worship is our weapon, and it's time we wake up and realize it.

Prayer

Dear heavenly Father, thank You for opening our eyes and helping us see that our weapons are right in front of us. Thank You for helping us realize our fight comes from inside of us. Let us not grow weary in the fight but let us build up our worship and our praise to do damage to the darkness that dwells near. In Jesus' Name. Amen.

Call To Action

There is power in your praise. Whether on the mountaintop or in the valley, always remember our worship is our weapon!

Zariah Watson

August 28

SO WILL I

Let everything that has breath…Praise the Lord. Psalm 105:6

When I think of praise and worship, I think about the song *So Will I* by Hillsong. Praise and worship have to come from a place of desperation, freedom and recognition because it's all about thanking God throughout our trials and tribulations, thanking God for where He has brought us from and thanking Him just for thanking Him sake. "Let *everything* that has breath…praise the Lord," every living creature. This Psalm even mentions that the rocks shall cry out unto His name. Could you imagine rocks crying out and not us, God's children? We need to get it together. Once we have breath in our bodies, we should be able to pour out our praise to God.

Think of it like this: What are you giving back to God when He has done an abundance of things for you? How are you thanking Him? God acts powerfully on behalf of those who believe in Him and praise His name. We can't grow tired of praising Him; we can't grow weary in worshipping Him because when we get to Heaven, we will be praising non-stop. The questions you must ask yourself are: Are you ready to praise the Lord your God until your last breath? Are you ready to thank God for all He has brought you through? Will you thank Him in the middle of the storm, in the middle of your trials? Will you still bless Him, will you still worship Him, will you still dance like David danced unto Him regardless of your circumstances? Will you?

God never gets tired of blessing you, so why get tired when it is your turn to thank Him? It's time to stop taking God for granted and worship Him with all you can. It is time, worshippers, let us worship!

Prayer

God, help us not to take the gift of salvation for granted, but with grateful hearts, remind us to continue to give thanks! In Jesus' Name. Amen.

Call To Action

Remember, fellow believers, let us not grow tired of blessing God because He never gets tired of blessing us! God bless.

Zariah Watson

August 29

THE FLOW

You make known to me the path of life; in your presence there is fullness of joy; at your right hand are pleasures forevermore. Psalm 16:11

Nobody else is there

It's only me and Him

He guides me along the stage with every step

I feel Him moving within me

The grace, the power, the flow of my movements

He takes over

It's an overwhelming feeling

But it's prepossessing

It's engaging, alluring

Absolutely heavenly

The beauty of it all is so appealing

Truly to become one with Him

To allow every part of your body to counterpart with His

When you worship, it's your mind, body and soul

You move wholeheartedly

You move with purpose

You move with a message

And most importantly, you move with a blessing.

Zenaida R. Mayers

August 30

ONE. ZERO. ONE

The Lord is my strength and my shield; my heart trusts in him, and he helps me. My heart leaps for joy, and with my song I praise him. Psalm 28:7

The title of today's devotion may seem a little odd, but if we take a closer look, we will recognize that these numbers represent the basic anatomy of a leap. In order to leap, a person must jump off of one foot and be carried in the air with zero feet on the ground before landing on one foot again. In Psalms 28:7, we are encouraged to leap for joy. Note that the psalmist did not say to walk or run for joy but to *leap*. Could it be that for either a run or walk, both feet remain on the ground, and perhaps joy is an expression of total dependence on God, especially in rough times? Also, isn't it interesting that the Psalmist didn't say to leap with joy but *for* it? To leap with joy could suggest that joy comes naturally, in and of ourselves, but to leap could suggest that joy is an expression we must put some effort into because it's contrary to how we may be feeling. To lay hold of such a posture means that we must rely on God to carry us above the raging waters. May we reach in the spirit toward joy!

Prayer

Father, we thank You for Your great and precious promises. You said in Your word that the joy of the Lord is our strength, and today, we lay hold of that strength by moving our bodies contrary to how we may be feeling. We leap knowing that joy is promised to us, and You will carry us over whatever we may face. Thank You for Your joy today. Amen!

Call To Action

Put a leap (big or small) in your step every day this week as a cognitive trigger of your reliance on God.

Pearl-Ann Bartlett

August 31

DANCING IN THE THRONGS OF GRATITUDE

I will thank you in the great congregation; in the mighty throng I will praise you.
Psalm 35:18

Praise is to express warm approval or admiration for someone or something. In the Bible, the Israelites were in battle against the Philistines. They were losing, so they brought the Ark of the Covenant into battle. The Philistines won and took the Ark of the Covenant, but when strange things started happening, they gave back the Covenant to the Israelites. The Israelites took the Ark and carried it back to the city. David was so excited that he was dancing in the streets. His wife was embarrassed and told him to stop. David basically said, "I am dancing to praise God. I can look like the biggest fool you have ever seen".

If you, like David, have a reason to praise God, do it! In Psalms, David praises God in a mighty throng. A throng is a large, densely packed place, filled with people. Imagine yourself in a throng praising God. Would you be able to do it?

Prayer

Heavenly Father, I thank You for everything You have done for me. I praise and honor Your name, Amen.

Call To Action

Take a few minutes out of the day to give thanks and praise. Thanks, is an expression of gratitude. So do not miss out on your chance today to say thank you to God. You can give thanks to Him by dancing, singing, and more.

Shaquonna Rock

September 1

EMBRACING GODLY CHARACTER

Do not be conformed to this world, but be transformed by the renewal of your mind, that by testing you may discern what is the will of God, what is good and acceptable and perfect. Romans 12:2

Godly character can be defined as "the ability to discern God's right way from the wrong, and to voluntarily surrender one's own will to do what is right in God's sight and, with the promised supernatural help, to resist the wrong even under pressure and temptation."

In Romans 12:2, Paul writes that we must no longer be conformed to the world. The word "world" is often used in the New Testament to refer to the world system or the way that every human being lives by default. John described this worldly way of living as "the desires of the flesh and the desires of the eyes and pride of life" (1 John 2:16). By instinct, all of us chase those things in pursuit of happiness and meaning.

Paul tells us to abandon the chase for pleasure, possessions, and status—to stop living like everyone else. Instead, he urges us to be transformed from the inside out. Specifically, he writes that we must change how we think and have our minds renewed so we can begin to understand God's will for our lives. We face trials and difficulties so God can know how committed we are to His way of life. He has to find out if we will endure hardship and suffering. Only then can He trust us with the powers that come with eternal life.

This life is not only for building character; it is for testing that character. Day by day, rededicating ourselves to His service is a lifelong process which we need to choose to do consciously. Transformation does not take place overnight but is dependent on the hidden values of the heart being translated into the active practice of our thoughts and motives. It is a free will choice to turn away from that which is evil and to honor the Lord in beautiful thoughts, beautiful words, and beautiful deeds by choosing to do what is right and holy.

Prayer

Father, help us live in ways that do not gratify our flesh but rather feed our spirit that is redeemed by the blood of the Lamb. You have given us the opportunity to make a positive difference in this degenerate world. May we, by word and example, bring light into this darkened, sin-indulged world. May the fruit of the spirit: love, joy, peace, patience, kindness, goodness, faithfulness, gentleness, and self-control, be evident in our lives so that these attitudes bring about good deeds which glorify You, Father. In Jesus' name, I pray, Amen.

Call To Action

When making big or small decisions, ask yourself if this decision is tied to having a Godly character, and that should steer you on the right path. Having a Godly character is not something that happens overnight, but if it is worked on, it can be fulfilled.

Danae Niles

September 2

FRUITS OF GODLY CHARACTER

But the fruit produced by the Holy Spirit within you is divine in all its varied expressions: joy that overflows, peace that subdues, patience that endures, kindness in action, a life full of virtue, faith that prevails, gentleness of heart, and strength of spirit. Never set the law above these qualities, for they are limitless.
Galatians 5:22-23

We, as Christ-followers, should aspire to have a Godly character as we look at what God did in the Bible. He committed to feeding the hungry, helping the poor, turning the other cheek, and sharing the Gospel. These are attributes we may think about when we consider what Godly character looks like. But how do we get there? Well, it takes the work of the Holy Spirit living inside of us to build our Godly character, and it is developed as we grow and mature in Christ.

As we grow in our walk with Christ, we will start to produce the fruits of the Spirit: love, peace, joy, patience, and more. These fruits become our characteristics when we consistently read the Word, pray and grow in our faith. So by having the fruits of the spirit, we will have Godly character.

Prayer

Dear heavenly Father, help us to be devoted to building our Godly character. Because this happens through the work of the Holy Spirit, we pray that our hearts and minds will always be open to what You have to say to us and that we will obey You immediately. I pray that we will examine ourselves to see what we can improve and take it to You in prayer. I pray that we will always want to be more like You every day. In Jesus' name, Amen.

Call To Action

I know that some people will self-reflect and think that they don't have Godly character. But remember, a Godly character takes time to build, and God will always continue finishing the good work He started in us.

Danielle Harewood

September 3

THE CHARACTER OF GOD

And he passed in front of Moses, proclaiming, "The Lord, the Lord, the compassionate and gracious God, slow to anger, abounding in love and faithfulness. Exodus 34:6

Our God is loving and has an eternal agape love for us. That means that His love is unconditional and compassionate, and He always cares for us. He cares about every part of our being: spiritual, mental, and physical. He is our mighty Healer, our Jehovah Rapha. He shows compassion for our hearts and souls. He even cares about our day-to-day activities, whether they're big or small.

He is our comforter who gives us peace in the middle of a storm and in times of distress. He is gracious and merciful in all of His ways towards us. He is glorious, magnificent, and excellent. He is faithful and stands true to His Word. He keeps His covenant and His promises towards us.

He is strong and mighty, the God of the angel armies. He fights our battles for us. He is slow to anger but also just. He brings down judgment upon the wicked.

He is a friend, our counselor, and a very present help in our times of need. These are some of the characteristics of our God, who is the same today, yesterday, and forever.

Prayer

Dear God, we thank You for being all that You are. You are wonderful, and we will forever praise Your matchless name. Thank You for being all these good things to us. Thank You for being everything that is good and true. I pray we'll continue to worship You for all that You are, in Jesus' name, Amen.

Call To Action

As you read the Word of God, you'll start to see more of God's characteristics. Sit and meditate on all that He is today.

Danielle Harewood

September 4

IN YOUR IMAGE LORD

And God said, Let us make man in our image, after our likeness: and let them have dominion over the fish of the sea, and over the fowl of the air, and over the cattle, and over all the earth, and over every creeping thing that creepeth upon the earth. Genesis 1:26

Can you imagine creating something or someone in your image? And not just limiting them to look like you, but giving them dominion over creation. Wow, that would be incredible and our God has already done it. When I look at being created in God's image, I think about all the characteristics He would have placed in man during creation. From this verse, we can see that God endowed us with a unique awareness and power that He did not give to animals, birds or fish. In other words, humans possess the capacity for intellect, emotion, will, personality and purpose. Also, like God, we have the capacity to experience and understand love, truth, and beauty because we are made in His image.

Prayer

Heavenly Father, thank You for making me in Your image. Thank You for endowing me with the capacity for intellect, emotion, will, and, most of all, purpose. Because I am made in Your image, I am truth, love and beauty. We bless You, in Jesus' name.

Call To Action

Take 5 minutes out of your day to take in God's creations. Listen to the birds or watch a flower bloom. Reflect on the things God has given you to enjoy.

Eslyn Taylor

September 5

SHINE LIKE A DIAMOND
(POEM)

Those who are wise will shine as bright as the sky, and those who lead many to righteousness will shine like the stars forever. Daniel 12:3

Shine bright like a diamond

No matter the time.

Be that beautiful sparkle,

That makes people marvel.

They might be some imperfections,

But know that you are God's creation.

So, you go on girl, dance to perfection, and shine like a diamond across the horizon.

Prayer

Heavenly Father, I thank You for forming me like a diamond with Your beauty and strength. Although the process is complex, and I may go through many trials and tribulations, I know that You are working them out for my good. Help my light to shine so that it may glorify You. In Jesus' name. Amen.

Call To Action

Find out the process a diamond must go through before it is created into jewelry. Compare it to God's love for us.

Eslyn Taylor

September 6

SINCERELY, ME

But the fruit of the Spirit is love, joy, peace, patience, kindness, goodness, faithfulness, gentleness, self-control; against such things there is no law. Galatians 5:22-23

This Galatians verse speaks of the acts of the flesh versus the fruit of the spirit. The acts of the flesh include sexual immorality, impurity, hatred, discord, jealousy, and anything that does not please God. Just as a sick or dying tree will bear bad fruit, so will people who are dead in sin. However, those persons alive in Jesus Christ naturally produce good fruit: the fruit of the spirit. Those fruits of the spirit are love, joy, peace, patience, kindness, goodness, faithfulness, gentleness and self-control. Once we possess the fruits of the Spirit and apply them to our Godly character, we will inherit the Kingdom of Heaven.

As dancers, it is important to bear good fruit and have a Godly character. It is not only important to our ministry that takes place on the stage, but the ministry that happens in our day-to-day interactions. Our fruits of the spirit help us relate better to our peers, supporting them to bring forth their own fruits of the spirit and Godly character. When our personal life follows the character of Christ, our ministry does the same.

Prayer

Dear heavenly Father, I pray that my character will become the fruit of the Spirit and that being like You will become my nature. May You be at the forefront of all that I do and that when people see me sincerely, they will also see You. I know that I will stumble and that some days will be harder, but may that never discourage me. Amen.

Call To Action

Assign each of the fruits of the spirit to a day in the week. Then, use that day to exemplify the fruit. Since there are 9 fruits and 7 days, you can do two fruits for two days of the week. Eventually, displaying these fruits of the spirit will come naturally.

Gabrielle Blackett

September 7

LOVE IS THE ANSWER

Beloved, let us love one another, for love is of God; and everyone who loves is born of God and knows God. He who does not love does not know God, for God is love. 1 John 4:7-8

Character is what defines us. We cannot say we love God and yet do not display love towards fellow believers and those in the same ministries as us. Our love towards others is an indication that God is within us.

The dance team should always dance in unity, not only physically but also spiritually. Worshippers are expected to prepare the congregation to assist in bringing them to a place of worship where their hearts and minds are ready to receive the Word. If we want to see worship happening in the sanctuary, it must begin with us. There's no place for bad-mouthing fellow dancers, bearing grievances, envy or strife, as we would only be dancing in our flesh. Whatever we are holding onto on the inside will be displayed on the outside when we dance. We can't fool God, for He sees our hearts.

Love is the answer. Satan wants nothing more than to disrupt the ministry. But when we walk in love and see ourselves and others as God sees us, He will be able to use us in a mighty way.

Prayer

Heavenly Father, Your desire is for us to be molded in You so that we may reflect Jesus to this world. Lord, remove whatever is in us that is not of You so that we can present ourselves as vessels of honor in Jesus' name, we pray. Amen.

Call To Action

- Clothe yourself with the presence of God.

- Be morally disciplined.

- Be the light of the world – be the example.

Gurlain Applewhaite

September 8

IMITATE JESUS CHRIST

But also for this very reason, giving all diligence, add to your faith virtue, to virtue knowledge, to knowledge self-control, to self-control perseverance, to perseverance godliness, to godliness brotherly kindness, and to brotherly kindness love.
2 Peter 1:5-7

We must emulate Jesus in our Christian walk because, in doing so, we draw others to Him. We do not change into all that God desires automatically. There must be a desire on our part and also a willingness to work with the Holy Spirit in bringing about change. Jesus said in Matthew 5:48 that we should be perfect as God is perfect. We know perfection seems unattainable in this life. However, we should aspire as much as we can to be like Jesus in our walk and our talk as we grow and mature. We don't do it in our own strength but in the power of the Holy Spirit.

Our ministry does not begin when we go on the stage or platform to dance. Ministry is not a garment to put on or take off. Our ministry is who we are and what we present to the world. If we are representatives of Jesus, our behavior must align with who He is. There is always room to grow for us to be better individuals, and the Holy Spirit will work with each of us to help us become who we aspire to be. Dance is about sacrifice. As we cut off undesirable people and behaviors from our lives, and keep our eyes focused on Jesus, those looking on will be drawn to the ministry we present, which reflects Jesus.

Prayer

Heavenly Father, help us to walk this Christian walk in a way that is worthy of being called by Your name, to walk in integrity and be the salt of the earth. In Jesus' name, we pray. Amen.

Call To Action

- Spend time studying the Word.

- Apply Scripture to your life.

- Align your behavior and attitude with the Word.

Gurlain Applewhaite

September 9

STAY CONNECTED

Put on therefore, as the elect of God, holy and beloved, bowels of mercies, kindness, humbleness of mind, meekness, long-suffering, forbearing one another and forgiving one another, if any man have a quarrel against any: even as Christ forgave you, so also do ye and above all these things put on charity, which is the bond of perfectness. Colossians 3:12-14

As elects of God, we should be merciful, kind, humble, meek, long-suffering and forgiving, but the greatest of these is love. With love, all the others will become easier. Our character is the sum of our disposition, and our choices influence and develop who we are. 1 Corinthians 13 speaks about the importance of love: "You may speak in tongues of men and angels and if you have not love, you become like a sounding brass or a tinkling cymbal." Love is most important to God, so our hearts will be in tune with God by committing to love.

Having a heart for ministry may not necessarily mean having a genuine heart for Christ, so building a relationship with God by spending time in His Word and in His presence is important. Godly character is the result of the Holy Spirit's work of sanctification. As dance ministers, let us see God as the tree and we as the fruits. If we are not connected to the tree, our fruit will not mature, and it will eventually die. Also, as dance ministers, we should show love and encouragement because our mission is to reach those in need and introduce them to the endless possibilities they can have through faith and God's love.

Prayer

Father, I am thankful we have You to stay connected to so we can come to maturity through our ministry and our walk with You. Amen.

Call To Action

- Stay connected to God.

- Build a relationship with God to develop Godly character.

- Allow yourself to grow through Godly character.

Jenifer Arrendell and Mandy Samuels

September 10

WE HAVE AN OWNER

Lord, I know that people's lives are not their own; it is not for them to direct their steps. Jeremiah 10:23

This verse was Jeremiah's prayer for the people of Israel. There is a lesson here to be learned in the reality that our lives are not our own and that a truly successful life is directed by the One who created us. To have a successful life requires complete surrender to the One to whom our lives belong. Our lives have an owner, but it is for us to recognize who that owner is. That owner is the creator of the universe, God our Father. We may think we know what is good for us, but our Father knows what is best for our lives.

As Christians, we should want to reflect our creator by possessing Godly character. We cannot rely on our strengths to get this done. Praying and reading His Word are needed to possess this character. To develop a Godly character, it calls for us to be in constant prayer. Our Father is the only person that helps us to possess His character when we ask for help. When we pray, we have to believe that He will help us. Reading and studying His Word is of the most importance. God's Word is our guide to be like Him. We should aim to spend as much time as possible being students of His Word.

Prayer

Heavenly Father, we ask for Your help in being like You, our owner. Forgive us for not spending time in prayer, reading, or studying Your Word. Thank You, Jesus, for helping us and forgiving us. In Jesus' Name, Amen.

Call To Action

I want to encourage you to spend time in prayer and study His Word as often as possible. God requires this from us, so let us sacrifice the time to develop Godly character.

Julie Greene

September 11

THE POTTER'S WHEEL

But the pot he was shaping from the clay was marred in his hands; so the potter formed it into another pot, shaping it as seemed best to him. Jeremiah 18:4

In verse 1 of this same chapter, Jeremiah, the prophet, was told by God to "go down by the Potter's House and there I will give you a message." The reality is that we are born in sin and shaped in iniquity. We need to be moulded by God often. God is the only person that knows everything about us. He knows every fault and every blemish. Our aim should be to allow Him to mould us into the people that He wants us to be for His Glory.

The refining process of shaping clay can be very painful. Hence, as Christians, we tend to avoid the shaping process, as the pain is necessary to have a Godly character. For many, displaying Christian attributes is easy when things are good, but these attributes become challenging to show under pressure. God said in His Word in 1 Corinthians 10:13, "I will not put more on you than you can bear." We must trust Him to help us through the refining process. God's goal is to have His vessels with holy and Christ-like characters. Therefore, we have to make a choice to allow God to mold us on His Potter's Wheel. However, God will not force us to get on His wheel. We must make that choice.

Prayer

Father, we place our lives on Your wheel. Mold us and shape us into the Godly vessels You have called us to be. We put our full trust in You that even though the process may be painful, You will help us through it. Thank You, Jesus, for the refined me. Amen.

Call To Action

I challenge you to do two things:

1. Allow God to be involved in the nitty-gritty details of your life, which calls for openness and complete surrender. This is step one to getting on the Potter's Wheel.

2. Allow Him to mould you into a vessel to be used by Him. This is when the shaping occurs. Trust Him to help you through the pain of the refining process.

Julie Greene

September 12

WHO WE REALLY ARE

This, then, is how you ought to regard us: as servants of Christ and as those entrusted with the mysteries God has revealed. 1 Corinthians 4:1

This is one of my favorite verses. It always keeps me focused on the bigger picture as a dance minister. It is so easy with enough technique, facial expression and passion to move the majority of a crowd, but this verse reminds us that who we are off the stage in our day-to-day lives is far more important to God than the snapshot in time when we are fulfilling ministry on stage on His behalf. God is like, "You better rep me all the time". You see, when we do that, He shows up. We then become the light and salt He has called us to be. Our Father is proud of us in these moments as we show up as His hands and feet on this earth to show forth His love and to draw men in. If our characters are inconsistent with what we do on stage, we cause a lot of damage; we confuse people and bring God's name into question. Let's aim to be consistent.

Prayer

Lord, help us to be authentic to our calling, and allow us to strive to be Godly in our walk. God, where we are flawed, strengthens us so we will not be stumbling blocks first for ourselves and then for others. Let us desire to be more like You every day. Amen.

Call To Action

Think of the last few ministry pieces you would have done. Think of the songs you danced to. Write them down, and if there is anything in you that does not line up with the message of these songs and the character God expects of you, commit to praying and asking God to change you on the inside.

Laina Jacob

September 13

BEING LIKE GOD

Be perfect, therefore as your Heavenly Father is perfect. Matthew 5:48

There is a song I would sing when I was a new Christian, "I want to be more like You…" To be more like God, we must exude love, for the Bible tells us that God is Love. 1 John 4:8 notes that "Whosoever does not love does not know God." Love is a part of God's character. Character refers to the mental and moral qualities distinctive to an individual, so love is a characteristic of God.

I have always aspired to not just dance but to make sure my lifestyle measures up to holy living. If I am to minister through dance, my character must speak for itself, on and off stage. My character also speaks to the kind of company I keep. The Bible tells us that "bad company corrupts good morals". Who my friends are can influence my behavior, so having good, Godly, positive friends helps me to develop a Godly character.

If I persevere in my battles and sufferings, the Bible says that this produces character, and character will produce hope (Romans 5:4). Sometimes, we want to run away from our sufferings, but sufferings shape our character.

Prayer

God, make me more like You. Please help me to conform to Your image in Jesus' name.

Challenge

Write down 5 things that you need to change to build Godly character and act on these things.

Maxine Butcher

September 14

SEARCH MY HEART

But put on the Lord Jesus Christ, and make no provision for the flesh, to gratify its desires. Romans 5:8

How is this possible when dealing with people? Let's put it this way: would you die for someone you love, much less your enemy? Someone who hates you and goes out of their way to make your life miserable? I'm guessing the answer is no. But let me ask you this: do you think you deserve better than anyone else? The way God sees you, that other person is a soul to Him as well, one He loves regardless. I know it's difficult to see past things when we've been hurt and mishandled or judged wrongly, but this is why we need not operate in the flesh. We must put Jesus Christ before us in words, thoughts and deeds.

The same chapter says that while we were yet sinners, Christ died for us. Saint or sinner, hurt or not, we all need the love, deliverance, restoration, mercies and grace of the Lord. When you think you can't do it, remember Him and look to Him for strength to display that Godly character. Ask Him for wisdom and to speak to Him about how you are feeling.

My Bishop said once, hurt people, hurt people. So do those who feel unloved, angry, bitter, used or discouraged; people lash out for various reasons. In some situations, you could be the salve they need. In other moments, God uses people or situations to extract what is hindering us from moving forward in our God-ordained purpose. It's not always about other people. It could very much be about you. Let Him be lifted high and shown.

Prayer

Heavenly Father, it's hard not to give in to fleshy desires, but I know with You, nothing is impossible, and I can display Godly characteristics. My heart desires to please You always and to do that, I ask for Your help. In Jesus' name, Amen.

Call To Action

I will train my mind and tongue to respond with Godly character.

Orissa Fitzpatrick

September 15

CHARACTER SKETCH

But know that the LORD hath set apart him that is godly for himself: the LORD will hear when I call unto him. Psalm 4:3

Set-apart	Ps 4:3		Sober	Ti 2:12
Devout	Ps 32:6		Righteous	Ti 2:12
Sincere	2 Co 1:12		Reverential	Heb 12:28
Edifying	1 Ti 1:4		Charitable	3 Jn 1:6

Some Descriptive Adjectives of a Godly Person

Character Sketch of a Godly Person

The Godly person is called and *set apart* by the Lord Himself to serve Him and His Kingdom. This person constantly lives in the presence of the Lord and is *devout* in their service to Him. The Godly person is *sincere* in all of their interactions and maintains an *edifying* and encouraging disposition. They remain *sober* (clearheaded) whether confronted with life's daily tasks or challenging situations. Being *righteous* is one of their hallmark characteristics, as they are guided by God and His Word. They are *reverential* when referring to God and the things of God and stay humble whatever their trials and triumphs may be. They also stay *charitable.*

Do you see any of the above characteristics in your life on a consistent basis? Are there other Godly attributes you can add to the list above? Write down a few of your own.

Prayer

Lord, help us to maintain a consistent Godly character in whatever we do and wherever we go.

Call To Action

- Write a "Character Sketch" containing the Godly attributes you desire to possess.

- Work on your "interpretation" of these attributes and try to display them in your facial expressions when ministering.

- Walk (dance) out some of these attributes in a choreography.

Pierre Rock

September 16

INFORMATION LABEL

Teaching us that, denying ungodliness and worldly lusts, we should live soberly, righteously, and godly, in this present world. Titus 2:12

Godly Characteristics Serving Size: 24/7		
Prayer	Psalm 32:6	100%
Praise	Psalm 145:10	100%
Posture	Hebrews 12:28	100%
Position	Psalm 4:3	100%

For this shall everyone that is godly pray unto thee in a time when thou mayest be found: surely in the floods of great waters they shall not come nigh unto him. Psalm 32:6

All thy works shall praise thee, O LORD; and thy saints shall bless thee. Psalm 145:10

Wherefore we receiving a kingdom which cannot be moved, let us have grace, whereby we may serve God acceptably with reverence and godly fear. Hebrews 12:28

But know that the LORD hath set apart him that is godly for himself: the LORD will hear when I call unto him. Psalm 4:3

The above information label shows just a few godly characteristics that we should aspire to possess one hundred percent of the time. **Prayer** - converse with God daily. **Praise** - exalt God for being just that, God. **Posture** - maintain a humble disposition before God, whatever our status or success in life. **Position** - stay in God's Kingdom and at the foot of the cross wherever life's journey takes us.

Prayer

Father, help us to cultivate Godly characteristics.

Call To Action

Prayer, praise, posture, and position - combine these four godly characteristics in a choreography.

Pierre Rock

September 17

MY FATHER'S CHILD

So God created mankind in his own image, in the image of God he created them.
Genesis 1:27

The first thing that is said about mankind in the scriptures is that God created us in His image. For as long as I have known myself, I've heard, "You look just like your father" or "Your father can't deny you, girl, you look just like him". Up to this day, I still hear it, and although I don't see it as others do, I suppose it is true. Just as I have a strong resemblance to my earthly father, I desire to have an even stronger resemblance to my heavenly Father. As His children, we should have His character; we should behave just like our Father, have His attributes, and be undeniably His.

But what is God's character? What characteristics does God have? What are His ways? The revelation of this is found in the Bible. By reading scripture, we become equipped with the knowledge of who God is: forgiving, compassionate, loving, and the list of positive attributes goes on.

When we minister, who do people see? Do they see God or do they see us? Do not be fooled; representing God authentically is not achieved by masking or faking it and thinking that we are fooling others. Realistically, we are only fooling ourselves. Dance has a way of showing us up. DNA determines our appearance, and the DNA of God's character, once it exists on the inside of us, will show up on the outside. It should not be something we put on and take off but that which is embedded within us. Do you look like you are your Father's child?

Prayer

Lord, as You reveal Your character to me in Your Word, help me to embody these Godly characteristics. Please help me look like You in my thoughts, speech, and actions. May everything about me be a good representative of who my Father is, and my resemblance to You be undeniable. In Jesus' Name.

Call To Action

Do your own research and write down the characteristics of God.

Rheanne Rock

September 18

YOUR CHARACTER LORD

The fruit of the spirit is love, joy, peace, forbearance, kindness, goodness, faithfulness, gentleness and self-control. Against such things there is no law.
Galatians 5:22-23

To have Godly character means you must possess the fruit of the spirit. There is one fruit of the spirit with nine segments:

Love - Love is more than a feeling; it is an action. Telling your friends and family on a daily basis that you love them is one way of showing love. We must not only say it, but we have to show it as well. Corinthians 13:13 shows us that love is the greatest commandment.

Joy - Joy is being happy. We display joy when we are excited. We should not walk around looking sad because our Father gives us an overflowing amount of joy.

Peace - Peace is living well with everyone. If at school the children in your class tease you, be at peace because you know you are doing what is right.

Forbearance - Forbearance is being patient. At times, we want things now, but we have to trust that our parents or anyone in charge of us know best. We can ask God to help us or show us how to wait.

Kindness - Kindness is when we help people when things are okay and also when things go wrong. When someone falls, we should aim to help them right away and not laugh.

Goodness - Goodness is the quality of being good. For example, vegetables are good for our health even though, at times, we may not want to eat them.

Faithfulness - Faithfulness is when we do what God wants us to do in every way. If God says to do something, then we should find a way to do it.

Gentleness - Gentleness is when we are not rough in actions or words. The Bible shows us in Proverbs 15:1 that a gentle answer turns away wrath, but a harsh word stirs up anger.

Self-control - Self-control is when we control ourselves. Controlling yourself can be a hard task but once we remember that we are always representing God, then it will not be so hard.

Prayer

Dear Lord, help us to show love, joy, peace, forbearance, kindness, goodness, faithfulness, gentleness and self-control to everyone always. Amen.

Call To Action

My challenge for you is to do all these things twice a day.

Rhema-Jae Greene

September 19

LIVING OUT YOUR GODLY CHARACTER

Let your light so shine before men, that they may see your good works, and glorify your Father which is in heaven. Mathew 5:16

You may be wondering what light this verse is referring to. You might say, "But I don't have a light." Oh yes, you do. The light this verse refers to is your character. It is what people see or receive when they interact with you. Your character defines who you are and who you are becoming. Through the salvation of Jesus, something inside of you is activated, which starts to influence your speech and behavior. You begin to look like Jesus, and the image seen is one of love, humbleness and kindness even when you have been treated unkindly. Your words are chosen carefully to ensure they don't leave a stain or a stench on anyone's heart. Remember, it is Jesus you need them to see, not you. As a dancer, your Godly character is necessary whether you are on stage or off stage because you are a minister for the Kingdom of God.

Sometimes, choosing to be of Godly character might seem challenging, but let us remember that Jesus showed Godly character in the garden of Gethsemane in Luke 22 when the servant of the high priest's ear was cut off. So, we have to follow His example. Godly character comes through practice, but it is done because of our love for Jesus. Matthew 21:37 says you must "love the Lord with all your heart, all your soul and all your might". In doing this, your life will begin to permeate light, shining from the inside out, and your Godly character will shine even brighter.

Today, let us examine ourselves and be sure we are exhibiting signs of God's character. Are we displaying love, kind words and good attitudes with determination and discipline? We must make this a priority so that people can see God's character in us and glorify our God who lives in heaven.

Prayer

Lord, may I always have my Godly character on display so You can be seen through my words and actions in Jesus' name. Amen.

Call To Action

- Spend time reading God's Word.

- Love God and show how much you love Him by developing your character.

- Examine the actions of your heart.

Rhonda. A. Babb

September 20

WHEN WE LOOK LIKE GOD

Since God chose you to be the holy people he loves, you must clothe yourselves with tenderhearted mercy, kindness, humility, gentleness, and patience. Colossians 3:12

Sometimes, we dress in our outer garments, forgetting to wear our Godly garments. God has chosen you not because He doesn't know any better but because He loves you. This love that He gives to us must extend to everyone we know. Love helps people to see Jesus through us. We who know Jesus Christ have a responsibility to wear these garments every day. Are you going to leave home naked? No! Therefore, our spiritual garments are to be worn just like our earthly garments. God didn't give us spiritual clothing to hang up in our hearts or to leave at home; He gave us them so people can know that God still exists and He is not dead.

Every garment spoken about in the verse above represents the character of God, so when we wear them, we, too, will represent God's character. I am sure some of us were in places where we thought there was no hope, but through God's tenderhearted mercy, kindness, humility, patience and gentleness, we were able to recover from our brokenness.

In ministry, in order for our lives to exhibit the character of God, every spiritual garment must be on display. People need to see that Jesus lives in and through us everywhere we go and every time we meet to fellowship. No longer are we to look like ourselves. We must be ambassadors for our heavenly Father. Without Him, we could not dance, so our spiritual garments must always be seen even when we dance.

Prayer

God, if we have not worn Your garments in a long time, remind us to put them on today so that we can bless others in Jesus' name. Amen.

Call To Action

- Be intentional about wearing your garments; they represent God's character.

- Let the character of God shine through your actions.

- Remember, we are chosen and loved by God.

Rhonda. A. Babb

September 21

TRAITOR!

And God said, let us make man in our own image, after our likeness; So God created man in his own image, in the image of God created he him.
Genesis 1:26-27

"Traitor! Traitor! Traitor!" they chanted. The crowd was in a frenzy. They had waited for this day to come when he sold them out. An injustice had been done and it was time to face the music. There was no escaping this outcome. After all, the manual was written and he showed his hand in the beginning.

Finally, he had someone he could count on. They say the apple doesn't fall far from the tree, but this was no small feat. He had big shoes to fill. He had to walk in His shadow, exhibiting His traits: honesty, integrity, and love. This traitor couldn't get it done, not in his own strength.

"Traitor! Traitor!" they still chanted. Everything was at his fingertips. There was no want for anything. Yet it was too much for him to handle, and he let it slip through his grasp. He followed the wrong crowd, who tricked him into believing that all that glitters was gold. All his morals and perks went down the drain because he didn't take a stand for anything and fell for everything. His word wasn't his bond, and he lied to get out of every bad situation he found himself in.

He needed to change his life and become the man he was destined to be. He was poured into so he could take on the nature and characteristics of one who is faithful. He was the first-born, made in an image that was larger than life itself. The day had come for justice. Another plan was in the works, for where sin abounds, grace abounds much more.

Prayer

Wonderful God, Your nature and character are upright and Holy, and we declare that we will walk like You and talk like You. We will not let our sinful nature win, and the world will see You in us in all that we say and do, in Jesus' name, Amen.

Call To Action

Represent God and walk uprightly in His image and likeness. Illuminate the world with His light; display His Godly character.

Sandra Britton

September 22

CALL ME GRACE

Through these he has given us his very great and precious promises, so that through them you may participate in the divine nature, having escaped the corruption in the world caused by evil desires. 2 Peter 1:4

Let me introduce you to Grace. You can call on her any time of the day or night, for her portion will never run dry. Despite everything we put our Heavenly Father through, rebellion, lies, or just being the downright opposite of all that He is, you can call on Grace.

When God created us, His nature became our nature, and we were so tightly entwined that you could not tell our shadows apart. We spoke what He spoke and He prepared us to take on the world. He had us prepped and ready to duplicate what He had begun, but sin stepped in and changed our nature and our image, removing us from His shadow, at least for a while, until Grace was ready. For all is not lost, and Christ shed His blood so we could reclaim our place and reflect the mirror image of God.

We tarnish God's name and character to the enemy when we walk contrary to all that God is. Do you know that righteous living upsets the enemy but pleases God? Displaying Godly character is a must, as our redemption gave us a fresh start, a new beginning that will lead us back to the presence of God. We can't do this alone. Through Grace, and with the guidance of the Holy Spirit, the enemy has no choice but to ask for permission to test us. Job was upright and displayed a Godly character like no other. Though we cannot all be like Job, we can try. We can put a dent in the enemy's kingdom. There is no need to be afraid because you are on the winning side.

Prayer

Holy One, Righteous Father, thank You for creating us in Your image and likeness. Help us to walk with Godly character; let our yea be yea and our nay be nay. Help us recognize that nothing can touch us without Your say so, and give us grace to continue on. In Jesus' name, Amen.

Call To Action

Walk with Grace daily.

Sandra Britton

September 23

GOOD GODLY HABITS

Do not be deceived: "Evil company corrupts good habits." 1 Corinthians 15:33

Paul speaks about the danger of deception in this scripture. He says that when you are deceived, it corrupts the good habits you have. The meaning of the word corrupt is to make someone dishonest, especially when they have important responsibilities. Your important responsibility is to not be deceived by the devil and to keep your good Godly habits.

Furthermore, Paul urges believers to "Awake to righteousness, and do not sin; for some do not have the knowledge of God. I speak this to your shame" (1 Corinthians 15:34). This underscores the importance of aligning our lives with God's righteousness and avoiding sinful behavior, especially when others may lack knowledge of God.

The characteristics of God should be reflected in our lives. Galatians 5:22-23 says, "But the fruit of the spirit is love, joy, peace, long-suffering, kindness, goodness, faithfulness, gentleness, self-control. Against such there is no law." This verse tells us that these are the characteristics of God we should practise.

Daniel is a great example of how we can possess a Godly character. When Daniel was thrown into the lion's den, he was not afraid; instead, he had faith and Godly character. I encourage you to have a Godly character and embrace good Godly habits.

Prayer

Lord, I pray that you will guard our hearts against evil things. May our lives reflect Your character, and may we face challenges with unwavering faith like Daniel. Amen.

Call To Action

Write a list of characteristics God has and practice doing them.

Shaquonna Rock

September 24

BLAMELESS

The one whose walk is blameless, who does what is righteous, who speaks the truth from their heart. Psalm 15:2

Godly character comes from God's Holy Spirit. Without God, our character is sinful. Psalm 15 explains that a Godly man is blameless, righteous, truthful, kind, keeps promises even when it hurts, despises evil, is a man of integrity and is unshakeable in his belief. A Godly man emphasizes his own integrity. He strives to be honest and just. He works to develop strong ethical foundations. He has an understanding of Godly behavior, and he lives life to please God. It doesn't matter what he *thinks* it means to be of a Godly character. What matters is the characteristics God *requires*.

Gifts and abilities may open doors, but character will determine what we do once those doors are opened. Man's character should be to conform to God's. Therefore, it must reflect graciousness, compassion, mercy and love. It is imperative that we listen attentively to the real us (who we are on the inside).

A blessed man is like a tree whose roots are nourished by a stream and are productively blessed. A blessed man does not keep company with bad crowds. Furthermore, the Word of God governs his thoughts both day and night as he thinks about what God has disclosed in His Word. Man's devotion to scripture produces fruit in his life, as stated in Galatians 5:22-23. As dance ministers, we align ourselves with God's character, and as we express our worship, we seek to articulate the Word and the Spirit of God through our bodies.

Prayer

Father, I humble myself to You, for Your mission and character matter. Your Word says if I trust You, I will not be disappointed. I know You are able, and I want to prove to You that I will serve You with an attitude that glorifies You. Help keep me humbled and focused on You in Jesus' mighty name. Amen.

Call To Action

- Allow the Word of God to take root in you.

- Align yourself with God's character.

- Confirm God's Holy characteristics.

Sophia Hazell

September 25

HIS HEART…THROUGH US

Put on therefore, as the elect of God, holy and beloved, bowels of mercies, kindness, humbleness of mind, meekness, long-suffering; Forbearing one another, and forgiving one another, if any man have a quarrel against any: even as Christ forgave you, so also do ye. And above all these things put on charity, which is the bond of perfectness. And let the peace of God rule in your hearts, to the which also ye are called in one body; and be ye thankful. Colossians 3:12-15

Do you know what it means to have a Godly character? A Godly character can be defined as the ability to discern God's right way from wrong. To voluntarily surrender one's own will to do what is right in God's sight and, with the promised help to resist wrong even under pressure is a perfect way to show Godly character in our day-to-day lives. A Godly character speaks to the attributes or traits of God himself. These include goodness, holiness, righteousness, compassion, kindness, faithfulness and love. These are just a few that speak to God's nature.

But how can we show a Godly character as dancers? The aforementioned characteristics are not only to be used in our daily interactions but also in our ministry; this does not necessarily speak to how well we dance but who we are both on and off stage. We must show Godly characteristics as dance ministers so that who we are does not cause a distraction to those we are ministering to. The goal is to let God's heart shine through us.

Prayer

Heavenly Father, we thank You for being a God who is kind, selfless and loving. You have proven this through scripture and Your presence in our daily lives. Lord, help us to be more like You, ever-growing into the image of Your only begotten son, Jesus Christ. Amen.

Call To Action

I challenge you this week to portray a Godly character. You can do this by being kind to others and being forgiving and helpful. Also, explain to a friend, teacher, parent or family member what a Godly character means to you.

Halal Teens

September 26

SHOWING THE LOVE OF CHRIST

Each tree is recognized by its own fruit. People do not pick figs from thornbushes, or grapes from briers. A good man brings good things out of the good stored up in his heart, and an evil man brings evil things out of the evil stored up in his heart. For the mouth speaks what the heart is full of. Luke 6:44-45

Having a Godly character means showing our love for Christ to others. Just like trees are recognized by their fruits, people that display Godly character are recognized by others. It is important that children of God walk and talk as Jesus would; this means we always tell the truth, follow the Ten Commandments and show compassion to others. Spending time with God will help us to develop a relationship with Him and help us to develop a Godly character.

Prayer

Father, help us to live our lives in a way that pleases You. May the fruit of the spirit, love, joy, peace, patience, kindness, goodness, faithfulness, gentleness, and self-control, show forth in our lives so that these attitudes bring about good deeds which glorify You. We pray this in Jesus' name. Amen.

Call To Action

Write out all the fruits of the spirit and practice these traits daily with everyone you interact with.

Trinitee Angus

September 27

THE FRUIT SHOWCASES GODLY CHARACTER

But the fruit of the Spirit is love, joy, peace, forbearance, kindness, goodness, faithfulness, gentleness and self-control. Against such things there is no law.
Galatians 5:22-23

The songwriter said, "To be like Jesus, to be like Jesus, all I ask is to be like Him." Having the fruits of the spirit allows us to do just that. It enables us to live holy and acceptable lives in God's sight. In the natural world, fruit is grown from the seed that is planted. You cannot have an apple seed and expect to have an orange as a fruit. In other words, whatever is put in the ground is what grows; this is the same in the spiritual world. If we seek to have a Godly character, then we must nurture our lives in such a way that the fruits that we bear are spiritual, as in Galatians 5:22-23. We nurture these fruits by reading the Word, praying, and executing our gifts in ministry, such as dancing, attending church and fulfilling our Christian duties. These activities help us to develop Godly character so that men will know that we are His Disciples.

Prayer

Heavenly Father, it is my desire to be like You. I want others to see the fruit of the spirit: love, joy, peace, kindness, goodness, faithfulness and self-control in me. Help me to read Your Word and spend more time with You so that these spiritual fruits will manifest in my life. Help me to live holy and acceptable in Your sight so that sinners will see my life as a testimony and come to know You as their saviour in Jesus' name. Amen!

Call To Action

Make a purposeful effort to do the things that nurture the fruit of the spirit in your life.

Tweann Layne

September 28

WHAT IS YOUR GODLY CHARACTER?

But the fruit of the Spirit is love, joy, peace, patience, kindness, goodness, faithfulness, gentleness, self-control; against such things there is no law.
Galatians 5:22-23

How do we, as Christians, portray our Godly character? How can we apply these fruits of the spirit to our everyday walk of life? Well, we need first to apply the pressure. Make sure you know these fruits of the spirit well. Write them down and check them off your mental list every day. Some of us get so caught up in our busy day-to-day lives that we don't have the time to stop and show love to one another.

The Lord said to love your neighbor as yourself, show love to one another, if you give unto one another give with a joyful heart, always have patience and peace that surpasses all understanding, show some act of kindness, do good and all things shall be added unto you, be faithful and gentle and always have self-control. These are all key elements for portraying Godly character. Let us not forget who we belong to or where we come from. We are royalty because we come from royalty, so it is only fair we act the way God expects us to and do the things that would make Him proud.

Within your different ministries, you should be able to take these fruits of the Spirit and apply them where they need to be applied. Be your brother's keeper, lend a helping hand, and be that shoulder to lean on because before you were the helper, you were the one in need. One good turn deserves another. Come on, brothers and sisters in Christ, make today the day we start to show these acts of kindness to one another. Make today the day we put self and pride aside and lean on each other because when we stand united, the enemy has to fall.

Prayer

Heavenly and most gracious Father, we thank You for showing us what it is to love, to have joy, peace, patience, kindness, goodness, faithfulness, gentleness and self-control. As a Christian community, we will lead by your example, God, and make You proud. In Jesus' Name. Amen.

Call To Action

Remember to always have the fruits of the Spirit planted in your mind so that when ripe and needed, you can take a bite out of them! God bless.

Zariah Watson

September 29

THE ABILITY TO DISCERN
(POEM)

Do not be misled: "Bad company corrupts good character". 1 Corinthians 15:33

To resist the wrong, even when you're under temptation

To resist the wrong, even when you're under pressure

The strength to say no

The strength to speak up

The ability to be a leader and not a follower

To surrender your own will to do what is expected of you in the eyes of Him.

That's what He wants

That's what He needs

That's what He desires

For you to surrender yourself of your own free will to be His humble servant.

To not allow yourself to be corrupted

But to be honest.

Zenaida R. Mayers

September 30

THE RIGHT THING
(POEM)

Seek good and not evil that you may live; so the Lord God of hosts will be with you, as you have spoken. Hate evil, love good; establish justice in the gate. It may be that the Lord God of hosts will be gracious to the remnant of Joseph.
Amos 5:14-15

The want

The need to be good

To be the example He so yearns for from you

To shun evil as you open your mouth

As you move your feet

Not just in dance, but in your spiritual walk with Him

To be the same person off stage, that you are on stage

The want

The need to be His daughter

His son

His servant

The want

The need to be genuinely, unconditionally, His.

Zenaida R. Mayers

October 1

ALIGNMENT

For "who has known the mind of the Lord that he may instruct Him?" But we have the mind of Christ. 1 Corinthians 2:16

Without the knowledge of Christ, the unsaved person cannot understand the teachings and revelations of God because he lacks something that only the redeemed person has—and that is "the mind of Christ".

As believers, we are aided by the Holy Spirit and are given the mind of Christ. In other words, we can think spiritual thoughts because Christ is alive within us. We no longer think the way we once did, but we begin to think in Godly ways. This mind of Christ is the source of true, godly wisdom. It is not worldly, it is not of men, and it does not divide. Instead, it is a wisdom that demonstrates the power of God.

Ephesians 4:23 states, "For if we do not die to self, we will not grow in the wisdom of Christ". This transformation is only possible through Christ and when the spirit of our mind and heart is renewed. This renewal continues throughout the believer's life as he or she is obedient to the Word and will of God. The process is not a one-time accomplishment but the continuous work of the Spirit in us. Our resources are God's Word and prayer. It is through these means that we gain the mind of Christ, and it is through that mind that we live the life of Christ.

As ministers, we should not portray negative thoughts. Remember, this is not reflective of the mind of Christ at work in us, for we are spiritually mature and guided by the Spirit. We have access to the heart and mind of God through the Spirit, who searches the depths of God.

Prayer

Lord, I want to be truly aware of the mind of Christ in my life. Help me to open myself only to know Your will and push away old mindsets. Strengthen and renew the spirit of my mind in Christ. In Jesus' Name. Amen.

Call To Action

Know that God alone is the bedrock on which to build, so build a strong relationship with God to gain the mind of Christ. Make God your only source and supply and filter all your thoughts through His mind.

Cherry-Ann Cumberbatch

October 2

TOTAL TRANSFORMATION

For who has known the mind and purposes of the Lord, so as to instruct him? But we have the mind of Christ [to be guided by his thoughts and purposes.
1 Corinthians 2:6

The Holy Spirit living in us transforms our entire being; He changes our hearts, souls, and our minds. Sin once ruled our minds, but with the transformation we experience, we can live freely, being guided by our savior, Jesus. Since we have the mind of Christ through the Holy Spirit, we are able to get new revelations. Whatever God wants to reveal to us, we will understand.

In dance, sometimes our moves can be symbolic. We can create these moves because of our understanding of scripture and God, especially the things He has done and continues to do for us. For example, moving our hands around our heads can symbolize Christ's blood covering us.

In your day-to-day life, let the mind of Christ influence all that you do. We know that Christ has given us tremendous mercy, so let us give mercy to others. Let us continue to understand the things of God through the mind of Christ that He has given us. When we operate this way, we will be ready and willing to love our enemies and do what God has asked of us.

Prayer

Dear God, thank You for who You are and all You have done for us. Thank You for already giving us the ability to understand You and Your Word. We pray that we will willingly obey and submit to You in our day-to-day lives as we begin to understand that Your will is good, acceptable, and perfect. Thank You for renewing our minds and giving us the mind of Christ so that we are able to understand Your will. In Jesus' Name, Amen

Call To Action

Let us live in light of Who God is and all that He has done for us, and ask Him to continue to reveal more of Himself to us.

Danielle Harewood

October 3

IN HARMONY

He that saith he abideth in him ought himself also so to walk, even as he walked.
1 John 2:6

As a child, you wanted to play dress up with your mother's clothes and wear her shoes. Although the shoes were big, you still put your feet in them and tried to walk. We believed that if we dressed and walked around in our mother's shoes, we would be like her. God is telling us that we can do the same with Him. This verse talks about walking in harmony with God. We live in harmony with God when we put our hopes, dreams and lives in Him. Being in harmony means having the same mindset. The way He lived while on earth, we should live.

Harmony means to be in one accord. Dancing is all about harmony. If the group does not have the same mindset or goal, the dance or ministry will not flow. When you watch a group dance, and one person messes up, you can see its effects on the dance. That happens when we are not walking in harmony with God. It affects not only us personally but also those lost souls we are trying to reach. If we say we abide with Christ, we should walk as He walked. We must have that same mind He had when He lived on earth.

Prayer

Let us walk, therefore, in Christ. Thank You that we can have the mind of Christ by walking in harmony with You. It is not always an easy walk, but it's rewarding. May I always look to You for my source of strength as I walk with You, Lord. I thank You that even when I am unable, You are there to carry me.

Call To Action

Read about the life of Jesus and reflect on His life. Put yourself in His shoes and write three descriptions of what His life means to you.

Eslyn Taylor

October 4

VOICES IN MY HEAD

Finally, brethren, whatsoever things are true, whatsoever things are honest, whatsoever things are just, whatsoever things are pure, whatsoever things are lovely, whatsoever things are of good report; if there be any virtue, and if there be any praise, think on these things. Philippians 4:8

We always hear that we should have the mind of Christ, but what does having the mind of Christ really mean? It's easier than we may think. To have the mind of Christ does not require any miracles or any special thoughts. It just requires that we be intentional in our pursuit of the mind of Christ. Therefore, we must read the Word, identify things that align with Christ, and think about those things. Philippians 4:8 tells us that we should think about things that are lovely, pure, honest, fair, and of good report.

How does this translate to our roles as dance ministers? Well, we can't be on the mission of spreading the Word of God and thinking ungodly thoughts; it's contradictory and will distract us from the work of the Kingdom. If we don't keep our intentions on the mind of Christ as dance ministers, we risk blurring the lines between secular and godly, which will confuse those we are trying to save.

Prayer

Almighty and heavenly Father, cover our minds with Your precious blood. May our minds be filled with Godly things that are pleasing to You. May whatever things are true, pure, lovely, and of good report forever flourish in our minds. May the mind of Christ not be isolated to just our thoughts, but may it also influence our actions. Amen.

Call To Action

Be intentional this week about possessing the mind of Christ. Every day, keep your mind focused on the Kingdom of God.

Gabrielle Blackett

October 5

THINKING LIKE JESUS

Let this mind be in you which was also in Christ Jesus, who, being in the form of God, did not consider it robbery to be equal with God, but made Himself of no reputation, taking the form of a bond servant, and coming in the likeness of men.
Philippians 2:5-7

We cannot know God through our own natural wisdom. However, we have the ability to know God when we have made the decision to surrender to Him. It is only when we have the mind of Christ that we are able to understand the deep truths of God. He reveals previously unknown things to us which can only be understood by the power of the Holy Spirit, and these things inspire us to teach others. So, what is the mind of Christ, and why should we yearn to have it?

Having the mind of Christ is thinking the way Christ thinks. Jesus is our perfect role model for the fruit of the Spirit. When we surrender our lives to God, the Holy Spirit will help rid us of all the past behaviors which did not glorify God. We are a new creation. Although this transformation is a gradual process, the more we recognize what is ungodly, humble ourselves, and ask God to remove our ungodly behaviors, the more He will.

It has been said that husbands and wives who have spent many years together begin to resemble each other. Their features start to look alike, they think alike, and sometimes they may even finish each other's sentences. Likewise, the more time we spend in the presence of the King, the more we will resemble Him. Can you imagine what our ministry would be like if everyone had the passionate desire to walk and talk like Jesus? Let us mirror Jesus' character.

Prayer

Father, break the chains over our minds and set us free. We submit our thoughts and all our desires to You. Wherever there is conflict and confusion in our minds, we declare that we have clarity and a sound mind. In Jesus' name, we pray. Amen.

Call To Action

- Walk in the Spirit so you do not fulfill the lusts of the flesh.

- Throw off your old evil nature and be born anew.

Gurlain Applewhaite

Call To Action

- Walk in the Spirit so you do not fulfill the lusts of the flesh.

- Throw off your old evil nature and be born anew.

October 6

DANCE EVANGELISTS

Finally brethren, whatsoever things are true, whatsoever things are noble, whatsoever things are just, whatsoever things are pure, whatsoever things are lovely, whatsoever things are of good report, if there is any virtue and if there is anything praiseworthy, meditate on these things. Philippians 4:8

The mind is the battleground. We all have a soul, which consists of our mind, emotions and will, and both the kingdom of God and the kingdom of Satan are battling for our souls. Therefore, it is important that we renew our minds daily with the Word of God so that we can become more Christ-like. The text here advises us to have a new mindset and replace unholy thoughts with the holy.

Emotions can affect our bodies, so just as Jesus glorified His Father through His perfection, we should set our eyes on Christ to glorify God through the perfecting of our dance. There is nothing wrong with having a passion for dance, but let our passion not be misdirected. It is not about us. Our dance on stage should be captivating as we commit each dance to God. Our relationship with God determines how we are able to impact an audience or congregation. We do not dance to show off how good we are. The aim is to draw men unto Christ, which can only be done when we empty ourselves of all self-gratification and fleshly motives. We then become living testimonies of who He is. What we fix our minds on will, undoubtedly, show up on the outside. So, let us fix our minds on who Christ is so we can showcase Him to the world.

Prayer

Heavenly Father, help us to turn away from what is ungodly and impure and fix our minds on what can build us up so that You can use us as a vehicle to spread the gospel of Jesus Christ through dance. In Jesus' name, we pray. Amen.

Call To Action

- Develop a devotional life and build an intimate relationship with God.

- Allow your mind to be conformed to the image of Christ.

- Identify things in your life that need changing so that you can start the process of change.

Gurlain Applewhaite

October 7

SETTING OUR MIND ON THINGS ABOVE

And do not be conformed to this world, but be transformed by the renewing of your mind, that you may prove what is that good and acceptable and perfect will of God. Romans 12:2

All, if not most of us, are familiar with What Would Jesus Do (WWJD). We as Christians must ask that each time we are up against a wall, we operate according not to worldly standards but to God's standards, aligning our actions with the Word of God. We can choose our thoughts, whether they be good or bad. However, we do not have to entertain those ungodly thoughts because we have the ability to "bring every thought into captivity to the obedience of Christ" (2 Corinthians 10:5). We can have a peaceful mind when we bring our thoughts under the control of Christ.

How we interact with each other in ministry demonstrates whether or not we have the mind of Christ. We do not just want to show off how well we can dance, but we want to represent Jesus in our behavior and attitude at all times. We should not compare ourselves to each other, which encourages envy and jealousy. Instead, let us see our true value and model God's love to those we minister to so that love will radiate. When you think like Christ, you will act differently. The more time we spend learning and becoming familiar with His way of living, the more we will change to His way of thinking and acting, and the more we will conform to His image. What a sight it would be to behold as we go out to minister with the love of Christ glowing all over us just as Moses shone from being in God's presence.

Prayer

Father, help us in whatever we do so that we glorify You in our actions and our thoughts. May we each be an example of Christ in our interactions with others. In Jesus' name, we pray. Amen.

Call To Action

Have a thirst and hunger for a deeper relationship with God. Submit your thoughts and desires to God.

Gurlain Applewhaite

October 8

DECLUTTERING OUR MINDS

But when He had turned around and looked at His disciples, He rebuked Peter, saying, "Get behind Me, Satan! For you are not mindful of the things of God, but the things of men." Mark 8:33

When Jesus explained to His disciples about His upcoming suffering, the crucifixion and the accession, Peter was annoyed and started to scold Jesus for saying these things. Jesus then rebuked Him. I honestly believe that Peter meant well. As a disciple, he would not want bad things to happen to Jesus. In life, we may think we know the best plans for ourselves, but we must have our minds in tune with God. On the surface, things may appear to be Godly, but they may run contrary to God's plans for us.

Having a mind of Christ begins with complete surrender to God. We must align our entire beings to the Holy Spirit, starting with our minds, as they control everything we do. The things we see and hear and the company we keep can all impact our mindset.

One may ask, "But how do I develop a mind of Christ?" Through the Holy Spirit, God has given us full access to all we need to live Godly lives. His Word shows us how we should live and interact. We Christians all have access to the mind of Christ through faith. However, we all still lapse into our old mindsets, so there's a chance we will give into sinful ways of life from time to time. To combat our sinful nature, consistency is key. As Christians, we need to renew our minds daily so that our minds can be filled with Christ-like thoughts.

Prayer

Jesus, we open our minds and hearts to You. We ask for forgiveness for not having our minds filled with godly thoughts. We ask You to renew our minds and thank You for granting us the opportunity for daily renewal. In Jesus' name, Amen.

Call To Action

I encourage you to keep your mind filled with things that are Christ-like. Let us allow God to declutter our minds and fill us with Godly thoughts.

Julie Greene

October 9

LESS TALK, MORE ACTION

Therefore everyone who hears these words of mine and puts them into practice is like a wise man who built his house on the rock. Matthew 7:24

Have you ever been in a conversation with someone who talks a good game, but when you watch how they live or behave, it does not align? That's how we appear when we preach the Word or profess our faith in Christ and then act outside of how the Word describes us. Does it mean we need to be perfect to serve God? Absolutely not.

What it does mean is that we have to be open to the sanctification that comes through reading and studying the Word, letting it change us into who God wants us to be. It means confessing our sins when we are in error, so we do not give ourselves or others permission to act out of character. It means falling in love with God so deeply that we want to please Him always. It's normal for us to feel bad when we fall short; it shows how much we care about pleasing Him. We must keep the Word in our hearts and act it out publicly in our lives.

Prayer

Father, renew our minds, let us know You thoroughly and let Your spirit guide us into obedience to Your Word. In Jesus' Name, Amen.

Call To Action

Spend time this week going over scriptures that share the mind of Christ. Just meditate on His Word. Then, get up and live it out.

Laina Jacob

October 10

LIVE UP TO WHO YOU ALREADY ARE

But just as he who called you is holy, so be holy in all you do; for it is written: "Be holy, because I am holy." 1 Peter 1:15-16

When we read this verse, it can be quite daunting if we assume that we are supposed to be perfect because we see so many flaws when we look at ourselves. We cannot even see anyone around us that is perfect. So, what are we supposed to do? The Word actually confirms that we are holy, set apart from the rest of creation. What God is calling us to do is to live up to who we already are.

We should strive to be set apart on this earth, knowing that when we fall, and we will, we just get back up and keep striving because of who we are in Christ. He has set the standard so that we know when we are not meeting it. This is not to make us feel bad but to remind us about what we are striving for and who we are. Let your mindset be what Christ has said about you, and make that your standard.

Prayer

Lord, I want to see myself the way You see me so that if I stumble or fall along this journey of obedience to You, I am clear on where I need to get back to. Lord, I know I can only do it with Your help, so help me, strengthen me. I look to You only in Jesus' Name. Amen.

Call To Action

Find five scriptures in the Bible that speak to who God says you are. Meditate on these scriptures over the week, and let them change your mindset.

Laina Jacob

October 11

GIVE ME THE MIND OF JESUS

Let this mind be in you, which was also in Christ Jesus. Philippians 2:5

What does it mean to have a mind of Christ? Jesus came to glorify the Father, to please God. He even said He came to do His Father's will in John 5:19. If you have not asked God these questions yet, you should: Is dancing Your will for me or am I just doing it because I am good at it? Am I glorifying You with my dance? Are you pleased with me, Lord, when I minister in dance? You see, all these questions point you to the mind of Christ. Jesus wanted to please the Father by doing His will.

According to Paul in 1 Corinthians 9:27, we must beat our bodies into subjection. He did not beat himself, literally, but he disciplined himself not to give in to fleshly desires so that he could do the will of God. We can only know the mind of Christ by reading His Word and doing His will, regardless of how hard it is. Jesus said, "We must seek to please the Father."

It's only through us Christians that the world will see what the mind of Christ is. We must live it out in our day-to-day lives. This is done with a renewed mind like Jesus when He was found in the form of man; he humbled Himself and became obedient unto death (Philippians 2:8).

Prayer

Give me, Lord, the mind of Jesus. Please help me to live it out for all to see.

Call To Action

Bless someone this week by giving them a word of encouragement and doing a favor for them.

Maxine Butcher

October 12

DANCE IN UNITY

In your relationships with one another, have the same mindset as Christ Jesus.
Philippians 2:5

Have you ever felt like you didn't like a dance, a song, or the group of people you're dancing with? You quickly realize that you are a team, and you need your team as much as your team needs you. The mind of Christ puts others first, which is clear to us because He came to die and sacrifice Himself for us.

I realized that I could not be selfish when having the mind of Christ. This mindset requires you to have a servant's heart and be humble and obedient to God. Yes, humility is the way up, and that's God's way. The world may say step on whoever you need to in order to make it to the top, but God taught me to treat others the way I want to be treated. Through His Word, I learned to be like Jesus, and I found that the best way to do anything is God's way. In His honor, we must value one another and put others before ourselves. Remember, Jesus was obedient even unto death.

Prayer

I pray that our relationships with others will demonstrate the mind of Christ. Teach us to put others first. Amen.

Call To Action

Find someone this week to demonstrate the mind of Christ to. Follow Jesus' example of obedience and selflessness, treating others with respect and value.

Maxine Butcher

October 13

MY MIND ISN'T MINE

Let this mind be in you, which was also in Christ Jesus. Philippians 2:5

For who hath known the mind of the Lord, that he may instruct him? But we have the mind of Christ. 1 Corinthians 2:16

My mind isn't mine, I allow the Word of God to renew my mind - "And be not conformed to this world: but be ye transformed by the renewing of your mind, that ye may prove what is good, and acceptable, and perfect, will of God" (Romans 12:2).

My mind isn't mine, I love the Lord with all of it - "Jesus said unto him, Thou shalt love the Lord thy God with all thy heart, and with all thy soul, and with all thy mind" (Matthew 22:37).

My mind isn't mine, I have the mind of Christ - "Let this mind be in you, which was also in Christ Jesus" (Philippians 2:5).

My mind isn't mine, I allow God to instruct me and my mind - "For who hath known the mind of the Lord, that he may instruct him? But we have the mind of Christ" (1 Corinthians 2:16).

My mind isn't mine, I allow the Word of God to guide my thinking - "Finally, brethren, whatsoever things are true, whatsoever things are honest, whatsoever things are just, whatsoever things are pure, whatsoever things are lovely, whatsoever things are of good report; if there be any virtue, and if there be any praise, think on these things" (Philippians 4:8).

Although we have a "mind of our own", our default setting should be one of giving the Holy Spirit the freedom to guide us and filter our thoughts. This way, we will be able to have the mind of Christ in us.

Prayer

Lord, let our disposition be one that looks to You for instructions as we live and dance, guiding our movements and choreographies.

Call To Action

- Submit to God (James 4:7) and allow the Holy Spirit to guide your thoughts.

- Resist the temptations of the enemy to use your mind. (James 4:7).

- Be persistent in your pursuit of God and Godly thoughts. (Philippians 4:8)

Pierre Rock

Call To Action

- Submit to God (James 4:7) and allow the Holy Spirit to guide your thoughts.

October 14

MINDING HIS BUSINESS

*So if there is any encouragement in Christ, any comfort from love,
any participation in the Spirit, any affection and sympathy, complete my joy by
being of the same mind, having the same love, being in full accord and of one
mind. Do nothing from selfish ambition or conceit, but in humility count others
more significant than yourselves. Let each of you look not only to his own interests,
but also to the interests of others. Have this mind among yourselves, which is yours
in Christ Jesus. Philippians 2:1-5*

This scripture sums up where our focus should be; it says it all. Now, let the church say amen. Imagine if our focus could shift from self to minding the things of God. God wants us to be of the same mind, the mind of Christ, putting aside selfish ambitions and conceit. What is the focus of your thoughts? Are they focused on fulfilling God's plan here on earth or have we become too caught up with the things of the world and ourselves?

God's Business:

Love and affection- Are we showing genuine love towards God's people? Are we loving the unlovable?

Sympathy- Are we harsh and unsympathetic towards others? Do we have any awareness of how our actions affect others?

Unity- Are we unified with our brothers and sisters and the members of our ministry? Are we in one accord?

Selflessness- Are we looking out for our brothers and sisters or are we looking out for ourselves? Are we willing to make sacrifices for them? Are our thoughts only about ourselves or about others?

Humility- Do we think too highly of ourselves, placing ourselves on a pedestal and putting others beneath us?

Let's start minding God's business, and if you already are, continue to keep His business at the forefront of your mind.

Prayer

Lord, help me focus on You always, despite all that happens around me. Realign my thoughts to match Yours. In Jesus' Name.

Call To Action

Anytime you realize your focus has shifted, realign your thoughts and remind yourself of what God's business is.

Rheanne Rock

October 15

CHANGE YOUR MIND…CHANGE YOUR LIFE

Casting down imaginations, and every high thing that exalteth itself against the knowledge of God, and bringing into captivity every thought to the obedience of Christ. 2 Corinthians 10:5

Our minds play a major role in our existence. If we could change our minds to having a Christ-like mindset, we could indeed change our lives. The number of thoughts we have in one day is countless. We can start thinking about one thing and then be entranced in a spiral of varying thoughts. But what consumes our thinking, exactly? Is there a pattern? Are we deliberate about what we allow to play out in the "secret life" of our thoughts?

We know that temptation is real, but we can help ourselves to move away from sin by capturing those ungodly thoughts. Only God knows our thoughts, and although we may hide from others, we are not hiding from Him. Don't let your thoughts and imagination get the better of you. Cast down anything that tries to exalt itself against the knowledge of God. Our way of thinking can make or break us.

If we allow ourselves to have a negative mindset, our lives will reflect such. Capture those thoughts…

If we allow ourselves to conjure up ways of revenge and deceit, our lives will reflect such. Capture those thoughts…

If we allow ourselves to take in ungodly information, soak it in and think on these things, our lives will reflect such. Capture those thoughts…

If we could but just change our minds and our thinking, we could change our lives.

Prayer

Lord, help me to change my mindset to be more Christ-like daily. Teach me how to capture every thought that is not of You. In Jesus' Name.

Call To Action

Work on not only capturing the ungodly thoughts but also how quickly you capture them. The longer they fester, the greater the temptation to keep them there.

Rheanne Rock

October 16

FILL MY MIND LORD

In your relationships with one another, have the same mindset as Christ Jesus.
Philippians 2:5

We should aim to think as the Lord thinks. When we think as the Lord thinks, we think good things and will behave in a certain way. As children, we must be careful with what we allow to enter our minds. We should watch Godly television shows and listen to Godly music. This way, we will fill our minds with Godly things. We should also have friends who encourage us to do the right things. The way we behave starts with our minds, so thinking as God thinks is important.

Examples of Godly behavior:

Loving others more than you love yourself - When someone is fretting you, still love them more than you love yourself. If someone falls, instead of laughing, you can help them. If someone is mean to your friend at school, you can be really nice to them. If your sibling teases you at home instead of teasing back, you can be kind.

Be obedient to your parents - If your parents say to clean your room, be obedient to them.

Doing things for God at church - Dancing, singing and preaching at church. Do anything that God wants you to do.

These things can seem hard to do, but once we ask God for help, He will help us. We also have to do our part by reading and praying to Him.

Prayer

Dear Lord, help us to think like You do. Help us to do the right things and don't hurt anyone's feelings. Fill our minds with Godly things and remove any bad things that may be in our minds. Thank You for doing it, Lord. In Jesus' name. Amen.

Call To Action

My challenge for you is to try to always think as God does. Fill your minds with Godly things, as this is the only way to have a mind like His.

Rhema-Jae Greene

October 17

A GODLY MIND

For as he thinketh in his heart, so is he: Eat and drink, saith he to thee; But his heart is not with thee. Proverbs 23:7

Your heart takes part in your thinking, so who or what is your heart focused on? If your heart is on things of the world, your mind will also think of ungodly things. God requires us to have His mind in everything we do or say. If our heart or mind is not on Christ, we will be dancing and not ministering. I heard someone once say, "Dance without God is exercise."

Our minds carry the power to change our outer appearance, and we can only do that if we allow our minds to think like Christ and not like the devil. When God controls our minds, He directs our hearts, and we behave like Him and fulfill His expectations.

I know you might say I have tried and tried, but Hebrews 12:11 says No discipline is enjoyable while it is happening—it's painful! But afterwards, there will be a peaceful harvest of right living for those who are trained in this way. Thinking on Genesis 1:27, as you begin to train your mind to become like the mind of Christ, remember that you will become the image and likeness of God. Use the mind of Christ today so your thoughts will be that of His ways.

Prayer

Lord, I pray my heart and mind will always be on You, and as I begin to look like You, my life will become what You have planned for it in the name of Jesus. Amen.

Call To Action

- Let your heart be of Jesus.

- Let your mind change your appearance.

- Be disciplined in keeping your mind on Christ.

Rhonda. A. Babb

October 18

A TALE OF TWO MINDS

For who hath known the mind of the lord, that he may instruct him? But we have the mind of Christ. 1 Corinthians 2:16

A mind is a terrible thing to waste, so often, my mind goes haywire. Sometimes, the most hateful things can come to mind during fits of anger, despair or rebellion, whether I am angry at God, a friend or a family member. I sometimes get despondent because God "took long" to "show up" or I didn't obey His words. I waste time thinking about how particular situations could have gone better and wishing they would have been another way and not God's way (which is always the better way). These thoughts are not pleasing to God, which tells me it is time to renew my mind.

It is time to think as God intended when I accepted Him into my life, for if I am born again, then the same spirit that raised Christ from the dead dwells in me. Christ is God's, and we are Christ's, so we should meditate on what is true, honest, just, pure and lovely. We cannot show who Christ is if we are angry without a righteous cause, show despair when our plans are not God's plans for us or rebel against God. God's plans and purpose for mankind should be our plans and purpose. We must win souls for His Kingdom and walk in His purpose for our lives so that He can receive all the glory, honor and praise. We must have the mind of Christ.

Prayer

Our loving savior, thank You for dying for our sins and sending your Holy Spirit to live in us. We ask You, Lord, to help us daily in this walk with You. Renew our minds. Help us as we read Your Word to discern what the Spirit of the Lord is saying, and help us to keep our minds focused on You. In Jesus' name, Amen.

Call To Action

Seek God daily for the renewing of your mind.

Sandra Britton

October 19

SHAPING OUR THOUGHTS

Be careful how you think; your life is shaped by your thoughts. Proverbs 4:23

In 1 Corinthians 2:16, Paul focuses on the change that has been made in a believer's life because we have received God's Holy Spirit. This change affects everything about us, including our minds! In addition, Proverbs 4:23 reminds us to be careful how we think because our thoughts can shape our lives.

We, as believers, must be mindful of our thoughts, as we know they can wander at times. If I am not mindful, I can often start to overthink very quickly, which means that I am not trusting and believing that God has me covered. As the loving Father He is, He needs us to depend on Him, just like we would depend on our earthly father. Having a mind of Christ encourages us to depend on His guidance and not lean on our own abilities.

Although I am in a dance group, I sometimes minister by myself at my church or with other groups within the church. I often had to lean on God's guidance when choosing a song to minister to. My mind would be all over the place, and I would second-guess if the song was suitable. So I would say WWJD, "What Would Jesus Do?" As I began to think about all that He has done for me and His promises, the clarity of my choice of song and dance moves would take shape. Having a mind of Christ is critical for shaping our thoughts and guiding us through life.

Prayer

Heavenly Father, I thank You for the gift of Your Holy Spirit. We pray that we will have the mind of Christ and be mindful that we do not take matters into our own hands as we depend on You daily. In Jesus' name, Amen.

Call To Action

Let us try to be intentional in letting go and letting God.

Shandi Browne

October 20

FROM OLD TO NEW

*Therefore if any man be in Christ he is a new creature, old things are passed away,
Behold all things are new. 2 Corinthians 5:17*

Our beliefs have died with Christ, and we no longer live for our worldly selves;
we have become spiritual. Our death is that of the old sinful nature, which was
nailed to the cross with Christ and buried. Just as The Father raised Him, so are
we raised to walk in the newness of life.

Our old nature includes pride, love of sin, reliance on work, former opinions,
habits, passions and mostly the supreme love of self in the forms of self-
righteousness, self-promotion and self-justification. We now desire to put away
those sins that we held onto, as in Ephesians 4:22-24. We renew our minds,
creating the new believer in verse 24.

A new creation is a wondrous thing formed in the Mind of Christ and created
by His power and for His glory. It looks outwardly towards Christ instead of
inwardly towards self. We receive this when we accept Christ into our lives
by faith. Our newborn souls are now delighted in the things of God, and our
purposes, desires, and understandings become fresh and Godly within our
minds. We are no longer slaves to sin. God changes our desires, outlooks and
priorities as we turn from self-worship to God-worship.

When ministering in dance, each minister should renew their mind, not only
when doing ministry but in everyday life. Our expressions, interpretations and
movements shall tell a story from old to new, from death to life.

Prayer

Beloved Father, please grant us Your peace. Help us to keep our minds fixed on
You so that we will experience a fully renewed body, mind and soul. Lord, I ask
that You remind us of Your love and forgiveness, which grant us a new life in
Jesus' mighty name. Amen.

Call To Action

- Renew your mind daily.

- Present your body as a living sacrifice.

- Focus on knowing God by surrendering yourself daily to the control of the Holy Spirit.

Timeless Ministers

October 21

IT'S IMPORTANT TO HAVE A MIND OF CHRIST

Be very careful, then, how you live not as unwise but as wise, making the most of every opportunity, because the days are evil. Ephesians:15-16

Having a mind of Christ means that we understand God's plan in the world and think like Him. It is important to have a mind of Christ because we were created in God's image, and He wants us to live our lives for Him. The more time we spend learning and becoming familiar with His way of thinking and living, the more our own thoughts and behaviors will change for the better. On the other hand, if we spend most of our time exposed to ungodly teaching and thinking, our behaviors will change to the ungodly ways we have learned. Two ways to keep our minds on God are to read our Bibles consistently and spend time with God. Dancing for Jesus also helps me to keep my mind on Him.

Prayer

Dear Lord, please help me to keep my mind on You and understand You. Set my paths straight, in Jesus' name, I pray, Amen.

Call To Action

When faced with certain decisions you are unsure of, ask yourself, "What would Jesus do?" This will keep you in the mind frame to always think like Christ and help you make wise decisions.

Trinitee Angus

October 22

WWJD (WHAT WOULD JESUS DO?)

And be not conformed to this world: but be ye transformed by the renewing of your mind, that ye may prove what is that good, and acceptable, and perfect, will of God. Romans 12:2

When you become a Christian, your mindset changes. You no longer think the way you used to or react to scenarios in the same manner because you now have a mind of Christ. Your morals and values change, you get a sense of redirection and renewal, and, in many situations, you often ask yourself: "WWJD" - what would Jesus do? The scripture above mentions not conforming to this world as we know it. It shows us that if we have the mind of Christ, we can be transformed and given a fresh mindset. This transformation is according to the perfect and acceptable will of God.

Many of us have sat down and contemplated our actions in certain situations with a friend, a family member or even a fellow minister. In those situations, we had to take a step back and realign our thoughts, words and actions. You see, to have a mind of Christ, we must walk in His shoes, show acts of kindness when someone has done us wrong, turn the other cheek, pray for our enemies and bless them. I know this way of life can be challenging, but every action *does not* deserve a reaction. I challenge you today to be the one who turns the other cheek, to be the one to walk away and let God do the rest. He sees and hears you, brothers and sisters, and He will work it out for you.

Prayer

Dear heavenly Father, help me to fill my mind to be like You, oh God, to understand Your Word fully. I will follow Your will and Your Word to be more like You. Renew my mind and heart, God, so that I may glorify You in everything I do. I pray this for each of my fellow ministers. In Jesus' Name. Amen.

Call To Action

Whenever you are faced with a situation, remind yourself to ask the question, "What Would Jesus Do?"

Zariah Watson

October 23

THAT SPIRITUAL CONNECTION
(POEM)

For who hath known the mind of the Lord, that he may instruct him? But we have the mind of Christ. 1 Corinthians 2:16

It doesn't just start on stage

It starts off

Who you are

What you've allowed yourself to become

Do you seek Him first?

In His word

Do you listen to Him?

A connection with Him has to start within you

You have to want it

Live it

Act on it

Show it

Put to death what is earthly and put on a new self

Your true self

A new foundation

Let Him change your mind and imagine the inevitable.

Zenaida R. Mayers

October 24

PUT IT ON

And do this, knowing the time, that now it is high time to awake out of sleep; for now our salvation is nearer than when we first believed. The night is far spent, the day is at hand. Therefore let us cast off the works of darkness, and let us put on the armor of light. Let us walk properly, as in the day, not in revelry and drunkenness, not in lewdness and lust, not in strife and envy. But put on the Lord Jesus Christ, and make no provision for the flesh, to fulfilll its lusts. Romans 13:11-14

All Christians and believers that are saved want to have the mind of Christ. Having the mind of Christ requires action from us. As the verse says, we have to put on Christ. God has given us guardianship over our minds. We have to cast off the works of darkness. We have to get rid of those things that blind us from the truth. It is like putting dirty clothes on a clean body. After a while, the body will pick up all the dirt from the clothes and will smell. Dancing requires us to put on Christ and have that mindset that we are glorifying God. We are not just doing movement, but we connect to Him when we dance. So, in order for us to put on the mind of Christ we must:

P- Pray daily for the mind of Christ

U- Utilise the Holy Spirt

T- Take off the old man

I- Immerse ourself in the Word

T- Talk to God

O- Obey

N- Never give up

Prayer

Father, today I pray for peace of mind and the gift of Your Holy Spirit. Help us to put on the mind of Christ You have given us as a gift. Let us make that conscious effort to guard our thoughts and lusts of our flesh. In Jesus' Name. Amen.

Call To Action

As we put on clothes every day, we need to put on the mind of Christ daily.

Eslyn Taylor

October 25

WHAT DOES HAVING THE MIND OF CHRIST MEAN?

I did this so you would trust not in human wisdom but in the power of God. Yet when I am among mature believers, I do speak with words of wisdom, but not the kind of wisdom that belongs to this world or to the rulers of this world, who are soon forgotten. 1 Corinthians 2:5-6

The mind of Christ involves wisdom from God, once hidden but now revealed. You and I have the mind of Christ right now! Some of us may realize this, some may not. Some of us may even be surprised by this statement. But if you have a saving faith in Jesus Christ, you have the mind of Christ. If we have been born again, we are a new creation. Yet, new creations that we are, many of us go around using our minds like we did before we came to know Christ.

We're not using the mind of Christ at all; some of us don't even realize that we already have access to this mind of Christ. After we are born again, the believer is under God's influence or at least should be. The Holy Spirit is very important in this process of spiritual development. Paul tells us in Romans 12:2, "Do not be conformed to the patterns of this world, but be transformed by the renewing of your mind".

As dance ministers, we should look at Psalms 150:4: "To rejoice and usher in God's presence". Through our dance and in all we do, we do it for the glory of God. We vow to teach, encourage and inspire others to worship God through the use of movement art. We are not here to entertain, only to minister to others.

Prayer

Father, You are god alone, and we give You all the praise and all the glory. Father, we ask that You renew our minds, and we pray that our minds align with Your will and Your purpose for our lives and our ministry in Jesus' name, Amen.

Call To Action

- Be committed to the ministry through a daily renewing of your mind.

- Develop the mind of Christ for total healing to take place.

- Focus on developing discernment as you connect with God and read the Word.

Laura Phillips

From the Heart of a Dancer

October 26

HAVING THE WISDOM OF CHRIST

Let this mind be in you, which was also in Christ Jesus. Philippians 2:5

When you have the mind of Christ, you think like God. We have access to His wisdom, but not all people tap into it. We can ask God to bless us with the mind of Christ. Another word for having the mind of Christ is having the wisdom of Christ. King Solomon asked God for wisdom, and He was known as the wisest man in the kingdom. In the same way King Solomon seeks God's wisdom, we can also seek it.

In Philippians 2:5, Paul said, "The same mind that is in Christ Jesus should also be in you." Some people might be wondering how they would know if they have the wisdom or mind of Christ. You will know because, in really difficult situations, having a mind of Christ empowers you with solutions. Let's take King Solomon as an example. In 1 Kings 3:16-28, King Solomon had two women, each claiming to be the mother of the same child. With God's gift of wisdom, King Solomon was able to discern the true mother.

Like King Solomon, God helps us through difficult situations, it is up to us to listen to Him or not. Sometimes, it can be difficult to listen to Him. For example, God could be telling you not to buy a house that you think looks wonderful and ticks most of your boxes. Even though that house may look good, God may have an even bigger and better house waiting for you. So, you should obey God no matter the circumstance, it will always turn out to be better in the end!

Prayer

Lord, I thank You for helping me make the right choices. Even though I might not want to, please help me to be obedient. Amen.

Call To Action

Write about any times you made a bad decision and what you could've done better with the mind of Christ.

Shaquonna Rock

October 27

TRANSFORMING THOUGHTS INTO CHRIST-LIKE ACTIONS

Let this mind be in you, which was also in Christ Jesus. Philippians 2:5

When you think like Christ, you behave like Christ. No mind operates on its own; it is fed by a source, just like electricity. Hence why, it is so important to be connected to the Holy Spirit at all times. He causes us to change our language, behaviors and attitudes. He renews our minds daily.

When our minds are not connected to God as its source, we behave in an unholy manner and justify it by saying I am only human. God created us in the image and likeness of Him, which means when people see us, there should be no confusion. We must look like Christ. When we look in a mirror at ourselves, we don't see a reflection of someone else; we see us. Matthew 7:17 says we shall be known by our fruits, and those come directly from God.

The Word of God says so a man thinketh, so is he. As dancers, our mindsets must be of Christ and not of ourselves or the world. God expects our words to reflect a Godly mindset because we are ambassadors for the Kingdom of Heaven. Let us as dancers change the way we think so it influences the way we live and minister. God has ordained us before time to live a life that is pleasing to Him, and in order to do this, we must have the mind of Christ.

Prayer

Lord, help us to change the way our minds work as we stay connected to the source of the Holy Spirit. We shall become better citizens of Your Kingdom as we walk the earth. Amen.

Call To Action

- Connect to the source of God.

- Let your life be a reflection of God.

- Renew your mindset.

Rhonda. A. Babb

October 28

WHO HAS THE MIND OF CHRIST?

For who hath known the mind of the Lord, that he may instruct him? But we have the mind of Christ. 1 Corinthians 2:16

The Apostle Paul, in the book of 1st Corinthians, provides a clear perspective concerning the mind of Christ: the mind of Christ is not like the wisdom of man (verses 5-9), the mind of Christ cannot be understood by those without His Spirit (verses 10-14), and the mind of Christ gives believers discernment in spiritual matters (verse 15).

Therefore, the natural man cannot receive the things of the Spirit of God because they will seem foolish to him, nor can he know them because they are spiritually discerned. In order to have the mind of Christ, one must first accept Jesus as Lord and Saviour by faith. After salvation, the Holy Spirit enlightens the mind of the believer. The believer bears a responsibility to yield to the Spirit's lead and allow the Spirit to transform and renew their mind.

As believers, we cannot assign human motives and understanding to God's actions, as we can develop wrong beliefs about His character and who we are. Our frustration of not understanding can lead us to places of wrong thinking. We must be willing to trade our thoughts, motivations, and attitudes to that of Christ by allowing the Holy Spirit to instruct us. There are many times I have had to surrender my plans, thoughts, and will to Him so that He could instruct me in the way of truth. Having the mind of Christ means sharing the plan, purpose, and perspective of Christ, and it is something that all believers possess.

Every dancer then must ask themselves, "What is filling my mind?" We must dwell on whatsoever is true, honest, just, pure, lovely, of good report, and if there be any praise. We must be willing to trade carnal thinking for spiritual thinking.

Prayer

Dear Lord, help me to think on that which is from and of You and allow the Holy Spirit to instruct me in everything I say and do. In Jesus' name, amen.

Call To Action

Today, I encourage you to align with God's plan for your life. Allow His Holy Spirit to renew your mind and instruct you in everything you say and do.

Sobrina Forde

October 29

UNLOCKING DIVINE WISDOM

For who has known the mind of the Lord, that he may instruct Him? But we have the mind of Christ. 1 Corinthians 2:16

Here, the Apostle Paul was addressing the carnal-minded Corinthians. His teachings were that when a person receives Jesus Christ as Lord, there must be a difference. There must be a change in the way one thinks or behaves. He noted that there is a difference between human wisdom and God's wisdom. His heart for them was that they know the mind of Christ that they may be instructed. Therefore, having the mind of Christ meant having the ability to maintain focus and values like Christ.

As dance ministers, our thoughts can have the power to paralyze us, push us into despair or propel us to victory. They can cause us to know the truth or lead us slowly but steadily down the path of destruction. Scripture tells us, human wisdom is faulty, leading mankind to call good evil and evil good. The ministry of dance calls for focus, so dependency on the Holy Spirit is critical. The dancer must hear God's voice and express His heart through every movement made.

Prayer

Heavenly Father, thank You for the opportunity to express our love to You through dance. We acknowledge, Jesus, that our wisdom alone is not enough, and we need Your wisdom. We thank You that our understanding has been enlightened, and we can now boldly say we have the mind of Christ. Help us to walk in this revelation. In Jesus' Name. Amen.

Call To Action

I encourage each dance minister to first bring every evil thought into captivity, spend time reading God's Word and pray in order to show forth the mind of Christ.

Kishara Green

October 30

BREAKING OLD HABITS

Therefore, if anyone is in Christ, he is a new creation. The old has passed away; behold, the new has come. 2 Corinthians 5:17

What comes to mind when you hear "mind of Christ"? Perhaps being kind to others, turning the other cheek when people hurt and disappoint you, maybe even being slow to anger and quick to extend grace to those around you who may need it. If you agreed with any of these, you'd be correct. But having the mind of Christ doesn't stop there; we can show the mind of Christ by cultivating new habits which enable us to act in a way that is pleasing to God. This means that any bad habits we had before, like lying, stealing, or getting angry, must be traded in for good habits like being truthful, not stealing, and extending grace to others; this is how the mind of Christ shines through us.

It is hard to authentically be dance ministers of God's Word without having the mind of Christ. Yes, we will make mistakes, and sometimes we will miss the mark, but without committing ourselves to actively replacing our bad habits with good ones, our ministry will always be at a disadvantage. Those we are supposed to minister to must not be distracted by our bad habits. We have a Godly role to fulfill. Don't allow yourself to be a distraction.

Prayer

Dear Heavenly Father, I thank You for the opportunity to change for the better and to model my life after You. I pray that I will hold Your actions to the front of my mind before making decisions so that I can be more Christ-like. I pray that through this, I will be a beacon bringing people closer to You; in Jesus' mighty and precious name, Amen.

Call To Action

This week, I challenge you to be aware of your old habits that may not be pleasing to God. Think of ways that you can transform and renew those habits into ones that will please Him.

Gabrielle Blackett

October 31

A KINGDOM MINDSET

For as he thinketh in his heart, so is he: Eat and drink, saith he to thee; But his heart is not with thee. Proverbs 23:7

Our mind is a powerful weapon; if used correctly, we will become like Christ. We sometimes use our thoughts to become evil, this is a representation of the devil. If we think like Christ, then we will behave in a way that models our king of kings, Jesus Christ. Since Christ's mindset was a sacrifice for us, we have to be ready to have a sacrificial mindset for Christ. A kingdom mindset.

Your mind and thoughts do not come from your own self. Your thoughts come from two sources: one is the devil, and the other source is God. To have a Godly mindset, we must ensure that our lives are plugged into the source that is God so we can renew our minds daily to become more like Him. Christ's mindset was one of His Father's will, doing His Father's work, and if we are made in the image and likeness of Our Spiritual Father, we too must be spiritually minded.

When dance ministers understand that how they think is who they become, they dance with knowledge and understanding of who they are in God. Their dance becomes one of God's mind and heart. When Christians put on the mind of Christ, they too become His foot soldiers on the earth for the Kingdom of God, bringing honor and glory to our Father's name wherever we go. There isn't only freedom when you are living with the mind of Christ, but you also become a channel fit for God to use as you walk your Christian journey.

Prayer

Lord, help us to have a mind like you and not ourselves. Let what we think daily in our hearts be pleasing to your heart in Jesus' name. Amen.

Call To Action

- Think like Christ.

- Become Christ's foot soldier.

- Always have on the mind of Christ.

Rhonda. A. Babb

November 1

CONQUERING THE WAR WITHIN

For the desires of the flesh are against the Spirit, and the desires of the Spirit are against the flesh, for these are opposed to each other, to keep you from doing the things you want to do. Galatians 5:17

If you are a child of God, there is a war going on within you, a battle between your natural flesh and the indwelling Spirit of God. Our natural flesh is twisted, corrupt, and opposed to God. The Spirit of Christ living in us is in the process of transforming our desires into holy ones. But our flesh is powerful; it would rather thrive than die. So, we feel the pull toward obedience and righteousness while also feeling the counterpull to appease our flesh with its cravings. Many Christians spend much of their lives struggling to repress their fleshly tendencies. The problem is flesh can't reform flesh. Our fleshly desires need to be put to death. Only by living by the power of the Holy Spirit can we overcome our flesh. The pull of our flesh is strong. But the Spirit is even more powerful. We must exercise faith in the power of the indwelling Holy Spirit to grant us victory over the flesh.

Although believers are made righteous in the sight of God and given the power of the Holy Spirit to overcome sin, all believers still have an old nature, which Paul calls the flesh. Paul says in Romans 7:18 that nothing good dwells in our flesh. Even so, we can still exercise our freedom to choose by obeying the flesh, and that does not mean we will be made unrighteous in the sight of God. It is impossible to undo Jesus' work on the cross by our behavior.

The contrast to making a poor choice to carry out the desire of the flesh is making a good choice to walk in the Spirit. What does that look like? It is when believers, through love, serve one another. Believers who walk by the Spirit won't carry out the desires of the flesh. The Spirit and the flesh are direct enemies; we can't pursue and follow the other. We get to choose, but our choice is binary: we can obey the flesh or the Spirit. There is no third option.

Prayer

Lord, help us to live by Spirit and not by flesh. Help us understand we cannot dwell in both, and we must make that important decision. I pray all believers and non-believers will dwell in the Spirit. In Jesus' name, we pray, Amen.

Call To Action

Have a long, intense conversation with yourself and decide whether you are going to follow the flesh or the Spirit and remember you cannot follow both.

Danae Niles

November 2

DEFEATING OUR FLESH BY GOD'S HOLY SPIRIT

If we live in the Spirit, let us also walk in the Spirit. Galatians 5:25

Crucifying our flesh is always hard, and sometimes it's even painful. Submitting to the desires of our flesh came naturally to us for such a long time, not thinking twice before we spoke or did something, not even feeling conviction about sin. After all, we were all born in sin and shaped in iniquity.

However, having been saved by the grace of God, submitting to our fleshy desires is in the past for us Christians. Holy Spirit now convicts us and shows us right from wrong. We know we will have temptations, but we also know that Christ Jesus has given us the power through him to overcome these temptations. While we may fall sometimes, it's important that we get back up and keep walking in step with the Spirit.

Prayer

Dear Heavenly Father, we call upon You, asking You to cleanse us from all that is not of You. We ask that You forgive us when we stumble or fall, and we thank You for being a loving Father who is there to pick us up. Thank You for sending Your Son to die on the cross so that we can receive the gift of Your Holy Spirit. In Jesus' Name. Amen.

Call To Action

Let us choose to always walk in the Spirit and not give in to our fleshly desires. I know those desires can sometimes be strong, but we know that our God is all-powerful. Remember that with every temptation, God has made a way of escape that will bring you out of it victoriously. God can help us through any temptations that we might be struggling with. All we have to do is call on Him, and He will guide us through.

Danielle Harewood

November 3

GUIDED BY THE HOLY SPIRIT

For if you live according to the flesh, you will die; but if by the Spirit you put to death the misdeeds of the body, you will live. Romans 8:13

According to the Oxford Dictionary, flesh is known as the soft part of a person or animal's body between the bones and skin. Dancing in the flesh is when dancers use choreographed movements because they are instructed to without any meaning behind them and because it goes well with the music. This type of dancing is normally associated with people who dance in the world. We, as ministers in dance, may succumb to the worldly music and movements of these types of dances. We may try these dances without knowing the meaning behind them.

We should dance in the Holy Spirit, such as in the presence of God, to carry out His message. Dancing in the Spirit is when a worshipper or dancer closes his/her eyes to allow the Holy Spirit to guide him/her. This dance is not usually choreographed. Dancing in the Spirit is a manifestation of the Holy Spirit in a believer. This experience happens once the worshipper is attuned to the presence of God, allowing the Spirit to take control of physical motion along with spiritual and emotional being.

Dancing in the Spirit is distinct from choreographed social dancing and orchestrated dancing. Dancers should know that they are picked out by God to change the atmosphere and to carry out a message, but within that, we must dance in the Spirit and not flesh.

Prayer

Heavenly Father, thank You for this talent that You have given us. We ask that You speak to us about how we should use dance according to Your will. Help us to dance only by Your Spirit so we can always carry out Your message. In Jesus' name, I pray, Amen.

Call To Action

As an individual in ministry, although you have a choreographed dance, always ask God for His guidance and let His will be done.

Denmarie Alleyne and Rianna Taylor

November 4

NOT ME, BUT YOU

*For the flesh lusteth against the Spirit, and the Spirit against the flesh: and these
are contrary the one to the other: so that ye cannot do the things that ye would.*
Galatians 5:17

Why is it so tough to live a Christian life? When you ask someone why he
or she is not a Christian, the response is that it is hard. As the verse says, the
flesh lusteth against the Spirit and the Spirit against the flesh. The word lust
describes the nature of humans that opposes the Holy Spirit. In essence, the
flesh and Spirit are always at war, which is why it's "hard" to live a Christian
life. It is not impossible, but the battle that rages between the flesh and the
Spirit is a daily one.

Fighting against our flesh can happen as dance ministers. I remember I was at
a birthday party, and I was a big hip-hop fan back in the day. So, this one song
came on and I found myself wanting to dance and sing. I had to check myself
quickly and remember what I was feeding my Spirit. I am not saying that you
cannot listen to hip-hop, but if we allow the flesh to lust after it more and more,
we are acting contrary to the will of God for our lives. Therefore, by growing in
the Holy Spirit, we can overcome the lusts of the flesh. Our lives should be one
of "Not me, but You Lord".

Prayer

Father, thank You for the Holy Spirit You have given us to finish the race. You
knew it would not be easy, so You left Your Comforter. Continue to be my
guide as my flesh wars against Your Spirit. I thank You for continually fighting
our battles. Not my will but Yours. Amen.

Call To Action

Every morning when you wake, say three times to start your day: "Not my will,
but Yours, Lord."

Eslyn Taylor

November 5

SPIRIT LEAD ME

Watch and pray that ye enter not into temptation: the Spirit indeed is willing, but the flesh is weak. Matthew 26:41

Temptation, Temptation, Temptation. There are about 28 verses about temptation in the Bible, which signifies that this is a major battle in any Christian's life. Because of this Flesh vs Spirit tug of war, Matthew says we have to watch and pray that we do not enter into temptation. The Spirit is always ready to ensure that we do not get into temptation, but the flesh is weak. Remember when Jesus asked the disciples to come and pray with Him? They said yes, but Jesus came and found them sleeping. That is the perfect example of a willing spirit against weak flesh.

God always has a plan to help us fight temptation. We have to watch out for temptation and not put ourselves in positions to be tempted. Nevertheless, if we find ourselves in a tempestuous situation, He says to pray that we may not enter into temptation. In this Christian life, we have to ask the Spirit to lead us. Even in dance and choreography, we must ask the Spirit to lead because our flesh might want to do something totally different.

Spirit lead me every day,

I know you will make a way.

For any temptation I may face,

With Jesus, I can win this race.

My Flesh and Spirit may be at war

But like a lion, I will roar.

Prayer

Abba Father, I thank You for Your Spirit that will lead me. I pray that as my Spirit is willing, You will strengthen my flesh. May You continue to be that source that guides every aspect of my life and whatever temptation comes my way that You, oh Lord, have a way of escape. In Jesus', name, Amen.

Call To Action

Allow the Spirit to lead you in any decision you make today. It might be as small as buying an item or as big as setting up a new business. Let Him lead.

Eslyn Taylor

November 6

DR. JEKYLL & MR. HYDE

Whoever sows to please their flesh, from the flesh will reap destruction; whoever sows to please the Spirit, from the Spirit will reap eternal life. Galatians 6:8

Who are you? No, who are you really? Who are you when the lights are off, and no one is watching? Is this person someone that God would be proud of? If the answer to the last question is no, then it's ok. You are in the right place. Life is a learning experience, and those who are committed to a life of bettering themselves and serving Christ are burdened with the knowledge of right and wrong and what makes Jesus proud. Keeping up appearances may seem like the right choice at first, especially if you are trying to straddle the line between following the world and following Christ, but in the end, you are severing your ties to the Spirit.

Consider the story of Dr. Jekyll and Mr. Hyde. Dr. Jekyll could be likened to our Spirit, the good side of us, while Mr. Hyde is our flesh, the parts of us that should cling to God a little tighter. In the end, Mr. Hyde is behind every bad event, and this consumes Dr. Jekyll because he is stronger than the good inside Dr. Jekyll. If we are not careful, we can fall into the same fate. It is important, as dancers and ministers, to always make sure that our hearts and spirits are tuned into the voice of God so that the moral and good parts of us outshine and consume what bad there might be inside of us because, let's be real, no one is perfect.

Prayer

Dear God, I know that I cannot serve two masters and that I must not have two faces if I want to be an asset to Your Kingdom. I pray that You will help me to only have one face and that one face is who You want me to be. Remove any hindrance. In Jesus' name, I pray, Amen.

Call To Action

This week, focus on who you are when no one else is looking. In your alone times with God, ask Him to remove any masks hindering your purpose.

Gabrielle Blackett

November 7

A TALE OF TWO CITIES

The heart is deceitful above all things, And desperately wicked; Who can know it?
Jeremiah 17:9

Right and wrong, good and bad, left and right, heaven and hell; these polar opposites seem to define our lives, how we interact with our environment and our choices. The world tells you to follow your heart in all your pursuits, and while this is good advice, we must not rely solely on our hearts. You see, our hearts are not innately "good," automatically knowing to follow the right path. Sometimes, our hearts can deceive us. Our hearts may not always tell us to do what God wants us to; instead, they may tell us to follow our fleshly desires. But how do we trust something that can deceive us at any point? The best we can do is submit ourselves to God, tune our ears to His heart, and follow His desires, not the desires of our flesh.

As ministers of God's Word, we must make sure that our hearts are always in alignment with His Spirit and heart instead of our own. We must be cognizant of the fact that what we do in our day-to-day lives affects the kingdom of God, not just our ministry. We should not be hypocritical as we do not want to be someone's reason for resenting the Kingdom of God.

Prayer

Gracious and heavenly Father, open my spiritual eyes and ears so that I can operate in my God-assigned ministry. May I never be a hindrance to Your Kingdom because my flesh is stronger than my Spirit, but may my Spirit be always stronger than my flesh. Amen.

Call To Action

Examine your daily practices. Are you leaning on your flesh or your spirit? Are you actively keeping your connection to God well-fed and strong? Look at how you could strengthen your connection to your spirit, and weaken the relationship with your flesh.

Gabrielle Blackett

November 8

PUTTING ON THE LORD JESUS

I say then: Walk in the Spirit, and you shall not fulfill the lust of the flesh. For the flesh lusts against the Spirit, and the Spirit against the flesh and these are contrary to one another, so that you do not do the things that you wish. Galatians 5:16

In any battle, the stronger side wins, the one in which we often have placed our trust and confidence. If we say the Holy Spirit leads us, then we must be prepared to hear, listen and obey. It takes practice, but the more we listen and pay attention, the more we can discern when the Spirit is speaking to us as opposed to our own thoughts. Everything that seems good does not necessarily come from the Spirit. It could be what we desire, but it may not be of the Spirit.

Dancers must be able to flow in the anointing, discern what God is saying to the group and the church as a whole, and intercede on its behalf. If there are any disagreements within the ministry, they must be dealt with as soon as possible, for it is impossible to minister unto the Lord effectively when there is hurt and disillusionment. Even if we are the injured party, we must not cause further conflict or division in the ministry. It should be our desire never to portray any behavior that does not glorify God and is certainly indicative of operating in the flesh. This also includes the way we move and how we dress when we are ministering. Make every effort to glorify God in all ways.

Prayer

Dear Lord, we thank You for giving us the Holy Spirit to teach us and show us how we should live. Lord, You say that Your sheep hear Your voice. You know them, and they follow You. Help us recognize Your voice and be obedient so we may please You in all ways. In Jesus' name, we pray. Amen.

Call To Action

- Be a house of prayer.

- Be sensitive to the promptings of the Holy Spirit.

- Imitate the life of Christ, so you don't follow your own desires

Gurlain Applewhaite

November 9

THE STRUGGLE IS REAL

I have been crucified with Christ; it is no longer I who live, but Christ lives in me; and the life which I now live in the flesh I live by faith in the Son of God, who loved me and gave Himself for me. Galatians 2:20

Some of us may have thought that with water baptism, all the cares, concerns, fears, bad behaviors and attitudes were also washed away. The truth is that when Christ was crucified, He took all of our sins with Him. And just as He rose from the dead, we also were raised into the newness of life. But the old desires did not just disappear, they resulted in a constant struggle because what the flesh desires is opposed to the Spirit's leadership in our lives.

We acknowledge that God's purpose is for us to be like Jesus, and we can work towards it through the power of the Holy Spirit. How do we get to be like Jesus? We immerse ourselves in God's Word and check that we are living a godly lifestyle in accordance with the Word. Being in the ministry is not all about skill and talent. It is about not yielding to our former lusts and desires but renewing our minds and having an intimate relationship with God.

The message which permeates throughout the Bible is love: love for God and love for our neighbour. When we operate in love, then we make no provision for our evil desires when they show up because our love for God transcends all. We have the ability to do what is right through the Holy Spirit, but we fail if we try to do it through our own strength. God is love, and when we walk in love, it creates an atmosphere that draws others to be what God desires of us all.

Prayer

Heavenly Father, we submit all our plans and decision-making and ask that You take charge so that everything will be done in accordance with Your will. Prune, purge, mould and shape us so that we may be vessels of honor and produce good fruit. In Jesus' name. Amen.

Call To Action

- Crucify your sinful desires and yield to the Spirit daily.

- Feed on the Word.

- Fellowship with believers regularly for support.

Gurlain Applewhaite

Call To Action

- Crucify your sinful desires and yield to the Spirit daily.

- Feed on the Word.

November 10

FILL ME WITH YOUR SPIRIT

For the flesh desires what is contrary to the Spirit, and the Spirit what is contrary to the flesh. They are in conflict with each other, so that you are not to do whatever you want. Galatians 5:17

This verse pushes us to examine our fleshly desires. What is it that you like to do that satisfies a particular desire? As Christians, we should desire the things of the Spirit and not things of the flesh. The verse ends by saying, "You are not to do whatever you want". This implies that there is a battle going on. In life, we want to do what is right, but because of our sinful nature, we have to ask God for continuous help in this battle.

We are both body and spirit. Unless we allow the Holy Spirit to help us and be transformed by Him, we will be operating in the old man. Thank God for His salvation that enables us to overcome the desires of the flesh. Matthew 26:41 shows us the Spirit is willing, but the flesh is weak. We need to fill our spiritual appetite and deny our fleshly desires. Whichever one you feed is the one that will dominate.

It is important that we say no to temptations and reject our sinful desires, whatever they may be. We then need to feed the Spirit daily by reading and obeying His Word and having daily conversations with Him. In fact, the more we allow God to be a part of our daily lives, the more natural it is to follow His leadership. So, even talking to Him multiple times a day strengthens that consciousness of living with God and choosing Spiritual upliftment over fleshly destruction.

Prayer

Father, in the name of Jesus, help us to die to flesh daily. Help us to resist the many temptations that will come our way. Forgive us for the times we gave in to the temptations. Hold our hands and guide us as You are so willing to do. Amen.

Call To Action

Let us make up our minds to die daily to flesh. Let us put aside time in our schedules to feed the spirit. The Holy Spirit is willing and ready to help us. Find at least one person who would offer support to help you when you feel weak.

Julie Greene

November 11

WHO'S REALLY IN CHARGE

Those who are dominated by sinful nature think about sinful things, but those who are controlled by the Holy Spirit think about things that please the Spirit.
Romans 8:5

If you're not fighting daily to keep your sinful nature under control, might I suggest you go deeper in God? As ministers, we cannot get "5 minutes", nor do we get a break from being a light, being salt, being Jesus' hands and feet. So what do you do when it is tempting to say that mean thing that would destroy the other person and cause you to win the argument? What about when someone hurts you deeply, and you want to hurt them right back? Are there situations where you could help but choose not to? Do you make the gifts God has given you available to His people, or does it depend on your mood and feeling at the time? These are daily questions and battles we face while striving to be more like Christ. It is difficult, but God has given us the Holy Spirit to help us in these situations; all we need to do is take the help that is offered.

We must let the enemy know who is in control of our lives, and he has to understand that it is not him. As we grow in Christ, the battles may get harder, but remember who you are and who is in control of you. Let the Holy Spirit do His work in you. He will always give you a way out, He promised.

Prayer

Father, You know it is impossible for me to fight the enemy on my own, but I thank You for sending me a helper. Help me to tune my ears to Your Holy Spirit so that I may listen and be obedient to His counsel. I declare that You are in control of my life. I give myself fully to You and leave no room for anything else, in Jesus' Name. Amen.

Call To Action

This week, go about your day conscious of the Holy Spirit; I mean, talk to Him aloud (don't mind what people think). Note over the week the times He helped when you asked and the ways He kept you from succumbing to your fleshly desires.

Laina Jacob

November 12

SELFISHNESS VS. SELFLESSNESS

Don't be selfish; don't try to impress others. Be humble, thinking of others as better than yourselves. Philippians 2:3

If you are in dance ministry, even one day, you know that ministry is not about you. You show up late, you abuse people's time, you don't show up, and some part of the choreography can't be finished, or the dancers in the piece must go over it because you missed it. The dance minister connected to the vine knows that you must think about others in ministry if God's glory is going to be shown and if you are really going to exhibit the selfless character of God. Similarly, if we operate by the Spirit, we follow the lead of the Lord, and the flesh does not have the opportunity to take control.

When we are Spirit-led, we think of others and don't focus on 'I' so much. We are clear that it is not about us but about His kingdom. Conversely, if we are not behaving in this manner, the flesh is reigning. The more we allow the spirit room to lead us, the less opportunity we have for the flesh to gain ground, and this is one of the ways we grow in Christ. It is not about how we look to others but how we please God.

Prayer

Lord, I ask that You remove every Spirit in me that would want to exalt self. I humble myself before You and ask that You lead me to always be of service to others as You lend me breath. I want to stay grateful, Lord. I want to stay humble, hear Your voice and allow Your sweet Holy Spirit to lead me. In Jesus' Name, Amen.

Call To Action

What things do you have on your agenda for this week? Give some advance thought to show your consideration for those you have to interact with. What are the practical ways you can put others first this week? Plan for it and put that plan into action.

Laina Jacob

November 13

PUT ON YOUR RUNNING SHOES

For he that soweth to his flesh shall of the flesh reap corruption; but he that soweth to the Spirit shall of the Spirit reap life everlasting. Galatians 6:8

Remember Joseph and Potiphar's wife? Joseph was of the Spirit, but Potiphar's wife was of the flesh. We have heard this story so many times, but have we ever stopped to think about how Joseph felt? He was a young man, far away from home, family and friends, and he was missing his father and younger brother Benjamin. Then, in steps Mrs Potiphar, offering herself to Joseph. You would think under these lonely circumstances, Joseph would give in, but he refused because he wanted to please God and have God's Word fulfilled in his life. His thought process may have been like Genesis 39:9, which says, "How can I do this great wickedness and sin against God?". He was walking in the Spirit and did not give in to the flesh. If we sow to the flesh, as the text says, we will, from the flesh, reap corruption.

As dancers, we must keep our bodies clean and live a Spirit-filled life because "Your body is a temple of the Holy Spirit, who is in you", according to 1 Corinthians 6:19. We must not give in to the flesh and defile our bodies so that we can dance from the Spirit. Remember the daughter of Herodias, in Matthew 14:6-8, who danced for the head of John the Baptist? This is dancing in the flesh at its highest because it was led by vengefulness. When we dance in the Spirit, we bring Glory to God. We can sow to the Spirit by reading God's Word, worshipping and praying daily, and building a relationship with God. Like David, let us please God by dancing in the Spirit.

Prayer

Lord, may You teach me how to walk in the Spirit, and may I walk accordingly.

Call To Action

Get to know the voice of the Holy Spirit and follow His leading.

Maxine Butcher

November 14

SOUL TO SURFACE

Watch ye and pray, lest ye enter into temptation. The Spirit truly is ready, but the flesh is weak. Mark 14:38

That which is born of the flesh is flesh; and that which is born of the Spirit is Spirit. John 3:6

It is the Spirit that quickeneth; the flesh profiteth nothing: the words that I speak unto you, they are Spirit, and they are life. John 6:63

Dearly beloved, I beseech you as strangers and pilgrims, abstain from fleshly lusts, which war against the soul. 1 Peter 2:11

Our senses generally have us thinking in the now. We want what we want in that moment. However, if we are denied that instant gratification or we decide to wait a little longer, the instant urge for that thing generally reduces or dissipates altogether. We can classify this way of thinking as *outside-in*, from surface to soul; our flesh is the dominant factor.

What we want is the reverse of this way of thinking. We need to go from outside-in to *inside-out* thinking. This way of thinking in a Spirit-dominant way leads to decision-making that accounts for factors beyond the now. It goes from sight and seeing what's in front of you to vision and seeing what's beyond you. It is not dominated by our senses or flesh, but by our Spirit when we submit to the Holy Spirit's leading.

We can nurture and prepare our Spirit for dominance by reading the Word, and watching and praying to avoid temptation when it tries to surface (Mark 14:38). We can accomplish Spirit dominance by abstaining from fleshly lusts while feeding our Spirit through the Word, prayer, devotions and worship dancing to list a few methods.

Prayer

Help us to watch, pray and feed our Spirit so that we may avoid and/or overcome temptations. Renew our thinking that it may be Spirit dominant going from soul to surface.

Call To Action

This week:

- Feed your Spirit with the Word of God.

- Follow the lead of the Holy Spirit regarding a song.

- Focus on a mini choreography of the song the Holy Spirit led you to choose.

Pierre Rock

November 15

LIFE IN THE SPIRIT

For to be carnally minded is death; but to be spiritually minded is life and peace.
Romans 8:6

Scripture	Flesh	Spirit
Romans 8:1	Condemnation	**No Condemnation**
Romans 8:2 & 6	Bondage/Sin/Death	**Freedom/Life/Peace**
Romans 8:14-15	Spirit of fear	**Spirit of adoption**
Galatians 5:16	Lust of the flesh	**Walk in the Spirit**
Galatians 6:8	Reap corruption	**Reap life everlasting**

"There is therefore now no condemnation to them which are in Christ Jesus, who walk not after the flesh, but after the Spirit" (Romans 8:1).

"For the law of the Spirit of life in Christ Jesus hath made me free from the law of sin and death" (Romans 8:2). "For they that are after the flesh do mind the things of the flesh; but they that are after the Spirit the things of the Spirit. For to be carnally minded is death; but to be spiritually minded is life and peace" (Romans 8:5-6).

"For as many as are led by the Spirit of God, they are the sons of God. For ye have not received the Spirit of bondage again to fear; but ye have received the Spirit of adoption, whereby we cry, Abba, Father" (Romans 8:14-15).

"This I say then, walk in the Spirit, and ye shall not fulfill the lust of the flesh" (Galatians 5:16).

"For he that soweth to his flesh shall of the flesh reap corruption; but he that soweth to the Spirit shall of the Spirit reap life everlasting" (Galatians 6:8).

In this battle of flesh versus Spirit, we must speak life at all times, "Death and life are in the power of the tongue: and they that love it shall eat the fruit thereof" (Proverbs 18:21). If we want to enjoy the things of the Spirit, we must speak the things of the Spirit. However, first of all, we must renew our minds (Romans 12:2) to create a healthy environment for thinking and speaking life.

Prayer

Help us, Lord, to speak life in our dancing movements so that we may enjoy the fruit thereof.

Call To Action

Practice speaking and dancing life in your choreographies through your stage positioning, facial expressions, and movements.

Pierre Rock

November 16

THIS IS HARD!

For I know that good itself does not dwell in me, that is, in my sinful nature. For I have the desire to do what is good, but I cannot carry it out. For I do not do the good I want to do, but the evil I do not want to do—this I keep on doing. Now if I do what I do not want to do, it is no longer I who do it, but it is sin living in me that does it. Romans 7:18-20

I don't know about you, but I can completely identify with Paul in this scripture. Every day is a battle, an ongoing battle of flesh vs spirit. Which will be defeated? We are human beings with a sinful nature, trying to be holy. No wonder Paul said he does not do the good he wants to do but does the evil he does not want to do. It is so easy to do what is sinful. It's easy to "tell off" that person who wronged us. It's easy to lie to avoid shame, to not forgive, to commit sexual sins, and to get angry. On the other hand, saying no to sin and ungodly living is hard. Unfortunately, this battle will continue as long as we live, so how do we survive? How do we get back up if we stumble?

Our relationship with God is paramount in overcoming sin. Because of our sinful nature, we need the one who is sinless to overcome. A relationship with God is what we need to help us in this daily fight. Imagine you have two cups, one called godliness, the other sinfulness. If we expose ourselves to the lusts of the world, we are pouring into our sin cup. However, if we constantly expose ourselves to the things of God, we will fill up our Godliness, and it will constantly overflow in us.

Truthfully, this battle never ends, and if you mess up, trip up and fall flat on your face, don't tap out in defeat. Start to fill up that Godliness cup. Read the Word, pray, worship, fast, fellowship with believers, listen to sermons, and keep refilling that Godliness cup.

Prayer

Lord, I thank You for always providing a way to escape when we are tempted. Cleanse our hearts, minds and bodies. In Jesus' Name.

Call To Action

Spend more time on the things of God and fill that cup up.

Rheanne Rock

November 17

YOUR SPIRIT LORD

So I say, walk by the Spirit, and you will not gratify the desires of the flesh.
Galatians 5:16

In this verse, God reminds us to walk in a Godly fashion. You can walk Godly by:

Being polite - When you ask for something, you can say please can I have this and when the person gives you, you can say thank you. When you don't say please and thank you, you can hurt the person's feelings, and the person might not give it to you again.

Sharing with others - If you get a toy from someone, you can share it with someone else who has always wanted one. If you do not share with others, you can make them angry, upset, sad, or you can hurt their feelings.

Being obedient - When an adult says that you can only go on a device for an hour, obey them. If you follow the flesh, you will want to be disobedient.

Loving others - When your sibling or anyone is sad, you can do things to make them happy. To walk in the flesh means you may ignore them, which is not Godly.

It can be hard to walk in the Spirit, but God gave us a Book which shows us how to get it done. His Word gives us guidance, so we have to read it and live what it says daily. This way, it will not be so hard, and it will be worth it in the long run.

Prayer

Dear Lord, help us to follow You and not the flesh. Help us walk in a Godly way and do the right things. In Jesus' name. Amen.

Call To Action

My challenge for you is to follow the Spirit and ignore the flesh. It may be hard, but it is way better to obey God and not please the devil.

Rhema-Jae Greene

November 18

THE STRONGER FORCE SHALL WIN

The sinful nature wants to do evil, which is just the opposite of what the Spirit wants. And the Spirit gives us desires that are the opposite of what the sinful nature desires. These two forces are constantly fighting each other, so you are not free to carry out your good intentions. Galatians 5:16-21

It says two forces are fighting against each other. These two forces are your flesh and the Holy Spirit. The Holy Spirit takes up His position after you receive salvation, which means you would have to fight alone if there was no salvation. There is a difference when you are connected with the Holy Spirit. Your life now has a new meaning and begins to transform. The former things you used to do now become distasteful as the Spirit begins to move in and through you. So, things like swearing, lies and sexual immorality, which are things of the flesh, begin to fight against holiness, righteousness and purity, which represent things of the Spirit.

Paul says in Romans chapter 7:19-20, when you do wrong, it's not you that does wrong it's the sin in you, so you need to get rid of the sin. This can only happen if the Holy Spirit is living in you. Jesus Christ gives you the power to win this battle against your flesh. In your own strength, you are weak, as Paul says. You want to do right, but that sinful nature keeps you in bondage.

Even as a dance minister, having your life controlled by sin can be very dangerous. When you begin to minister, whatever you pour out is what each person will receive. They receive what your flesh produces and not what the fullness of the Spirit produces, so you must keep your temple clean at all times. Feed your Spirit with the Word of God so it will win the battle over the flesh.

Prayer

Dear God, help us to obey the Spirit of God so we can live in the Spirit. Let our flesh be subject to Your Spirit in Jesus' name, Amen.

Call To Action

- Be connected to the Holy Spirit.

- Obey the Spirit.

- Keep your temple clean.

Rhonda. A. Babb

November 18

THE BATTLE IS REAL

So I say, let the Holy Spirit guide your lives. Then you won't be doing what your sinful nature craves. Galatians 5:16

The one who is the strongest wins, and he must be both physically and mentally strong. Endurance and stamina are key components for your Spirit to win this battle. These characteristics give you the strength to get up and go again when you have fallen, though this is no excuse to sin repeatedly. Your flesh becomes weaker if you don't give in to it. It is very important to allow the Holy Spirit to be in charge of your life.

Heed the word of James 1:22. But don't just listen to God's Word, you must do what it says. Otherwise, you are only fooling yourself. In order for the Spirit to win this battle, you must not only hear the Word, but you also have a responsibility to obey the Word. Do not become foolish, but be wise in choosing which side will win in the battle between the flesh and the spirit. The side you feed the most will win, so decide today what you will do.

A dance minister must live a life pleasing to God in order to win this battle. Let the Holy Spirit be the person in charge of you and not your flesh, so when you worship, you will worship in Spirit and in truth, according to John 4:24. You can win this battle.

Prayer

Lord, enable me to win the battle against the flesh. Give me the strength to fight when I am weak. In Jesus' name, Amen.

Call To Action

- Obey the Word of God.

- Be wise and not foolish.

- Feed your spirit regularly.

Rhonda. A. Babb

November 19

DEAD OR ALIVE

For when we were in the flesh, the motions of sins, which were by the law, did work in our members to bring forth fruit unto death. Romans 7:5

WANTED! The warrant has been posted for all to see. He can run, but he can't hide, and sooner or later, the law will catch up with him, especially if he continues living this way. Choosing the wrong path in life can lead to destruction, and it brings turmoil along with it. From the time he knew himself, he made one bad choice after another. It didn't matter who he hurt, he just wreaked havoc wherever he went with no regard for life or even death when it stared him in the face. Once his cravings were satisfied, you could "talk chalk"; he was in hog heaven.

But no one is above the law, and he thinks he can do as he pleases without repercussions. He wants to become a law unto himself. Hmmm, there is no way that he can get away with this. He must answer to someone who is above the law, above reproach and blameless. Who is that perfect one? Who will be his redeemer? He is still alive and all is not lost. Once there is life, there is hope, and there can be a turnaround. He just needs to see it and recognize that he can change and get over that slave mentality that has him bound to repeat his mistakes. There must be someone who is rooting for him, someone who can look at him with love and open arms to let him know that change is possible. I know who he can call, Trinity.

All of his troubles will vanish away. There is a way to turn things around. He just needs to see it their way, and once he repents and brings himself under subjection to their way of doing things, the law cannot hold him. Let's hope that he says yes to Trinity. I did.

Prayer

Father, everything is perfect in You; without You, we are nothing. We bring our bodies to You as a holy and acceptable sacrifice in Jesus' name. Amen.

Call To Action

You can overcome the flesh, so pray and will it under subjection to the will of God.

Sandra Britton

November 20

QUIERO VIVIR (I WANT TO LIVE)

But now we are delivered from the law, that being dead wherein we were held;
that we should serve in newness of Spirit, and not in the oldness of the letter.
Romans 7:6

To live in Christ and to die is gain. Living in the Spirit is not an easy task. Then again, this walk with God is not easy either, but it sure beats living a life that will bring nothing but damnation. I thought that when I accepted Christ into my life, it would be a breeze, but I was wrong on all fronts. Everything seemed hard, and I felt like I had made the wrong decision. I can boldly say today that I did not! Through trials, errors and a determined attitude, I chose to live and not die.

Let's be real for a moment. Killing your flesh daily is no easy task, but it is necessary if we call ourselves children of God. God is Spirit, and if we indeed are children of God, then we must let the Spirit push through that mass of flesh and live according to what God already had planned for us long ago. We must choose whom we will serve. Will we let the flesh get the better of us and, when we die, go to the pit of hell, or will we strengthen our spirit man by doing the things we ought to do? We know right from wrong, but some of us want to give credence to the flesh, let it control us, and then ask God to forgive us. God is not mocked; we are still living in the flesh. Now, don't misunderstand me; things happen, and everything is a process, but at some point, the milk stops curdling, and the scent is unbearable, so it is discarded.

We serve a God who is forgiving, loving and merciful and still wants you in His kingdom. Accept Him today, and He will help you in this walk.

Prayer

Father, I am a sinner and believe that Your Son Jesus Christ died for my sins. Forgive me, Lord, and come into my heart and make me new in Jesus' name, Amen.

Call To Action

Repent to live.

Sandra Britton

November 21

BEAUTY IS ONLY SKIN-DEEP

For all who are led by the Spirit of God are sons of God. Romans 8:14

Some people are just a pretty face. I know it may sound harsh, but sometimes there is nothing more to a person than their looks. Have you ever met someone so pretty, but when you spoke to them, their personality was unkind? That's exactly what I mean. Their flesh does not match their spirit. Truthfully, just because someone is pretty on the outside doesn't mean they are pretty on the inside. But what does it mean to be pretty on the inside? Well, that could look like possessing the fruits of the Spirit: love, joy, peace, patience, kindness, goodness, faithfulness, gentleness and self-control. It could even look like putting others before yourself. Having a pretty inside means being led by the Spirit of God and following His 10 Commandments.

Before we can minister effectively, we should ensure that our Spirit aligns with God's will. If not, we risk our "ugliness" becoming a hindrance and distraction from what God is trying to do through our ministry. When we get on the stage to dance, we don't want someone in the congregation to say, "How are they trying to tell me about Jesus when they are so mean on a daily basis?" We always want to make sure that our flesh and spirit align to bring God the glory in every situation.

Prayer

Dear Heavenly Father, I come before You humbly asking You to align my flesh and my spirit with who You want me to be. May I possess all the fruits of the Spirit, and may my beauty not only be skin deep. Reveal any issues within me that are hidden, and allow me to get one step closer to being who You want me to be.

Call To Action

Soul searching is a beneficial part of life. Search your soul today and see how you can align your flesh and spirit with the will of God.

Halal Teens

November 22

EMPOWERED BY THE SPIRIT

For the flesh desires what is contrary to the Spirit, and the Spirit what is contrary to the flesh. They are in conflict with each other, so that you are not to do whatever you want. Galatians 5:17

When I think about the flesh versus the Spirit, fasting or dancing comes to mind. When you are fasting, sometimes you get so hungry that you have to fight the temptation not to eat a snack. I have to forget about my physical flesh and focus on the Spirit in worship to God. It is very easy to depend on ourselves and our abilities.

I love this Bible verse which says, "And because we belong to Christ Jesus, we have killed our selfish feelings and desires" from Galatians 5:24. We sometimes forget that without God, we are nothing, and we need to remember to allow the Spirit of God to move in us as we honor Him through our dance. When we act in the flesh, we carry things like anger, hate, jealousy and envy in our hearts, but when we act in the Spirit, the love of God shines through us.

Prayer

Dear God, today we acknowledge that sometimes our flesh may fail us, but you will never fail us. Help us to always depend on you in everything that we do. May we think and walk by the Spirit.

Call To Action

Make a decision today to always be guided by God's Holy Spirit.

Trinitee Angus

November 23

THE WAR WITHIN

*For the flesh lusteth against the Spirit, and the Spirit against the flesh: and
these are contrary the one to the other: so that ye cannot do the things ye would.
Galatians 5:17*

As a young Christian growing up in a world that can heavily influence you,
you have to be strong, or you will lose yourself every time. There is always a
constant war between what you want to do and what you should do. Take it
from me, you have to be strong-minded in following your chosen path. We
can't be lukewarm Christians; we can't say we want to serve God and then fall
back into our fleshly antics. Easier said than done, right? I have been there, and
to be honest, I'm still working on it.

We have to take steps in our walk with God to not fall back into old habits and
behaviors that would normally consume our souls. Certain steps like feeding
your spirit man are beneficial. When you feed your spirit man, your spirit
becomes equipped to fight off any backlashes of the enemy you encounter.
Whether it is reading the Word or spending time with God, these activities
should always be a number one priority.

Have people around you who won't allow you to slip through the cracks, have
people there to push you, to motivate you to do better, persons with whom
you can spend time together with God. We need to be our brother's keeper. I
know saying these things and putting them into practice can be difficult, but
we need to start somewhere. Even if it is a small step, it is a step closer than
you were before. We need to be in a season now where we must make ourselves
uncomfortable to be comfortable.

Prayer

Dear God, my prayer today is this: we must choose which side we are on as
believers. I pray that we no longer have to fight off our fleshly ways, but if
we do manage to slip through those cracks, we always come out of this fight
victorious. I pray that You will be our guide and guide us according to Your will
and Your ways. In Jesus' name, I pray. Amen.

Call To Action

Let us fight this battle and come out victorious!

Zariah Watson

443

November 24

THE BATTLE FOR DOMINANCE
(POEM)

For the desires of the flesh are against the Spirit, and the desires of the Spirit are against the flesh, for these are opposed to each other, to keep you from doing the things you want to do. Galatians 5:17-21

I don't think they understand

I think I should make them understand

The war that's happening starts within

The decisions you make come from within

The stronger you feed your flesh

The more conflicted you become

The further you drift from your Spirit

Don't weaken your Spirit

Don't lose yourself wanting fleshly desires

Don't lose yourself wanting human artifacts

Don't lose yourself chasing what you know is wrong

Don't let your flesh win

Don't let it consume you

Control you

Make your decisions

Do you feel that?

Feel that weight dragging from your ankles

Free yourself from those chains

Have a mouth-watering desire to grow your Spirit

Can't you see the battle?

The battle for dominance between the two within

One has to be higher

One has to be smarter

One has to be stronger

Has to overpower the other

Don't let that be your flesh.

Zenaida R. Mayers

November 25

DROWNING
(POEM)

And you He made alive, who were dead in trespasses and sins, in which you once walked according to the course of this world, according to the prince of the power of the air, the spirit who now works in the sons of disobedience, among whom also we all once conducted ourselves in lusts of our flesh, fulfilling the desires of the flesh and of mind, and were by nature children of wrath, just as the others.
Ephesians 2:1-3

My internal battle wants to weigh me down

Trying to drag me deep into waters that were once blue

But has slowly twisted itself into black as I inhale more water

And at that moment

I can hear it

The flesh keeps speaking to me

I don't want to feel like this

Be like this

Have this feeling of giving up

On the one thing I truly love

The one thing I believe God bestowed upon me

My mind is fighting with my heart, that's fighting with my flesh, that's fighting with my Spirit

That's encouraging me to keep going

There's a light and with that light comes a hand

Comes a promise

A feeling of safety

The warmth of His hand enveloped around mine

I feel lighter

I'm floating up

The waters look blue again

My heart feels warm again

The desire, the need to worship again it's back

To move my limbs to the sound, the beat, the words

It's back

It's so refreshing

I never thought I would be here again

The heavy feeling of doubt I once felt

It's replaced with a voice

The voice that saved me from
drowning

The voice that assured me

The voice that promised me

He will never put me through
anything I cannot bear

The voice of God saved me

Zenaida R. Mayers

November 26

WALK BY THE SPIRIT

But I say, walk by the Spirit, and you will not gratify the desires of the flesh. For the desires of the flesh are against the Spirit, and the desires of the Spirit are against the flesh, for these are opposed to each other, to keep you from doing the things you want to do. But if you are led by the Spirit, you are not under the law.
Galatians 5:16-18

As I started to write and think about this topic, the said flesh vs spirit started their battle (it reminded me of how siblings fight). I started doubting myself and asking, "Should I share this, or should I not share that? What would people say and think if I opened up too much about myself? These questions are normal and expected because the flesh vs. spirit battle started from the beginning of time (Adam and Eve).

In our everyday lives, from the smallest decision to the biggest, we all try to decide if to move with #TeamFlesh (which is mostly based on an emotional reaction) or #TeamSpirit (which is based on prayer, reading the Bible and meditating which is spiritual). And if we are truly honest with ourselves and tapping into God as we should, we would be well aware by now that spirit is actually faster than flesh. It is always best to operate in the spirit first then manifest what was downloaded from spirit to flesh. This allows God's will to be done through you and within you.

Prayer

Dear Lord, we give You thanks and praise always. Let us practice tapping into the Holy Spirit first on a regular basis, so it becomes a norm in our everyday life. With His help, our decision-making will be made easier, and our crooked paths will be made straight. We ask these things in no other Name but Jesus Christ, who is Lord and Saviour. Amen.

Call To Action

Let's meditate on the song *Spirit Lead Me* by Hillsong.

Keisha Batson

November 27

IT'S JUST A BREATH AWAY

And the LORD God formed man of the dust of the ground, and breathed into his nostrils the breath of life; and man became a living soul. Genesis 2:7

God made the flesh form of man then breathed into him to give life. By the time man was formed, the earth was already filled with all that he needed. All that was previously created was seen as good, but like Adam, functionality and purpose came when the earth received its life source, the rains. A similar transformation occurs at salvation –a "new life." The Holy Spirit is given to man, who should then function with a different understanding of purpose, to worship God in all He does.

With our bodies being the temples of God, it is necessary for every believer to constantly renew their body, mind and spirit. However, where a singer may singularly focus on training the vocals, a dancer uses their entire body, from facial expression to the position of the feet. So, preparation may be more intense to keep the flesh at bay.

You can have the raw ability to dance, teach, choreograph, design and/or construct, but when you tap into the Holy Spirit, it gives way to a strong connection to the heart and needs of others. It is just like the earth before the rains, Adam before the breath of life, and mankind before the Holy Spirit. A choreographer may put some moves together and create a well-executed choreography, but until he/she connects with the Holy Spirit, the purpose and function will not take place. Flesh can produce an entertainment piece while the Spirit executes ministry. As you come to dance, always remember to gear up armed to enter a battlefield. True, not every piece is a warfare dance, but anything done for the Lord will meet opposition.

I recall my first dance piece as a member of the Halal Dance Ministry. We practiced and practiced; it was a struggle because I couldn't connect the movements, but it was only when I read, understood and internalized the lyrics of the song that those movements gained life. A life was breathed into my understanding, and I was truly able to "step pun de enemy."

Prayer

Father, You created everything we needed before You placed us in any position. As we worship You in dance, may our bodies imitate Your creation so that we may freely bow like the trees, move with the grace of the swans, extend like the wings of eagles in flight and leap like gazelles. May our feet trample the enemy like a herd of elephants as we move rhythmically and spiritually in sync. Amen.

Call To Action

As you dance, allow the Spirit to breathe life into every motion, connecting spirit with flesh so that you may glorify the name of the Lord.

Kathy-Ann Pile

November 28

THE BATTLE TO DO RIGHT

For the desires of the flesh are against the Spirit, and the desires of the Spirit are against the flesh, for these are opposed to each other, to keep you from doing the things you want to do. Galatians 5:17

It's tough, isn't it, to do what is right daily and efficiently manage the situations we may be confronted with? However, we have to set our minds on the Lord and not only on what a great example He is, but also determine in our hearts to represent Him. Of course, this is easier said than done, as we tend to be selfish and want to satisfy fleshy emotions. Giving into selfishness and desires of the flesh are not actions we are called to do, nor do they represent who we are.

When we came to Christ, we became a new creation. This means we should move from operating in the flesh to operating in the spirit. Though this will not happen overnight, it can happen if we are intentional. Our hearts' aim is to please the Lord and be good to each other. How do we do this? By actively engaging the Holy Spirit to help us and thinking before we speak or do things. We can also spend time reading the Word and praying, even simply reflecting on the nature of our Saviour, Jesus Christ. If you do this, if you really want to change, you can. You will be pleasantly surprised by the progress you made.

Prayer

Dear Lord, thank You for being such a great example for me to follow. You are awesome. As I awake each day, help me remember who I am serving, and may my heart always seek to honor You. In Jesus' name, Amen.

Call To Action

Declare over your life: "I shall not let flesh override my morality. I must always choose to do the right thing."

Orissa Fitzpatrick

November 29

NO TWO MINUTES!

Don't you know that when you offer yourselves to someone as obedient slaves, you are slaves of the one you obey—whether you are slaves to sin, which leads to death, or to obedience, which leads to righteousness? Romans 6:16

Sometimes, we really want to beg the Lord for two minutes, just two minutes, to tell off that person who just got under our skin. We cannot ask the Holy Spirit for an excuse. What do we expect that the Holy Spirit will leave and come back after we have finished giving that person a piece of our mind? It doesn't work that way.

Everyone has fleshly desires, some of which are more of a challenge to overcome than others. What is a temptation for one person, may not be a temptation for another. Some struggle with honesty, drugs, alcohol, fornication, adultery, rage, and the list goes on. The devil will tempt us in an area he knows we have a challenge in, but we have to be more strategic than him, not asking God for a two-minute excuse so that we can sin.

The Strategy:

Be honest with yourself; who are we trying to fool? We know the truth, and so does God. Know what fleshly desires are most challenging for you.

Be proactive, do not allow yourself to get into a situation that you know is a challenge, then try to get out. Example: If you have a problem with alcohol, don't go to a bar, then try to be strong.

Be intentional; kill flesh daily. A gardener does not pull up weeds and then expects that to be the end. Daily maintenance is critical.

Be focused on the right things: righteous living, prayer and the Word. What we give attention to is what consumes us.

Prayer

Lord, you know I struggle with (*name the struggle*). Help me to apply Godly strategy daily to overcome this hurdle.

Call To Action

Do you have an accountability person? If you don't, consider getting one and choose them wisely.

Rheanne Rock

November 30

REMOVING ALL FLESH

But I say, walk by the Spirit, and you will not gratify the desires of the flesh.
Galatians 5:16

In the Bible, "flesh" refers to bad thoughts. These thoughts come from the things we watch, listen to and read. If you watch things with people using bad language, you will find it creeping into your vocabulary. If you watch things that lift you up spiritually, you will be inspired to put what you learn into practice. Instead of watching bad things, watch something Godly or read your Bible. Watch a church service you may have missed or listen to gospel songs, new and old.

Although I love to listen to jazz songs, I have to be mindful about what the words are saying. I once read a book, and there were unpleasant things in it. Unfortunately, I started to do some of those things. I realized the bad influence it had on me and stopped reading the book. Romans 8:6 says, "For to set the mind on the flesh is death, but to set the mind on the Spirit is life and peace". This verse is saying if you meditate on bad things, you will be put to death; in some cases, this may be physical death, and in others, it may be spiritual. If you think good things, you will have life and peace. Therefore, you should think, watch and read Godly things and not those that are sinful.

Prayer

Dear Lord, I thank You for Your Holy Spirit. I pray You will remove all fleshly thinking. Amen.

Call To Action

Find books, shows and songs that are more wholesome.

Shaquonna Rock

December 1

THE HONORABLE THING TO DO

Repay no one evil for evil but give thought to do what is honorable in the sight of all. Romans 12:17

At some point in our lives, we've all had to forgive someone. A negligent barb hit its mark and now replays in our minds, scraping open the scabs. Perhaps it's a deeper wound caused by someone's abuse, abandonment, or assault. The ache of these injuries can linger for years, decades or even a lifetime. Forgiving someone can be one of the most difficult things we will do in our lifetime. Yet, through forgiveness, God heals our deepest wounds and frees us from our prisons of anger, hate, self-pity, and self-contempt.

There can be confusion around forgiveness. Firstly, Jesus has not said that our forgiving others would lead Him to forgive us. We can't earn forgiveness. Instead, He said that just as He offers forgiveness to us, we are to do likewise to others. We are encouraged to imitate Him.

Some seem to think forgiveness is all about being nice and moving on from hurt, but we can't move on unless we deal with the hurt. Forgiveness is not leniency, excusing or dismissing. When God forgives us, He does not ignore our sins. He deals with them by inviting Jesus to bear the load. And so forgiveness is quite compatible with seeing justice being done. I may forgive someone who acts in a criminal way towards me but, at the same time, take steps to ensure the crime is punished. When I forgive, I decide not to let the hurt done to me shape my life and cause me to hit back personally. I don't forget it, but I choose not to let the memory dictate the rest of my life.

Prayer

Dear Lord, I thank You for the power of forgiveness, and I choose to forgive everyone who has hurt me. Help me set my enemies free and release them to You. Help me bless those who have hurt me. Help me walk in righteousness, peace, and joy, demonstrating Your life here on earth. I choose to be kind and compassionate, forgiving others, just as You forgave me. In Jesus' name, amen.

Call To Action

Forgiving others (and yourself) is sometimes easier said than done. However, it doesn't have to be. So the next time you find yourself feeling hurt by someone's actions or overwhelmed with frustration over a situation that occurred, turn to the Bible for advice.

Danae Niles

December 2

RELEASE OF FORGIVENESS

Forgive us the wrongs we have done, as we ourselves release forgiveness to those who have wronged us. Matthew 6:12

We all want to be forgiven when we do or say something wrong. Sometimes, we say something wrong without even thinking about it, and by the time we say it, it's too late. The person we are saying it to has already heard, and we can't take back our words.

Sometimes, we even do what we think is right for someone, but it comes across the wrong way to that person. Then, we ask the person whom we unintentionally hurt to forgive us. If they do, that's great, but if they don't, then we might have lost an excellent friend because of unforgiveness. Can we blame them for not forgiving us? We, too, find it hard to forgive people who have hurt us.

I've learned from personal experiences that forgiving the people who hurt you is extremely important. It says in Matthew 6:15 that if you withhold forgiveness from others, your Father withholds forgiveness from you. I believe that forgiveness is one of the many things that help us to be truly free.

Prayer

Dear Heavenly Father, help us to learn to forgive others when they've wronged us. I pray that we will be able to give grace to them. Help us not to hold unforgiveness in our hearts towards any person. We know it isn't easy, but with You, all things are possible. In Jesus' name, Amen.

Call To Action

Let us focus on truly seeing who we have on our minds and in our hearts that we have not forgiven, whether it be a friend, family member, co-worker, or acquaintance. If we can't think of anyone, we can ask our Heavenly Father to show us. Let us forgive that person or persons. It might take some time, but eventually, we'll get there.

Danielle Harewood

December 31

CONFESSION

If we confess our sins, he is faithful and just to forgive us our sins, and to cleanse us from all unrighteousness. 1 John 1:9

No one wants to have a sinful Christian life. We want to walk righteously and be in tune with the Holy Spirit, and all God has for us to do in His will. We want to have a strong prayer life and get closer to God daily. But sometimes, sin can enter our lives, and we often need help understanding how it entered and how we can prevent it from entering in the future.

When I think of sinful thoughts or say something that is sinful, I ask God to forgive me right away. I ask Him to continually cleanse my mind and help me control my tongue. Feeling remorseful about sinning shows that you know you did wrong, and hopefully, you want to make it right. In the Bible, we see that many popular Biblical figures encountered sin. Yet they always ask their Heavenly Father to forgive them, and that's what we should also do. As the verse above says, He is always faithful and just to forgive us.

Prayer

Dear heavenly Father, thank You that we can always come to You and ask for forgiveness. I pray that we will not be ashamed to come to You as a Father after we have done something wrong. I pray that we will always remember Your agape love for us because we know that nothing can separate us from Your love. Thank You for Your love, Father. In Jesus' name, Amen.

Call To Action

May we always know that we have a loving Heavenly Father who will forgive us when we mess up and fall into temptation. When we sin, we should confess it to God, ask Him for forgiveness, and continue to walk in righteousness. Remember that His grace is sufficient for us, and His power is made perfect in our weakness.

Danielle Harewood

December 4

WHAT IS FORGIVENESS?

Then I acknowledged my sin to you and did not cover up my iniquity. I said, "I will confess my transgressions to the LORD." And you forgave the guilt of my sin.
Psalm 32:5

The definition of forgiveness is essentially the act of pardoning an offender. In the Bible, the Greek word translated as "forgiveness" literally means "to let go," as when a person does not demand payment for a debt. Jesus used this comparison in His parable of the unmerciful slave (Matthew 18:23-35) as well as when He taught his followers to pray: "Forgive us our sins, for we ourselves also forgive everyone who is in debt to us" (Luke 11:4). Forgiveness is a tough thing to do, especially when the offender isn't sorry or doesn't seem to care. The Bible teaches us that no matter the mindset of our offender, we should forgive.

Jesus sets the ultimate example of forgiveness that we should follow. The next time you feel yourself getting bitter and angry at someone who has betrayed or done you wrong, step back and read what the Word of God has to say about forgiveness. You can't have bitterness and unforgiveness in your heart and be walking with Christ at the same time. The two can't coexist.

We can forgive by taking these steps: acknowledge the pain, think through the situation, imagine being on the other side, remember God's forgiveness and mirror it, reflect on our Biblical command, let go of the hurt, forgive, and pray for the person who hurt us.

Prayer

Dear Lord, You are a forgiving and merciful Lord, abounding in love to all who call upon You. Thank You for granting forgiveness so freely to us who are so undeserving. I pray that You overwhelm us with awareness of the clean slate that Your forgiveness grants us so that we may grant the same mercy to others who have wronged us. Open our eyes to the trap caused by bitterness and enable us to find freedom by following Your example. In the name of Jesus Christ, we pray. Amen.

Call To Action

Many times, the need for forgiveness will result from small acts of thoughtlessness or unkindness from another. At other times in your life, you will be called upon to forgive, and it may feel like a bigger task than most. It will be a forgiveness that goes beyond your ability to understand, but you will be able to provide it, nonetheless. Are you open to developing the humility and the courage to forgive?

Destiny Niles

December 5

ALL BECAUSE OF YOU

For by grace are ye saved through faith; and that not of yourselves: it is the gift of God. Ephesians 2:8

What does it mean to be saved? For me, it means rescuing from harm or danger. Because of God's grace, I have been saved and not of myself. This wonderful gift was not given easily or cheaply. On the cross, as Jesus died, He asked His Father to forgive those executing Him because they did not know what they were doing. Imagine if that were us. I am not sure how forgiving we would be, but because of the love of Christ, we do not have to make that decision.

Some people say that they can forgive but not forget. That is not true forgiveness. Though you would remember what that person had done to you at some point, many people hold on to the hurt even though they claim to have forgiven the person who did them wrong. Unforgiveness is a sin that can eat away at our souls and affect our ministry. Today, many health issues that people face are a result of unforgiveness. We develop unexplained symptoms and go to doctors seeking remedies only to find out nothing physical is really wrong. Then, the Holy Spirit reminds us to forgive someone, and when we obey, the symptoms disappear.

I always ask the Lord to forgive me of any sin before I minister. Sometimes, when He tells me I need to forgive someone, my dance is a struggle if I do not obey at that particular time. Still, as soon as I obeyed and asked the person for forgiveness, the dance flowed. I know that it was all because of Jesus and not of myself. The gift that is given freely should be cherished.

Prayer

I will always be thankful for Your death, oh Lord. Thank You for Your forgiveness of my sins. I do not know what my life would be like had it not been for You. Thank You! What a wonderful gift you have truly given humankind. May we never forget. Amen.

Call To Action

Forgiveness can be challenging, but forgive someone today and truly mean it.

Eslyn Taylor

December 6

FORGIVENESS, CAN YOU IMAGINE?

Blessed are the merciful, for they shall receive mercy. Matthew 5:7

Forgiveness is such a touchy subject. It plays a bigger role in life than we think or may even be willing to acknowledge. Had God not sent His Son Jesus to die for our sins as the ultimate act of forgiveness, who knows where we would be today. God sent His Son to give us a chance at a better life through forgiveness. If God could give up His only Son for us, we can forgive those around us. It was not easy for Him, but He did it anyway; we should take a leaf out of His book.

Unforgiveness hardens our hearts and makes it difficult for God's love to flow freely through us to everyone around us. It could have consequences in both the physical and spiritual world. Forgiveness does not only apply to those who have wronged us, but sometimes we must also forgive ourselves. Truthfully, it can be harder to forgive yourself than it is to forgive others. In these cases, we must extend the grace God has given us to ourselves. Acknowledge that we are only human and that as we forgive ourselves, we allow ourselves to grow.

For example, if we as dancers don't appreciate our gifts and talents from God, we may not always give them the attention that they deserve, causing less than satisfactory results in our ministry. We may beat ourselves up about this, but it does not have to end there. Forgive yourself, learn from your mistakes and honor God with your gifts.

Prayer

Father God, I humbly ask for Your help as I learn to forgive others. Touch my heart so that I will forgive others just as You have forgiven me. You are the God of forgiveness, and I thank You for sending Your Son, Jesus, to pay for my sins. May that same Spirit guide me on my path to forgiveness as I release all harbored pain. Amen.

Call To Action

Release all unforgiveness you harbor in your heart; this may be towards others or yourself. Do not let unforgiveness stop you from being the best version of yourself as God ordained it.

Gabrielle Blackett

December 7

LOVE COVERS ALL OFFENCES

For if you forgive men their trespasses, your heavenly Father will also forgive you. But if you do not forgive men their trespasses, neither will your Father forgive your trespasses. Matthew 6: 14-15

Sometimes, we say that people are not sorry for what they did, so we live with a grudge against them. And even those who ask for our forgiveness, it is so hard for us to grant it to them, especially if we are replaying what they did to us in our minds. But in that Bible verse, Jesus says that God's forgiveness for our sins is tied to whether or not we have forgiven others. If we really give it some thought, we would acknowledge that we, too, have hurt others at some time or the other in our lives.

If we have anything against anyone, we should confess it to the Lord before we start praying. Unforgiveness is a sin, and it causes separation between us and God. Persons have been known to say, "I could forgive them, but I could never forget them." Really? Is that true forgiveness? What do we gain by holding on to the sins and mistakes of others? Doing that also stops our progress in our ministry, for the only person we are actually hurting is ourselves. And it is difficult to minister in unity when we are at loggerheads with someone. We would find that the person has moved on whilst we are stuck in a rut. When we show love to those who least expect it, it has a profound effect on them, which also radiates to those looking on. Love covers sin. Every time someone hurts us, let us tell ourselves that the love of God is deep enough to cover it.

Prayer

Lord God, cleanse our hearts of all bitterness and revenge towards others so that we can move ahead and enjoy the fullness of this life. Give us the grace to forgive and love those who have hurt us. In Jesus' name, we pray. Amen.

Call To Action

- Get rid of all malice and bitterness towards others.

- Allow God to root out all unhealthy habits.

- Acknowledge your faults and failures before God.

Gurlain Applewhaite

December 8

WHO THE SON SETS FREE IS FREE INDEED

Brethren I do not count myself to have apprehended; but one thing I do, forgetting those things which are behind and reaching forward to those things which are ahead. I press toward the goal for the prize of the upward call of God in Christ Jesus. Philippians 8:13-14

We have an enemy, Satan, who is actively working to discourage believers and cause doubt. One of the biggest hindrances to getting ahead in this life is unforgiveness of ourselves, insecurities and the belief that we don't think we are good enough or deserve better. God has provided a way out of sin for us: confess, ask forgiveness, and make a turnaround. For most of us, there is no problem accepting that God has forgiven us, but sometimes we are so disappointed in ourselves, appalled at what we have done that it is ever before us. Why do we hold on to what God has already forgiven and said He will remember no more? God has given the free gift of salvation and every benefit that comes along with it. We are no longer under condemnation. It's time to rid ourselves of guilt and walk in that freedom!

It is difficult to minister effectively in dance if we are imprisoned by past and present sins. Why are we still in the loop of guilt? How can we minister to others that God is a forgiving God, that we are a new creation in Christ, yet burden ourselves with the wounds of past hurts? When we forgive ourselves and then step out to minister, we can do so in the light of saying to others, "This is who I was. This is where I have been. This is where God has brought me from." Hallelujah!

Prayer

Heavenly Father, thank You for forgiving us of all our sins and welcoming us into Your kingdom. We need Your help, Lord, in forgiving ourselves so that we can live in that freedom You have given us. In Jesus' name, we pray. Amen.

Call To Action

- Accept God's forgiveness and forgive yourself.

- Let go of past guilt.

- Walk in the freedom that Christ has given us.

Gurlain Applewhaite

Call To Action

- Accept God's forgiveness and forgive yourself.

- Let go of past guilt.

December 9

I CHOOSE TO FORGIVE

Be kind and compassionate to one another, forgiving each other, just as in Christ God forgave you. Ephesians 4:32

The three commands shown in this verse go hand in hand. We can't show kindness and be compassionate to each other and not forgive. Forgiveness is the third command that Paul gave to the believers. He ended this verse by saying: forgive each other, just as God forgave you. We are always ready to ask God for forgiveness, but are we always ready to forgive others?

Forgiveness is the act of releasing someone that did something bad to you. When someone's actions hurt us, we can easily write off that person and move on. But this is not how God wants His children to be. Forgiving can be one of the hardest things to do in life, especially if you were hurt deeply. Sometimes, things that happened in our past are very difficult to forget and overcome. At the same time, holding onto those deep, hidden hurts can easily hinder what God wants to do in our future. We must learn to forgive even though people may not always accept that forgiveness. Let's ensure that we have done our part by honoring God's commandments with sincerity.

The two benefits of forgiveness are:

When we forgive, we will be blessed as we are obeying God's commands. Luke 11:28: "Blessed, rather are those who hear the word of God and obey it."

Freedom will be ours. If unforgiveness can keep us in bondage to the point of making us sick, forgiveness will free that weight physically, mentally and spiritually.

Prayer

Jesus, I thank You for forgiving us for all the wrongs we did to You. We commit to forgiving anyone who did or will do us wrong. We know that this is one of Your commands, and we will obey. In Jesus' Name, Amen.

Call To Action

I encourage you not to hold anyone in your heart, no matter what. As hard as it may be to forgive someone for the pain they caused you, be obedient to our Father and forgive them.

Julie Greene

December 10

OUR FORGIVING FATHER

If we confess our sins, He is faithful and righteous to forgive us our sins and to cleanse us from all unrighteousness. 1 John 1:9

As His children, we have direct access to God's forgiveness, but it comes with a condition. In this verse, we can see God's willingness to forgive us of our sins. There is a key that can gain us *access* to His forgiveness. The key is called confession. Confession is a formal admission of our sins. At times, we may be ashamed, reluctant, embarrassed, proud or in denial. However, once we understand that sin separates us from God, we should be even more urgent about our need to use the key of confession, which leads to forgiveness and reconciliation.

The verse also says that God is faithful and righteous. In other words, He is committed to getting us back on track to following our desire for reconnection, which we show with the confession of our wrongdoings. As one who is righteous, God alone is able to make us right with Him again. The result is us being cleansed from all unrighteousness.

Prayer

Father, we come to You. We confess (*name your sin*). We thank You for being faithful and righteous. We know that we can place our trust in You. Please forgive us for the sins that we have done. Thank You for cleansing us. Amen.

Call To Action

Be open, ready, and willing to confess your sins to God. Put everything aside that may hinder you from going to Him. Trust that God will stick to His Word. He is loyal and faithful. Accept His forgiveness. Once you confess, you can be assured that He did forgive you.

Julie Greene

December 11

LIVE FREE!

For if you forgive other people when they sin against you, your heavenly Father will also forgive you. But if you do not forgive others their sins, your Father will not forgive your sins. Matthew 6:14-15

Forgiveness doesn't mean that nothing happened; forgiveness means you can move beyond what happened, beyond what you did and beyond what the other person did. It allows you to live freely. Don't you want to live freely?

The word says that all have sinned and fallen short. We all have a mess. This is a good thing to remember, especially when we are faced with situations that seem unforgivable. It is so important that when Jesus taught us to pray, He made sure that "forgive us our trespasses as we forgive those who trespass against us" was a part of it.

We will all need to embody forgiveness, so God requires that we all do the work of forgiveness. God was the first to show us the way and give us His Holy Spirit to help us through those times when forgiving seems hard. Our love for God and our desire to please Him must always outweigh the obstacles.

Prayer

Father, help me to forgive (*call the person's name*) because this is what You require, and I want to be obedient. Show me what to do, give me the words to say, help me heal my heart, Lord. I want to be obedient, and I want to be free, in Jesus' Name, Amen.

Call To Action

Search your heart. See if there is anything you have not forgiven yourself for. Write it down and pray about it. Actively give it over to God.

Now, is there anyone you need to forgive? Ask God to show you. Enter into the process of forgiveness. Commit to making one step towards forgiving that person or persons. Let God guide you on how to reach out. Let Him do the healing work. Step out because you love God. Step out because you want to be free.

Laina Jacob

December 12

FORGIVE AND IT SHALL BE FORGIVEN YOU

Be kind and compassionate to one another, forgiving each other, just as in Christ God forgave you. Ephesians 4:32

Do you remember the story in Luke 7:36-50, which tells us about the woman who washed the feet of Jesus and wiped His feet with her hair and expensive perfume? She was showing how grateful she was for God's forgiveness. She showed it in the way she knew how. Oh, the love and grace of feeling God's forgiveness! Sometimes, when we mess up and sin, we cannot hold our heads up high, and sometimes we don't want to dance anymore. We can feel ashamed and unworthy, and this is exactly how this woman felt until she met Jesus. He is the one who offers us forgiveness because He loves us and will restore us if we are truly sorry for our sins.

God will forgive us. We must accept God's forgiveness and get back up again, knowing in our hearts that God loves us. Remember Peter, who denied Christ not once but three times? Jesus told him, "When you are converted", or, in other words, when you are restored, "feed the brethren". God wants to restore us to continue to do His will. You will fall, but you will also get back up again, dance again, worship again, and sing again. You are forgiven; the Father says so. If we confess, "He is faithful and just to forgive us our sins" (John 1:9).

Prayer

Father, forgive me for any sin in my life and help me to forgive others as You forgive me.

Call To Action

Think of someone to whom you need to offer forgiveness and do so.

Maxine Butcher

December 13

70 TIMES 7

Jesus said: "Even if they sin against you seven times in a day and seven times come back to you saying 'I repent', you must forgive them". Luke 17:4

The question was asked: "How many times must we forgive?" You see, even as God forgives us, we must forgive others. If we do not forgive, our heavenly Father cannot forgive us. Holding unforgiveness in our hearts can make us bitter and hateful. We must always forgive when we are offended by others.

As a dance team, you can imagine what can happen if there is offense among us; there will be no unity, and it will be seen by others who watch us dance. Yes, we can hurt each other over the smallest things and wound each other deeply by things said and done to each other. Working with different personalities can sometimes cause disagreements and challenges, but no one is perfect. We will make mistakes. As a child of God and a minister in dance, we must forgive each other for the sake of our souls and our ministry.

There was a time when it was hard to forgive others, but I realized that my fight was not against my sisters but the enemy of our souls who wanted to keep us apart. When we forgive and unite, we can do great things for God.

Prayer

I pray for unity and forgiveness among us as a People of God.

Call To Action

Find a person you offended and ask for forgiveness.

Maxine Butcher

December 14

HELP ME JESUS

But if you do not forgive others their sins, your Father will not forgive your sins.
Matthew 6:15

Even as I was pondering on this, I had, in mind, an image of a tree shaking, and I heard the words "shake it off". If this applies to you at this moment, let it go. I am not saying this with ease in my heart, for I know the depths of pain others can cause. I know the cruelty you can suffer from careless words and hurtful experiences. While enduring that kind of pain, we often think we may never forgive the person who has hurt us, but I say to you, you must.

It might be painful, and you may cry or have a burst of anger, and that is okay. You've got this. Do you know why? Because you don't want to hurt anymore. It's time to free yourself from that bondage, because that is what it is, and you deserve to live as the Lord called you to live. There is work for you to do and people you have to help. I don't want you to suffer in silence anymore; even more, Jesus does not. Give Him a chance to heal your heart.

The eye-opening part of this is what the scripture says, "if you don't forgive, He won't forgive you your sins". That's right. You also sin and would like Jesus to forgive you. Know this; by the same measure you forgive, it will be measured unto you. The Lord knew what He was doing when He said this because He's a fair God.

You are more than the hurt, anger, trust issues, and even your horrible experiences. You, my beloved, are a child of God. Let your heart beat again and be free. Those things no longer have a hold of you.

Prayer

Daddy, my Lord and Saviour, my help, You know what's in my heart and what I have been through. I ask You to help me through this, for I know as long as I hold unforgiveness in my heart, I am giving (*say the name and/or the situation*) power over me. Deliver me from this burden. Amen.

Call To Action

I will forgive (*say the name of the person*) and walk in my deliverance.

Orissa Fitzpatrick

December 15

CLEAN HANDS! PURE HEART!

If we confess our sins, he is faithful and just to forgive us our sins and to cleanse us from all unrighteousness. 1 John 1:9

There is a song by Kathryn Scott that starts with the words: "Search me, know me, try me and see every worthless affection hidden in me. All I'm asking for is that you cleanse me, Lord". Such words portray a heart that wants to be right with God. The heart can be very deceitful, and I am sure that is one of the reasons the Psalmist wrote: "Create in me a clean heart". We store so much inside of us for many reasons, but a big weight on us is shame for things we have done. We are embarrassed or feel as though we will be judged for our mistakes and sins committed. This is why it is so important to have Godly people around to help and pray us through.

Unforgiveness is such a major obstacle in our lives. It can make us sick when we harbour it in our hearts. It definitely is not a Godly thing to do and should not be part of who we are as Christ believers. The good news is that we are encouraged to confess our sins because His promise is that He will forgive us. There are times we will need to forgive ourselves. Do it now. He's waiting for you.

Prayer

Lord, You are such a good and compassionate Father. Thank You for opening my eyes and helping me to see that forgiveness isn't an action that always involves others. I can forgive myself, too. Cleanse me from all unrighteousness, in Jesus' name. Amen.

Call To Action

Forgiveness is also for you. Say and believe in these words, "I shall forgive myself."

Orissa Fitzpatrick

December 16

FOR YOU TO GIVE

To the Lord our God belong mercy and forgiveness, though we have rebelled against Him. Daniel 9:9

Forgiveness belongs to the LORD our God. Forgiveness does not belong to us. Forgiveness is a gift from God to be opened, used and shared with others. It is not for us to hold on to; it is for us to give, just as God gave, "For God so loved the world, that he gave his only begotten Son, that whosoever believeth in him should not perish, but have everlasting life." (John 3:16).

"And whenever you stand praying, if you have anything against anyone, forgive him, that your Father in heaven may also forgive you your trespasses (Mark 11:25). Our forgiveness of one another is tied directly to God, who forgave us for Christ's sake, "And be ye kind one to another, tenderhearted, forgiving one another, even as God for Christ's sake hath forgiven you" (Ephesians 4:32).

Other passages that speak to forgiveness include Matthew 6:12: "And forgive us our debts, as we forgive our debtors," and Matthew 6:14, "For if ye forgive men their trespasses, your heavenly Father will also forgive you".

Now that we have a proper perspective of forgiveness and its rightful owner, let us stop holding on so tightly to it for Christ's sake. Let us release it to be received by not only us, but those around us who may have "offended" us, remembering that not only have we too "offended" others, but we are all guilty before God and in need of His forgiveness.

Prayer

Lord, help us to remember that forgiveness belongs to You and that You have freely given it to us for Christ's sake. Help us to share it with each other, as we are all in need of forgiveness.

Call To Action

Let us aim for a minimum of three persons to forgive this week/month.

Give your all in worship next time you dance, knowing that forgiveness is a shared gift.

Pierre Rock

December 17

FORGIVE AND BE FORGIVEN

And when you stand praying, if you hold anything against anyone, forgive them so that your Father in heaven may forgive your sins. Mark 11:25

We all want to be forgiven when we do something wrong. We should ask ourselves, when others have wronged us, if we are also quick to extend that same forgiveness we often desire. We cannot put a limit on the number of times God forgives us. Still, we tend to limit our forgiveness of others or withhold forgiveness if we deem them unworthy. The idea of forgiving others so that we may be forgiven is mentioned several times in the Bible, so take note. I know people can do some pretty horrible things to us or our loved ones, and it's not easy to forgive them, but let's take a page from our Father's book and forgive them anyway.

As dance ministers, we need to be able to move freely without the weight of unforgiveness. We cannot minister as effectively with a load on our backs. We may have even experienced hurt within a dance group we belong to. Yet, we have to find it within us by the power of the Holy Spirit to forgive the person we believe wronged us. Forgiveness is not an easy task, but it's a necessary one.

Prayer

Lord, You know in my heart I want to do what is right, but it is hard. Help me to forgive (*say the name of the person*) and release myself from all ill feelings towards anyone who has hurt me. Show me how to love them. Give me the strength to do this, Lord, because I cannot do it on my own, in Jesus' Name.

Call To Action

Write a list of those persons you have not forgiven. Pray about that list often as you seek God's help in getting you to a place of forgiveness.

Rheanne Rock

December 18

READY TO FORGIVE

But if you do not forgive men their sins, your Father will not forgive your sins.
Matthew 6:15

This verse means that when people do wrong things to you, you should forgive them. We all make mistakes, so we must remain understanding and be willing to forgive others, as our Father will forgive us. It hurts badly when people do us wrong, but God can and will heal that hurt.

Examples:

1. At home - When your sibling takes one of your things without asking, you will feel angry or upset, but you can forgive them and explain to them not to do it again.

2. At school - When you are in a line for lunch, and someone pushes you, instead of shouting or screaming, you can forgive them.

3. At school- When a girl is mean to you, instead of doing the same thing to her, you can forgive her.

4. At church - When you trip while walking and your friends laugh at you, don't respond and say, "I am not your friend anymore". Instead, you can forgive them.

In the Bible, when Jesus explained forgiveness to His disciples, Peter asked how many times we are supposed to forgive others, "Up to seven times?" Jesus said, not seven times but 70 times 7 (Matthew 18:21-22). So, God expects us to forgive others. If we do not forgive others, God will not be pleased. We will then have to suffer the consequences of being unforgiving. No one knows what those will be, but whatever they are, God will still love us and will continuously provide chances for us to forgive.

Prayer

Dear Lord, help me to forgive others, help me do the right things, and love others no matter what, in Jesus' name. Amen.

Call To Action

My challenge for you is to forgive people just like the Lord forgave you.

Rhema-Jae Greene

476

Call To Action

My challenge for you is to forgive people just like the Lord forgave you.

Rhema-Jae Greene

476

December 19

A HEART OF FORGIVENESS

If we confess our sins, he is faithful and just to forgive us our sins, and to cleanse us from all unrighteousness. 1 John 1:9

It doesn't matter what you and I did, we can be forgiven according to 1 John 1:9. God can clean our souls and make us brand new. This happens when we confess our sins. The Merriam-Webster dictionary says confession means disclosure of one's sins in the sacrament of reconciliation. If we confess today, we can reconcile with God and make everything right.

Our sins might seem like we did the worst thing, but if David can be forgiven for committing adultery and murder, what does this say to us? Genesis 18:14 says there is nothing too hard for God. God can take things of evil and make them into things that are wonderful. We can sometimes enable the enemy to hinder our forgiveness by allowing him to speak negative things to us. God made us, not the devil, so there isn't anything too hard for God to do in our lives.

1 Samuel 16:7 says God looks at the heart, not the outer appearance of a man's life. He knows everything you have done; you only need to surrender your heart to Him, and He will forgive you right now. You must never let unforgiveness fester in your heart. As a dancer, it can plague your life and stop God from accomplishing His work inside your heart. That is where everything is hidden, and only God has the power to remove any unwanted things.

Prayer

God, my life is Yours. My heart is Yours. I come before You, confessing my sins daily as I live, in Jesus' name, Amen.

Call To Action

- Confess your sins to God.

- Never let forgiveness fester in your heart.

- Turn your life over to God.

Rhonda. A. Babb

December 20

HEARTFELT FORGIVENESS

If you forgive those who sin against you, your heavenly Father will forgive you.
Matthew 6:14

Forgiveness begins with you but can only happen through God. He requires us to forgive like Him and gives us the power to forgive everyone. According to Matthew 6:14, God says if you don't forgive, He will not forgive you, point blank. So we have no choice but to forgive each other. Yes, I know it's hard, but God is more than able to help. He created us with the ability to function under His authority as we allow His Holy Spirit to lead and guide our lives.

Forgiveness must be of the heart and not just the mouth. Saying I forgive you and not meaning it from your heart is not of God. You need to free your heart of all malice and anger when you are a child of God. Forgiveness produces a fruit of freedom and joy. It gives you the power to know that nothing will stop you from being what God has called you to be. A forgiving heart keeps you from living a life of bondage. It allows you to show how the fruits of the Spirit work, which is spoken about in Galatians 5:22. Your life must bear fruit in order for your heart to bear fruit. Never let unforgiveness hinder you or your ministry to God.

When you forgive as a true minister, your ministry will be connected to the heart of God and come from a place of freedom and love. Always forgive so that your dance brings freedom to someone else.

Prayer
Lord, please give me a heart of forgiveness and help me always stay connected to You, in Jesus' name, Amen.

Call To Action
Forgive all the time

Remember that forgiveness begins with God and it bears healthy fruits.

Rhonda. A. Babb

December 21

OPEN ARMS

Bear with each other and forgive one another, if any of you has a grievance against someone. Forgive as the Lord forgave you. Colossians 3:13

It's the year 1947, and two best friends fall into a lifelong spiral of demoralizing, destructive behavior that breaks apart what God put together. How did this happen? How did it get this far? Wasn't anyone looking on, interested in the events that were taking place leading up to this? They vowed never to speak again, dance again, praise again. Forgive, who her? Never!

What a blow to the kingdom of God! The enemy is ecstatic; he has been planting seeds for a long time now. Individually and as a team, he knew this would harden their hearts, and forgiveness wouldn't come easy or maybe it would never come. This was part of his plan; they were too powerful together and he was having none of it. Lives were being transformed and God was receiving all the glory. He was losing, and his pride couldn't handle that, and just like that, his efforts paid off; only God could sew up a rift like this.

So often, we open cracks and let the enemy make them into doorways that he walks through without even a blink. As individuals, keeping close to God on this walk is paramount. If we don't, the enemy can eat us alive and spit us out. Many times, he tries to sift us like wheat, that when we come together, we cannot be united because we are broken pieces of a puzzle.

When we do not forgive, we are not showing kindness and living according to the standard God has set, for He forgives us. He is the Almighty God, and if He can forgive, we can forgive, too. We are spirits, which gives us the capacity to forgive, for our spirit wills us to do the right thing, but our flesh does not. We cannot serve two masters, so choose today which one you will serve and forgive!

Prayer

Heavenly Father, help as we open our arms in brotherly love, by showing forgiveness, in Jesus' name, Amen.

Call To Action

Resist the devil and he will flee. Show him that your God is bigger. Go, open your arms and forgive. Read Isaiah 55:7

Sandra Britton

December 22

WHEN FORGIVENESS MATTERS

Forgive one another freely even if one has a cause for complaint against another. Just as God freely forgave you, you must also do the same. Colossians 3:13

Two definitions of forgiveness are choosing to let go of anger and resentment towards yourself or someone else, and surrendering thoughts of revenge and moving forward with your character intact. Forgiveness brings peace of mind, frees the individual from anger and helps repair relationships and release hurtful negative feelings that often cause pain and suffering. Forgiveness does not mean condoning the offense or the offender or pretending nothing happened. When we choose to forgive someone who wronged us, we let go of the need to carry that hurt anymore. We also free ourselves to seek peace of mind. Forgiveness is a spiritual grace that costs the individual nothing but pride that can stand in the way of reconciliation.

It has been proven that unforgiveness causes physical, mental and spiritual strain on the body and soul. As dancers, we must always seek or forgive anyone we might have offended in any way to ensure that we remain in good standing with God, other ministers and the people we are called to minister to. Forgiveness does not mean that we accept or approve of the wrong that has been done or that it minimizes the damage that has been caused. It means that we decide with God's help to let go of resentment, although we might have been hurt deeply. None of us deserve forgiveness, but God always forgives us through His love for us. We have a loving, forgiving God! And we should follow His example.

Prayer

Father, thank You for Your daily forgiveness, even when we are unaware of when or how we may have inflicted pain on others. Open our hearts to love each person we meet daily. Father, keep us covered in Your blood by Your grace as we continue this walk of faith. In Jesus' name. Amen!

Call To Action

- To live each day as unto God.

- Live peaceably at all times while evading contentious situations, and be ready to admit when you erred in preference to others.

- Keep God-focused and let God be the object of your love every day.

Gloria Gooding

December 23

FORGIVE AND LET GOD

And be ye kind to another, tenderhearted forgiving one another even as God for Christ sake had forgiven us. Ephesians 4:32

Have you ever wondered why it is so hard to forgive? Not partial or conditional forgiveness but like God forgives us. A lot of times, we want to forgive on our terms and when it suits our needs. How can we say we love God, who we cannot see but hate our brothers and sisters who we can see according to 1 John 4:20. God has called us to put away bitterness, indignation, bad temper and resentment for others who we think might have done us wrong so that when we stand before the courts of heaven, our prayers can be answered.

If we forgive others, we can reap the benefits of improved relationships and improved quality of life. The better we are at forgiving others, the better our relationships become with them. Sometimes, the people we are closest to are the ones that experience our shortcomings. Forgiveness is healthy because it relieves you from the bitterness, hate and anger you carry that can lead to sickness.

As a dance minister, forgiveness is important because when we go to minister, we are showcasing God, the wonderful characteristics He embodies and what He does for His children. How can we show love when we have hate in our hearts or peace when all we can think of is revenge? What we have on the inside is what we will send forth in our ministry. When you come before God in prayer, and a person comes to mind that you have an issue with, stop and pray for that person, seek to forgive them and then continue with your quiet time.

Prayer

Lord, help us forgive anyone we need to forgive as we seek fellowship with you; in Jesus' name, we pray. Amen.

Call To Action

- Always seek forgiveness before ministry.

- Make forgiveness part of your lifestyle.

- Set your heart free by forgiving.

Timeless Ministers

December 24

I FORGIVE YOU

And when you stand praying, if you hold anything against anyone, forgive them, so that your Father in heaven may forgive you your sins. Mark 11:25

Sometimes, it can be extremely hard to forgive someone who wronged or mistreated you somehow. The Bible advises against holding unforgiveness in our hearts. If we do not forgive others, our heavenly Father may not forgive us our sins. God showed us that He was a forgiving God when Jonah disobeyed Him by not going to Nineveh, and God gave him a second chance to do the right thing.

I have been in situations many times when classmates did things to me that I did not like, and it took me a while before I decided to forgive them. I try to think about what God would want me to do in each situation. Doing what God requires of us is sometimes very difficult, but it is the right thing to do.

Prayer

Father, You have forgiven me and You inspire me to forgive others. Yet, it is hard for me to forgive. Please give me peace and compassion toward everyone, especially those who have done me wrong Amen.

Call To Action

Practice forgiveness by writing letters to everyone who did something bad to you with the words "I forgive you" and deliver the letters to them directly.

Trinitee Angus

December 25

A TWO-WAY STREET

And forgive us our debts, as we also have forgiven our debtors. Matthew 6:12

Forgiveness is a two-way street. We must not only seek to be forgiven, but we must also forgive others. Jesus told a parable about a servant who owed his master 10,000 bags of gold. He begged his master's forgiveness and his master forgave him. This same servant went out and saw a fellow servant who owed him 100 silver coins and demanded that he repay him. The fellow servant asked his forgiveness, and he refused, having him thrown into jail. The servant with the debt of 10,000 bags of gold chose not to forgive the servant who owed him 100 silver coins; he did not forgive as he was forgiven. When those around saw what he did, they reported back to the master, and the master, outraged, asked him why he did not extend mercy like he extended mercy to him. The master punished him by having him thrown in jail.

Prayer

Father God, as we approach Your throne, we ask You to forgive us of our wrongdoings. We pray also that You will give us a heart of compassion so that we will forgive others as You have forgiven us. Help us not to be like the servant who would not forgive his fellow servant. Help us learn our lesson from this parable and be merciful to others, knowing that forgiveness is a two-way street. In Jesus' name, Amen!

Call To Action

It is very important that we forgive others. Jesus said forgive them 70 times 7; this just means to forgive over and over again. Like the servant who owed his master 10,000 bags of gold, if we do not forgive those who wronged us, God will not forgive us either, so remember to have mercy, because forgiveness is a two-way street.

Tweann Layne

December 26

SEVENTY X SEVEN

Then came Peter to him, he said, Lord, how often shall my brother sin against me, and I forgive him? Till seven times? Jesus saith unto him, I say not unto thee, Until seven times: but, Until seventy times seven. Matthew 18:21-22

Forgiveness is something we, as Christians, struggle with and also deny. We say we forgive others when they have done us wrong, but still, we can't hold a conversation with them, pass them without giving harsh looks, or even be in the same room as them. Why is that? Why can we not forgive our brothers and sisters in Christ, but we expect God to forgive us when we sin and fall short? God said to us in this verse that we must forgive our brothers seventy times seven no matter what they have done to us. You must be reading this and asking yourself, how can I forgive someone who has done so much damage to me? Easy, because we follow the laws of the Bible and what God says is right.

In our ministries, unity is everything; the devil thrives on discord. There is strength in numbers. Once we are unified, the enemy will have no room to linger or to distract us from doing what we are called to do. Being in a ministry is like being in an extended family; we grow together, we love together, we cry together, we fall down together, but we also pick each other up. Holding unforgiveness in our hearts can stop the work that needs to be done to better the people around us and to reach the people who need it the most. In this world we live in now, it is so hard to find people who love each other and look out for one another. Let us not be like that, my brothers and sisters. Let us forgive one another, grow together, and lead by example.

Prayer

Dear merciful Father, thank You for Your gift of forgiveness. I pray that peace will overflow my life, Lord, keeping out any doubt and anything hindering me from forgiving others around me. Help me forgive those who hurt me, and I pray that you bless them 100 times over! In Jesus' Name, Amen.

Call To Action

Repeat after me, "Thank you, Lord, for setting me free of unforgiveness."

Zariah Watson

December 27

DON'T LET THE SIGNAL BE CUT

If we confess our sins, he is faithful and just to forgive us our sins, and to cleanse us from all unrighteousness. 1 John 1:9

When we sin against God, we tend to let our connection with Him cut out, just like a bad Wi-Fi signal. Have you ever noticed that when you are far away from your Wi-Fi box, the signal becomes weaker and weaker? Well, that's how it feels when we sin against God; our connection to Him weakens, and we lose touch with Him. In this scripture, God is saying if we confess our sins, He is faithful and just to forgive us and cleanse us from all unrighteousness.

Let's say we begin to notice our signal is weak; we begin to notice that we are sinning against the laws of God. We then have to look for the source of our strength and begin to draw closer to it. So, we search for this "Wi-Fi box", and as we search, we find it and begin to move towards it for that stronger connection.

When we confess our sins to God, who is true to His promises, He will forgive and restore us and our connection to Him. We must always remember that God is the source of our strength. Don't let people tell you that your sin is too big and that God will never forgive you. God is not like man; he stays true to His promises, and He will forgive you for all your transgressions, but you need to be able to confess. We all need to be able to run back to the key source of our strength so our signal won't be cut off from Him. Today, I challenge you believers to always hold on to that strong connection between you and God, always confess your sins to Him and let nothing weaken your walk with God.

Prayer

Everlasting Father, we come before You, asking that You forgive us for our sins. Wash my sins away, Oh God, purify me and help me to learn how to walk towards a stronger connection with You. In Jesus' Name. Amen

Call To Action

Always remember, confession is one step closer to a stronger connection with God!

Zariah Watson

December 28

IF I HAD YOUR EYES
(POEM)

And when you stand praying, if you hold anything against anyone, forgive them, so that your Father in heaven may forgive you your sins. Mark 11:25

Do I have to?

Forgiveness

An act that starts with you

An act that involves putting your personal feelings aside

You choosing not to hold on, but to let go

It's hard

It's hard to see past why you weren't chosen for this dance.

Why not me?

Have I not done everything that has been asked of me?

"Why wasn't I asked to choreograph?"

"Why wasn't I chosen to speak?"

"Why wasn't I put in a certain position that I think I deserve? "

Look at me making this about me

Look at me thinking I'm more than anyone here

Forgive me

Forgive me Father

Please understand

It would be easier to understand if I just saw it from your point of view

It would be easier to let things go

It would be easier to be okay with decisions being made

It would be easier to understand I don't have to be included in everything

It just would be easier

If I just

If I just had your eyes

Zenaida R. Mayers

December 29

BE KIND TO YOURSELF!

And be ye kind tenderhearted , forgiving one another , even as God for Christ's sake have forgiven you. Ephesians 4:32

What happened in your past stays in the past! If your first response to a negative situation is to criticize yourself, it's time to show yourself some kindness and compassion. The only way to begin the journey to forgiveness is to be kind and compassionate with yourself. Think of each mistake as a learning experience. Our experiences are stepping stones for growth and the keys to unlocking ourselves from our personal prisons. This takes time, patience, and a reminder to yourself that you're worthy of forgiveness.

If we can't forgive ourselves we continually build walls which block us from receiving God's forgiveness and the ability to forgive others. Forgiveness is for our own growth and happiness. When we hold on to hurt, pain, resentment and anger, it harms us far more than it harms offenders.

To improve in this area of my life, one of the critical steps I had to take was to quiet the negative messages of my inner critic. Always remember, identify what you're feeling, give a voice to it and accept that mistakes are inevitable. You'll begin to see how freeing forgiveness can be, and this will lead to greater ministry in your life.

Prayer

Abba Father, we thank You that You are the one who first loved us. Help us to be more kind and compassionate to ourselves, for there is no more condemnation in Christ Jesus.

Call To Action

Reflect on your thought patterns and encourage yourself in the Lord.

Trena Milllar

December 30

FORGIVENESS IS FREEDOM

For if you forgive others when they sin against you, your heavenly father will also forgive you. Matthew 6:14

The definition of forgiveness is to stop feeling angry or resentful towards someone for an offense, flaw, or mistake. This sounds simple, but forgiveness is very hard for some people; we think if someone does us wrong, they should be punished and made to suffer forever. But God told us to forgive others as Christ forgives us in Ephesians 4:32. We repeat it daily in the Lord's Prayer, "Forgive us our sins as we forgive those who sinned against us" Luke 11:4, but do we mean it or are we just repeating a prayer taught to us as children? Christ gave a perfect example of forgiveness on the cross; being crucified, he said, "Father, forgive them for they know not what they do." Luke 23:34.

When you are praying, first forgive anyone you are holding a grudge against. Colossians 3:13 says, "Bear with each other and forgive one another if any of you has a grievance against someone". Proverbs 17:9 shows how love prevails through forgiveness, "Love prospers when a fault is forgiven, but dwelling on it separates close friends."

Forgiveness is important in dance ministry because to be unforgiving is a sin, and if we go before God with the sweetest piece of ministry while harboring unforgiveness or any other sin in our hearts, the dance will be tainted. If we are not pure in heart, the dance is not pure either, and God, our audience of one, is not pleased. Before ministering, pray, repent, forgive.

I have learned that forgiveness is not for the person who wronged me; it is for me to free myself of the pain, lift that burden and move on with my life. I've had to forgive a good friend in the past. It was easy to forgive from afar, but not easy to communicate again. That took time, but I did it eventually, and now I'm free.

Prayer

Father, we thank You for forgiving us of our sins and accepting us as Your own for all eternity. We pray that you will give us a heart of forgiveness and obedience. Lord, when someone asks us for forgiveness, may we do it eagerly.

Thank You for giving us examples to follow in Your Word. Strengthen us oh Lord, in Jesus' name, amen.

Call To Action

Let us forgive. We learn from scripture that nothing can be achieved unless we first clean our hearts, and this is done by repenting and forgiving others and ourselves. Practice the steps to forgiveness: 1. Acknowledge the hurt; 2. Consider how the pain has affected you; 3. Accept that it is already done and you cannot change the past; 4: Determine that you have to forgive; 5: Repair the relationship with the person; 6: Learn what it means to forgive; 7: Forgive the person.

Lylah Browne

December 31

MEND WITH FORGIVENESS

Though we are overwhelmed by our sins you forgive them all. Psalms 65:3

God forgives us when we ask Him to. We need to mirror that same forgiving heart and forgive others. It can be really hard at times to forgive, especially when the person keeps repeating the same offense over and over. One of Jesus' disciples, Peter, asked Jesus, "How many times shall I forgive my brother when he sins against me? Up to seven times?" Jesus replied, "I do not say to you, up to seven times, but up to seventy times seven." Seventy times seven is 490. That is a big number! But God does not want us to count all the times we say, "I forgive you." God wants us to forgive the person just as He forgives you.

There are so many different Bible stories on forgiveness. God forgives you your sins, but you are not to purposely do something wrong because you know that He will forgive you. The Bible speaks about not taking God's grace for granted. God sent His only Son down to die for us and forgive our sins so that we may be able to live with God. The Lord is merciful and just, and He will always forgive you your sins.

Prayer

Heavenly Father, I pray that You will show me how to forgive just like You. Amen.

Call To Action

Repeat the Lord's prayer every day.

Shaquonna Rock

The Authors

HALAL DANCE MINISTRY
OF SANCTUARY EMPOWERMENT CENTRE
(*BARBADOS*)

Akia Brathwaite

Alicia Olton

Charlene Hinds

Cherry-Ann Cumberbatch

Danae Niles

Danielle Harewood

Denmarie Alleyne and Rianna Taylor

Debra Marshall

Destiny Niles

Eslyn Taylor

Gloria Gooding

Gabrielle Blackett

Gurlain Applewhaite

Halal Teens

Jaida Roberts

Jenifer Arrendelll and Mandy Samuels

Julie Greene

Kathy-Ann Pile

Keisha Batson

Kishara Green

Laina Jacob

Laura Phillips

Lylah Browne

Maxine Butcher

Orissa Fitzpatrick

Pearl-Ann Bartlett

Pierre Rock

Rheanne Rock

Rhema-Jae Greene

Rhonda Babb

Sandra Britton

Shandi Browne

Shaquonna Rock

Shiloh Springer

Sobrina Forde

Sophia Hazell

Trena Millar

Trinitee Angus

Tweann Layne

Zariah Watson

Zenaida Mayers